Microsoft®

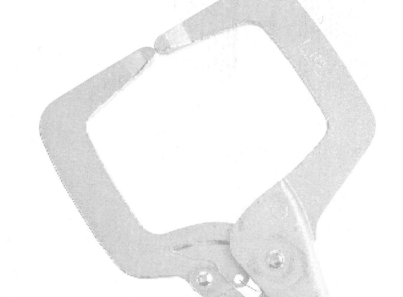

FUNDAMENTALS OF PROGRAMMING
THE MICROSOFT®
WINDOWS MEDIA® PLATFORM

Seth McEvoy

PUBLISHED BY
Microsoft Press
A Division of Microsoft Corporation
One Microsoft Way
Redmond, Washington 98052-6399

Library of Congress Cataloging-in-Publication Data
McEvoy, Seth.
    Programming the Microsoft Windows Media Platform / Seth McEvoy.
        p. cm.
    Includes index.
    ISBN 0-7356-1911-5
    1. Interactive media--Programming   2. Microsoft Windows (Computer file).   I. Title.

    QA76.76.I59M337   2003
    005.4'3--dc21   2003051278

Printed and bound in the United States of America.

1 2 3 4 5 6 7 8 9   QWE   8 7 6 5 4 3

Distributed in Canada by H.B. Fenn and Company Ltd.

A CIP catalogue record for this book is available from the British Library.

Microsoft Press books are available through booksellers and distributors worldwide. For further information about international editions, contact your local Microsoft Corporation office or contact Microsoft Press International directly at fax (425) 936-7329. Visit our Web site at www.microsoft.com/mspress. Send comments to *mspinput@microsoft.com*.

Acquisitions Editor: Danielle Voeller Bird
Project Editors: Lynn Finnel, Steve Hug
Copyeditor: Steve Hug
Electronic Artist: Greg Lovitt
Desktop Publishers: Greg Lovitt, Henry Bale
Indexer: Terrence Dorsey

Body Part No. X09-59417

To my wife, Laure Smith, with love, respect, and grateful appreciation
for all your invaluable help organizing and editing this book.

Contents at a Glance

Table of Contents

Introduction

The Windows Media platform is a comprehensive software system for the professional development of digital media content and solutions. This platform provides extensive programmability features that enable a developer to easily create custom software for a wide range of uses. This book explains the platform's components and programming principles with a series of 21 stand-alone sample applications that you can modify and reuse. Each application covers a different aspect of the Windows Media platform, including Windows Media Encoder, Windows Media Services, and Windows Media Player. Detailed step-by-step instructions for every line of code will help you learn how to use these components, customize their features, and make them work together effectively.

The concepts of the Windows Media platform will be demonstrated through the development of small applications that begin with the basic principles of the encoder, server, and Player. Next you will learn how to combine these components by using this book's unique automation techniques to simplify the process. The last chapter puts all these principles together into one large radio station application that is a complete Internet broadcasting workstation running on the Windows Media platform. This radio station application and all the other programs in this book can be easily adapted to develop your own digital media solutions in the future.

The 21 sample applications were designed to both explain the components of the Windows Media platform and provide automation procedures to make the components operate together more efficiently. All these applications include two techniques to automate the process of combining the encoder, server, and Player. The first technique will show you how to simplify each user interface in order to save steps by reducing the number of operational procedures. The second technique will provide ways to automatically trigger repetitive tasks that would ordinarily need to be performed by hand. These automation procedures have been specifically designed for this book, and each one can be used to reduce the complexity of your digital media applications, making them run faster, easier, and more proficiently.

How This Book Is Organized

This book is divided into five parts and an appendix. Part I discusses the architecture principles of the Windows Media platform. Parts II, III, and IV present sample applications that explain the programmability features of the platform's three major components: Windows Media Encoder, Windows Media Services, and Windows Media Player. Part V ties it all together by providing one large program that combines techniques from many of the book's previous sample applications. This large program will demonstrate how the encoder, server, and Player can be integrated to develop complete digital media solutions. In addition, the appendix presents advanced programming techniques for developing custom encoding profiles.

Although the material in this book focuses primarily on the three major components of the Windows Media platform, other platform components will be discussed, but not covered in detail. For information about the Advanced Systems Format (ASF) file specification, see the ASF specification on the companion CD. For more information about Windows Media Format, see the Windows Media Format SDK. Windows Media Digital Rights Management is not discussed in this book but can be used to protect the digital rights of content created with Windows Media. The Windows Media Rights Manager SDK and the Windows Media Digital Rights Management documentation will provide you with more information.

For your convenience, this book has a companion CD that contains all the program code and forms for the applications in each chapter, songs you can use to test those applications, and other useful programs and utilities. In addition, the companion CD includes the SDKs for the encoder, server, and Player, as well as the Windows Media Format SDK, white papers, and other documentation.

Part I: Windows Media Architecture

The first part of this book explains the components and programming principles of the Windows Media platform. Chapter 1 discusses how the encoder converts digital media to Windows Media Format, how the server broadcasts encoded media over a network, and how the Player receives and plays the media on a user's computer. You will also learn how Windows Media Format is used by all three components to build digital media solutions for content delivery to your home, school, or office.

Part II: Encoding Windows Media

The second part of this book has eight chapters that focus on the conversion of digital media into Windows Media Format files and streams by using Windows Media Encoder. Each chapter explains how to use Visual Basic to create encoder software applications, starting with simple programming concepts and code samples. Subsequent chapters add new concepts and reuse code from previous chapters to explain how the encoder can be automated to work more efficiently with the server or the Player.

Chapter 2 creates an application that encodes a file by using a streamlined user interface to simplify the operation of the encoder.

Chapter 3 demonstrates how to make Windows Media Encoder and Windows Media Player work together in the same application. Instead of running two separate programs, the application you create will run both components from the same window and, as soon as a file is encoded, you can play it in the Player.

Chapter 4 explains the techniques needed to create a network connection between the encoder and the Player. With this application, the Player will begin playing the streamed output of the encoder as soon as the encoder begins encoding. This chapter also uses the concept of event handling to trigger the Player when the encoding starts.

Chapter 5 explores the concepts of how to add attributes to the media that the encoder is converting. By adding attributes, you can embed text data into the audio and video stream. This chapter shows you how to use events in Windows Media Player to display the embedded attributes.

Chapter 6 creates an application that combines the encoder with the server to demonstrate how the encoder can push a stream of data to the server for transmission over a network. This application shows how the encoder converts digital media to a stream and sends it to the server, which then broadcasts it over the network to a Player. This application demonstrates how the three components of Windows Media can be operated from a single window.

Chapter 7 uses many of the same concepts as the previous chapter, but changes which component controls the flow of the digital media stream. This chapter covers the technique of encoder pull, in which the server requests a stream from the encoder and then relays the stream to a Player. This application includes two Players, one playing the output of the encoder and the other playing the stream from the server, demonstrating that you can add Players to your program to monitor the flow of the media stream at any point.

Chapter 8 shows you how to use the encoder to embed script commands in a Windows Media Format file or stream. You will see how to use script commands to operate a Player by remote control. The application for this chapter combines the encoder, a Web browser, and the Player embedded in a Web page in the browser. With this program, you can send color names to the Web page through the media stream to change the background color of the page.

Chapter 9 concludes the encoder part of the book by creating an application that uses a webcam to feed live audio and video into the encoder. The encoder then broadcasts directly to the Player in a pane that changes size to match the encoded height and width of the video signal.

Part III: Serving Windows Media

The third part of this book has five chapters that focus on how a server running Windows Media Services uses Windows Media Format to stream digital media across a network. Each chapter provides a Visual Basic application that covers one aspect of streaming digital media with the server. The first chapter will start with simple programming concepts and code samples. Later chapters will then discuss the three different methods that the server uses to deliver digital media to Windows Media Player. The last chapter will focus on how the server uses playlists to choose files to send over the network.

Chapter 10 explains on-demand publishing, the most popular method of streaming from the server. You will be shown an application that automates the server's selection of a previously encoded file and streams it out to the network with the push of a button.

Chapter 11 adds to the simple server application you created in the previous chapter by including Windows Media Player. This program allows the Player to play the content automatically, as soon as the file is ready for streaming. The Player also displays the protocol used by the media stream by using an event handler that detects when the Player starts running.

Chapter 12 demonstrates the principles used to broadcast a stream over the Internet or a corporate intranet. In this program, when the server starts a unicast broadcast, the Player automatically launches inside your application to play the digital media and display the protocol used.

Chapter 13 shows another way to broadcast a media stream over a network, by using multicasting. Instead of sending a stream to each Player on request, the server sends out one stream to all Players simultaneously. This application creates a multicast broadcast and publishes an announcement that the Player can use to receive the stream when it arrives on the network.

Chapter 14 explains the principles of how to program XML playlists to send out sets of files over the network. Playlists provide a powerful way to automate the output of a server. You can use playlists to choose what file or stream is transmitted next, and you can modify playlists through programming techniques. You will also see how to use Windows Management Instrumentation (WMI) to relay events from the server directly to your application.

Part IV: Playing Windows Media

The fourth part of this book has four chapters that explain how to automate Windows Media Player by creating custom user interfaces that modify the look and operation of the Player. Each chapter focuses on a different programming language to show you how to embed the Player in an application, modify its user interface, or change it completely.

Chapter 15 uses Visual Basic to create a custom version of the Player that reduces the user interface to a few buttons and text boxes, and displays the name of the song that is playing, the duration, and the position in the media.

Chapter 16 embeds the Player in a Web page in order to create a custom user interface. The automation concepts are the same as in the previous chapter, but instead of using Visual Basic, the programming languages will be Microsoft JScript and HTML.

Chapter 17 customizes the user interface of the Player by using Player skin technology. This application uses the skin's programming mixture of XML, Microsoft JScript, and layers of artwork to create unique interactive buttons, sliders, and knobs to control the Player.

Chapter 18 adds three more ways to customize the Player with banners, embedded Web pages, and borders. Each of these techniques uses XML and Windows Media metafiles to add graphic elements to the Video and Visualization pane of the Player. Banners modify the Player banner-bar pane to provide links to Web pages that can be synchronized with the digital media that is playing. You will also be shown how to embed Web pages and skins in the Video and Visualization pane to add custom elements while keeping the rest of the standard Player user interface.

Part V: Complete Radio Station Application

The fifth part of this book has one chapter, which will show you how to use Visual Basic to create a comprehensive application that will make the three major components of the Windows Media platform work together. This application is an Internet radio station that can be used as a complete broadcasting workstation, because it has everything you need to stream a playlist of songs over the Internet.

The user interface needed to run your workstation is combined into a single window that will let you configure the server, encode songs with the encoder, listen to them with the Player, and add the songs to a master playlist. After you audition the playlist, the final step is to allow users to connect to the server in order to listen to your radio station.

This application demonstrates the principles of automation by simplifying the user interface and reducing repetitive steps. These techniques are extremely useful because instead of using the buttons, menus, and dialog boxes of all three Windows Media components, you reduce the operation to a handful of buttons and text boxes that are all on one form. And by using a master playlist, you add further automation and save time by not having to wait for one song to end so you can begin streaming the next. The Radio Station application can be adapted easily for use with streaming video to create a complete audio and video digital media solution.

Programming Considerations

This book is written with the assumption that you will type the programs for each chapter and run them on your computer. However, you can also copy the same programs from the companion CD to study them in operation. They are listed in the Programming Notes document on the CD. For the programs that are written in Visual Basic, the companion form file is also included. In addition, if any program requires special files, such as a custom encoding profile, those files are also included on the CD in the same folder as the program.

Because there are so many different kinds of computer configurations possible, you may need to modify some of the default values that the programs provide for file names and paths, digital media file names, or publishing-point names. The code makes the assumption that the root folder of your Web server is C:\inetpub\wwwroot and that the root folder of your media server is C:\wmpub\wmroot. Several applications also assume that a folder named C:\media exists on your computer that will contain sample songs that you will encode with the encoder or stream with the server. Each chapter uses different names for publishing points and songs so that the publishing-point and song names from previous chapters will not create conflicts. Depending on the configuration of your computer, you may need to change the code to match the network name and port of your Web server.

> **Note** For information about the programs included with this book, please read the Programming Notes file on the CD. The file contains a list of the applications in this book, a list of which applications are built on other applications, and a list of the songs and other non-program files and which chapter they will be used in. The file also lists trouble-shooting tips that may help you run the programs more effectively in a networked environment.

Operating System Requirements for This Book

Some of the components of Windows Media are part of specific Microsoft operating systems. For example, Windows Media Player is part of many different versions of Microsoft Windows because it is intended for use in the home or office by end users. (There are also versions of Windows Media Player for Apple Macintosh and Sun Solaris.) Windows Media Encoder, however, is an application that you must install. You can download the encoder from the Windows Media pages of the Microsoft Web site at *http://www.microsoft.com/windowsmedia,* or you can install it from the companion CD. Windows Media Services, the media-server component of the Windows Media platform, is included in all the operating systems of the Windows Server 2003 family except Windows Server 2003, Web Edition. Each chapter of this book explains which operating systems are suitable for the sample application of that chapter.

You may want to choose which version of the Windows Server 2003 family to install before you start working through the examples in this book. The choice you must make is whether you want to run the multicast application in Chapter 13. If you do not, you can use Windows Server 2003, Standard Edition, for all the other applications in the book. But if you want to do multicasts, you must install either Windows Server 2003, Enterprise Edition, or Windows Server 2003, Datacenter Edition, both of which will work for all the other chapters as well.

However, if you want to work only with the programs from the chapters that do not use Windows Media Services (Chapters 2, 3, 4, 5, 8, 9, 15, 16, 17, and 18), you can run them on the operating systems explained in the Minimum System Requirements section later in this introduction.

Programming Language Requirements for This Book

This book uses several different programming languages to teach the principles of automating the components of the Windows Media platform. Each chapter tells you which languages are needed for the sample application in that chapter, and how to set up your programming environment.

Visual Basic was chosen for most of the sample applications in this book because it is one of the most popular programming languages in the world. By using Visual Basic in this book, the focus can be on the concepts that the application shows you how to perform, and not on the complexity of the code. (Even if you are not familiar with Visual Basic, but use other programming languages, you can quickly learn what you need to know by reading books like *Microsoft Visual Basic 6.0 Professional Step-by-Step,* by Mike Halvorson, from Microsoft Press.) Each chapter in this book that uses Visual Basic tells you what controls to add to the forms and what names to give them. Many of the chapters build on Visual Basic forms and code from earlier chapters, and you will find it easiest to use the Save Project As and Save Form As commands from the File menu to create a new project, taking care to rename the form and project when you have copied them to a folder different from the previous application.

Some of the chapters use scripting languages such as Microsoft JScript, XML (Extensible Markup Language), and the Player skin programming language. For these you need only a simple text editor to create the programs, and detailed instructions are provided on how to run the programs. Be sure the editor you choose can save code as plain text without any formatting.

Media Requirements for This Book

This book comes with several audio music samples that can be used with the programs in this book. Each chapter requires songs with different file names so that you can be sure that songs from previous applications are not playing instead. You must read the code in each chapter to see where the songs for each chapter need to be copied to from the CD, but most of them should be copied to C:\media. You also will need to copy some songs to the root folder of your Web server (typically C:\inetpub\wwwroot) or to the root folder of your media server (typically C:\wmpub\wmroot). Each song has the number of the chapter it is to be used with in its file name.

The songs on the CD are copyright Microsoft Corporation. All rights reserved.

> **Important** A copyright gives certain exclusive ownership rights to the person who creates an original work. These rights are protected by U.S. and international laws. It is illegal to reproduce copyrighted material without the permission of the copyright owner.
>
> Whenever you copy music or a video that you did not create, consider that it may be copyrighted. Ownership of a CD or licensed digital media files that you downloaded from the Internet does not necessarily constitute the right to redistribute or share the content. If you intend to redistribute or share content, be sure you have the necessary permissions to do so.

What's on the Companion CD?

The CD that is included with this book provides the following software, tools, and information that will get you streaming in no time with Windows Media 9 Series.

- **Windows Media Player 9 Series** Create or edit dynamic playlists that automatically update to reflect additions or changes to your Media Library, and enjoy the instant-on, always-on streaming experience with no buffering delays. Requires Windows 98 Second Edition or later.

- **Windows Media Encoder 9 Series** Take advantage of advanced capture abilities, powerful server integration for live broadcasts, and improved flexibility to optimize compression for a wide range of delivery scenarios, including multiple bit rate (MBR) streaming and delivery on CD or DVD.

- **Windows Media Load Simulator 9 Series** Create a real-world load on a Windows Media server by simulating Windows Media Player connections. View load-test results in log files and Windows Media Performance Monitor. Requires Windows XP or later.

- **Windows Media 9 Capture** Capture high-bit-rate, uncompressed audio and video to an AVI file.

- **Windows Media Services 9 Series Playlist Editor** Create server-side playlists that enable you to organize advertisements, audio, and video content into a single stream. Requires Windows XP or later.

- **Windows Media Player 9 Series SDK** Change the personality of Windows Media Player by creating custom skins and visualizations and embedding the Player into Web pages.

- **Windows Media Encoder 9 Series SDK**   Automate the encoding process for custom applications and solutions, and enable remote encoding. Requires Windows 2000 or later.

- **Windows Media Services 9 Series SDK**   Administer a Windows Media server programmatically, dynamically create and modify server-side playlists, set and retrieve properties for the system plug-ins included with the server, and create custom plug-ins when the system plug-ins do not satisfy your requirements.

- **Windows Media Format 9 Series SDK**   Enable software applications, such as players or content creation applications, to read, write, edit, and transfer files with Windows Media Format. Requires Windows 2000 or later.

- **Windows Media ASF Viewer 9 Series**   Inspect the contents of files such as .asf, .wma, .wmv, and .mp3. The objects within these files include header, data property, and codec objects.

- **Microsoft Producer for PowerPoint 2002**   Create rich-media presentations or corporate training sessions that you stream to users' desktops.

- **Sample code and digital media**   Complete sample code and digital media samples are provided for every sample application described in the book.

- **White papers and demos**   Learn more about Windows Media from how-to white papers, demos, backgrounds, and lots of extras, also included on the CD.

System Requirements

The minimum system requirements will work for using the companion CD and for the chapters that do not use Windows Media Services. If you want to create the sample applications that do use the server, you will need to use the recommended system requirements.

Minimum System Requirements

The following hardware and software are the minimum required to use the tools and content provided on the companion CD and to create the sample applications that do *not* use Windows Media Services (Chapters 2, 3, 4, 5, 8, 9, 15, 16, 17, and 18).

- Microsoft Windows 2000 with Service Pack 1, or Microsoft Windows XP.

- 400 megahertz (MHz) processor. A processor speed of 600 MHz or higher is recommended when capturing from a digital video device.

- 128 megabytes (MB) of RAM.

- 2 gigabytes (GB) of available hard disk space.

- An audio capture device.

- A video capture device (DV or analog).

- Microsoft Windows Media Player 9 Series.

- Microsoft Internet Explorer 6.0 or later.

- Adobe Acrobat or Adobe Reader is required to read the eBook.

Recommended System Requirements

The following hardware and software are required to create the sample applications that use Windows Media Services (Chapters 10, 11, 12, 13, 14, and 19). These requirements are also suitable for the sample applications in all the other chapters of the book.

- Microsoft Windows Server 2003, Standard Edition; Windows Server 2003, Enterprise Edition; or Windows Server 2003, Datacenter Edition. (If you want to create the multicasting application in Chapter 13, do not use Windows Server 2003, Standard Edition. For more information about which of these operating systems to choose, see the section "Operating System Requirements for This Book" earlier in this introduction.)

- 733 MHz or faster processor.

- 256 MB of RAM minimum (32 GB maximum for x86-based computers, 64 GB maximum for Itanium-based computers).

- 2 GB of available hard disk space.

- An audio capture device.

- A video capture device (DV or analog).

- Microsoft Windows Media Player 9 Series.

- Microsoft Internet Explorer 6.0 or later.

Acknowledgements

I want to thank the following people for their blood, toil, tears, and sweat: Kari Rosenthal Annand, Henry Bale, Terrence Dorsey, Katherine Enos, C. Keith Gabbert, Mark Galioto, Denys Howard, Greg Lovitt, Emily Moon, Kelly Pittman, Karen Strudwick, and the *entire* Windows Media team. The following people took time out of their busy schedules to read parts of the book and I thank them: Rajesh Deshpande, Chris Knowlton, Pandian Krishnaswamy, Jorge Novillo, Michael Patten, Brandon Pai, Ravi Raman, Dave Roth,

Yibin Tai, Nick Vicars-Harris, Shiwei Wang, Rui Wu, and Lan Zhao. I want to extend a special thank you to: Dagmar Shannon for fitting this project into our busy schedule; Michael Patten for writing the appendix; Juliana Aldous Atkinson, Danielle Voeller Bird, Julia Stasio, and Lynn Finnel of Microsoft Press for keeping on top of all the complexities involved in acquiring and producing this book; Steve Hug for his endless hours of editing and his breadth and depth of knowledge about Windows Media; and my manager, Tom Woolums, for accepting my proposal to develop this project, greenlighting the resources, and supporting the book every step of the way. (I still say whoever hired him made a good choice!)

Further Resources for Windows Media Programming

This book covers the three major components of the Windows Media Programming platform. For more programming information about these components, see the Windows Media Encoder SDK, the Windows Media Services SDK, and the Windows Media Player SDK. The Windows Media platform also includes other programming components, which are listed below. The latest version of the entire Windows Media SDK can be found at the Audio and Video node of the MSDN Web site at:

http://msdn.microsoft.com/nhp/default.asp?contentid=28000411

or by following the SDK links under Technologies and Tools on the Windows Media pages of the Microsoft Web site at:

http://www.microsoft.com/windowsmedia

Windows Media Format SDK

The Windows Media Format SDK will help you add Windows Media support to your own digital media playback or encoding applications written in C++. This SDK is used by both Windows Media Player and Windows Media Encoder for playback, encoding, and live streaming of Windows Media files.

Windows Media Rights Manager SDK

If you are encoding content whose distribution you want to restrict in any way, you can protect the content from unauthorized access through digital rights management (DRM). The Windows Media Rights Manager SDK enables you to apply DRM encryption to files and to distribute licenses to end users, based on usage terms that you determine.

Windows Media Device Manager SDK

Windows Media files, especially Windows Media Audio files, are supported on many portable devices. The Windows Media Device Manager SDK is intended for use by original equipment manufacturers (OEMs) who produce portable audio players, and independent software vendors (ISVs) who create software that downloads digital media onto those portable audio players. The SDK provides OEMs and ISVs with a way to securely transfer data, including files protected by DRM, between a personal computer and a portable device.

Windows Media Audio and Video Codec Interfaces SDK

When you use the Windows Media Encoder or an application based on the Windows Media Format SDK to encode Windows Media content, the resulting file or stream is wrapped in a container file format called Advanced Systems Format (ASF). ASF is optimized for both network streaming and for local playback, but it is not ideal for all scenarios. The low-level audio and video codec interfaces enable developers to compress and decompress audio and video content with the Windows Media codecs when using other file-container formats.

Windows Media Video 9 VCM

The Microsoft Windows Media Video 9 VCM is a plug-in compressor that works with the Windows Multimedia video compression manager (VCM) to encode Windows Media Video. VCM is typically used to encode content for use in Audio-Video Interleaved (AVI) files, but you can use other container formats as well. The Windows Media Video 9 VCM provides the quality and flexibility of Windows Media Video without requiring the ASF container.

Additional Technical Articles

The Audio and Video node of the MSDN Web site also contains many useful technical articles for developers on topics related to the use of audio and video on Windows. These topics not only cover Windows Media technologies, but also include information about Microsoft DirectShow and DirectSound.

Licensing Information

Certain aspects of Windows Media programming may need a separate license. You can learn more about licensing at the Windows Media Licensing page of the Microsoft Web site:

http://www.microsoft.com/windows/windowsmedia/create/licensing.aspx

The programs in this book do not need additional licensing except the End User License Agreements (EULA) needed to use the operating systems or software that make up the major components of the Windows Media platform (Windows Media Encoder, Windows Media Services, Windows Media Player).

If you want to redistribute Windows Media Player 9 Series or the Windows Media Player ActiveX control with your software, you can obtain a royalty-free license to do so from the Windows Media Licensing page. You do not need to do this if your software depends on the Player being already installed on the user's computer as a feature of the operating system.

Communities

The Microsoft newsgroup server hosts several newsgroups devoted to Windows Media. For more information about Microsoft newsgroups, visit the Communities page at the Microsoft Web site:

http://www.microsoft.com/communities/

The most relevant of these for developers is:

news://microsoft.public.windowsmedia.sdk

A public LISTSERV community, WMTALK, is devoted to Windows Media and related topics, both for developers and end users. To join this discussion group, go to:

http://discuss.microsoft.com/archives/wmtalk.html

Corrections, Comments, and Help

Every effort has been made to ensure the accuracy of this book and the contents of the sample files. Microsoft Press provides corrections and additional content for its books through the World Wide Web at the following address:

http://www.microsoft.com/mspress/support

To connect directly to the Microsoft Press Knowledge Base and enter a query you have, visit the following address:

http://www.microsoft.com/mspress/support/search.asp

If you have problems, comments, or ideas regarding this book or the sample files, please send them to Microsoft Press. Send an e-mail message to:

mspinput@microsoft.com

Or send postal mail to the following address:

Microsoft Press
Attn: Fundamentals of Programming the Microsoft Windows Media Platform Editor
One Microsoft Way
Redmond, WA 98052-6399

Please note that product support is not offered through the preceding addresses. For help with Windows Media products, you can connect to Microsoft Product Support Services on the Web at *http://support.microsoft.com*.

Visit the Microsoft Press World Wide Web Site

You are also invited to visit the Microsoft Press World Wide Web site at the following location:

http://www.microsoft.com/mspress

You'll find descriptions for the complete line of Microsoft Press books, information about ordering titles, notice of special features and events, additional content for Microsoft Press books, and much more.

Part I

Windows Media Architecture

Windows Media is a complete programming platform that can be used to create a wide variety of digital media options for your home, school, or office. This part of the book introduces you to the platform's three categories of components and their four underlying technologies. You will learn how they all work together, and you'll be shown the programming principles you will need to integrate the components more efficiently. This part of the book covers the features of three major components: Windows Media Encoder, Windows Media Services, and Windows Media Player. The material on the encoder describes how it inputs, outputs, converts, and customizes digital media. The Windows Media Services section explains the three ways a server can stream audio and video and how playlists automate the content selection process. The information about the Player includes many programming techniques you can use to customize its appearance and operation.

1

Understanding Windows Media Architecture

This chapter will introduce you to the Windows Media platform, explain its basic components and technologies, and show you how they work together to make a complete end-to-end digital audio and video programming system.

Introducing the Windows Media Platform

The Windows Media platform is a programming system designed to create, distribute, and play digital media. This platform is composed of three integrated categories of components: authoring, services, and playback. Authoring is the process of creating and editing audio or video content. Services components are used to control how content is distributed. Playback is the process of receiving distributed content and playing it for the user.

The authoring, services, and playback components are built with four technologies that are presented in the Windows Media Format Software Development Kit (SDK). The four technologies are Advanced Systems Format (ASF), Windows Media codecs, Windows Media digital rights management (DRM), and the Windows Media protocols. These technologies are the building blocks that power the operations of the components. The Advanced Systems Format defines file containers that store the digital audio and video content. Windows Media codecs are the mathematical formulas that compress the audio and video. Digital rights management is a content monitoring system that encrypts media files and protects the legal rights of content owners. The Windows Media protocols are a networking language that enables the distribution of digital media over a network.

Figure 1.1 shows the relationship between the three categories of components and the four underlying technologies of the Windows Media platform.

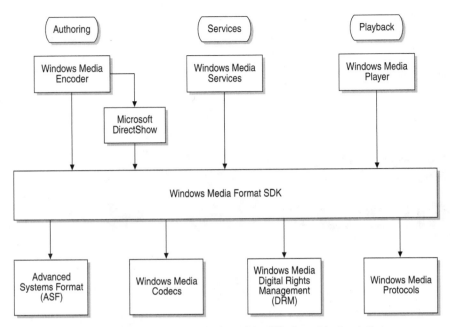

Figure 1.1 Components and technologies of the Windows Media platform.

The following sections present a brief overview of the basic components and technologies of the Windows Media platform presented in Figure 1.1.

Windows Media Authoring Components

The authoring components of the Windows Media platform allow users and developers to create and edit audio and video content. The Windows Media platform includes three authoring software packages: Windows Media Encoder, Windows Movie Maker, and Microsoft Producer for PowerPoint. There are several other authoring packages that are built with the Windows Media Format SDK that can be used with the Windows Media platform.

Windows Media Encoder is a software program that is the main developer authoring component of the Windows Media platform. It has been designed for developers and professional content creators to convert digital media or process live audio and video for distribution to servers and playback systems.

The encoder is the focus of Chapters 2 through 9 and is also discussed in more detail later in this chapter.

Windows Media Services Components

Windows Media Services is a set of technologies that are used to distribute Windows Media-based audio and video content from a file or a live encoder stream through a network to a playback system. Windows Media Services is the main services component of the Windows Media platform.

Chapters 10 through 14 focus on servers running Windows Media Services, which is also discussed in more detail later in this chapter.

Windows Media Playback Components

Windows Media Player is the main playback component for receiving and playing audio and video on the Windows Media platform. The Player is a software feature of Windows that uses the technologies in the platform to decode digital media that it receives from an encoded file or a server stream.

The Player is the focus of Chapters 15 through 18 and is also discussed in more detail later in this chapter.

Microsoft DirectShow

Microsoft DirectShow is a component of Microsoft DirectX, the multimedia programming interface of the Windows operating system. The Windows Media Format SDK provides information about how to use DirectShow to encode digital media. DirectShow is not covered in this book; for more information about DirectShow, see the Windows Media Format SDK on the companion CD.

Windows Media Format SDK

The Windows Media Format SDK is a software development kit of tools and technologies that enable developers to create authoring, serving, and playback components for the Windows Media platform. The Windows Media Format SDK covers four technologies that work together to provide the underlying programming systems for all the components of the Windows Media platform. These technologies are: Advanced Systems Format (ASF), Windows Media codecs, digital rights management (DRM), and the Windows Media protocols. These technologies are not covered in detail in this book; for more information, see the Windows Media Format SDK on the companion CD.

Advanced Systems Format

The Advanced Systems Format (ASF) is a file container specification for storing compressed or uncompressed synchronized digital audio and video. This format can be used for authoring, storing, and distributing digital media. The ASF file format is designed to package audio and video content, but an ASF file can include nearly all types of computer data. ASF files can have an .asf file name extension, but if an ASF file contains audio encoded with a Windows Media audio codec, it can have a .wma file name extension to specify that it is an audio file. In addition, when encoded with a Windows Media video codec, an ASF file can have a .wmv file name extension to specify that it is a video file.

For more information about ASF, see the ASF specification on the companion CD.

Windows Media Codecs

Codecs are mathematical formulas that are used to *co*mpress and *dec*ompress digital data. Codecs reduce the size of digital media files and lower the bandwidth required for distributing the files over a network. The Windows Media codecs compress audio, video, and images into the smallest possible file size while retaining the highest quality available.

Digital Rights Management

The Windows Media platform has an optional end-to-end programming system for the secure encryption and decryption of digital media files that are distributed to consumers. Digital rights management (DRM) is the system that enables content owners to distribute media only to users that have the proper licenses. Using DRM prevents illegal use and reproduction of intellectual property. For more information about DRM, see the Windows Media Rights Management SDK, which is available on the Windows Media Web site at *http://www.microsoft.com/windowsmedia*.

Windows Media Protocols

The Windows Media protocols are a networking language that facilitates the communication between the authoring, serving, and playback components of the Windows Media platform. Protocols identify the type of delivery system used to stream content over a corporate intranet or the Internet.

Understanding Windows Media Encoder

Windows Media Encoder is the main developer authoring component in the Windows Media platform. The encoder is a software authoring program that converts digital media into Windows Media Format in order to create, store, edit, and play Windows Media files and streams on your computer or distribute them over a network. The encoder is built with the technologies in the Windows Media Format SDK and Microsoft DirectShow.

About Windows Media Encoder

In order to transfer data from one source to another, the data must often be converted from its original form into a new format appropriate for the situation. Windows Media Encoder converts and compresses audio and video content into Windows Media files and streams. When the encoder processes a file or stream, the data is converted to the Advanced Systems Format by using Windows Media codecs. By using these Windows Media Format SDK technologies, the files and streams can be distributed and played on a wide variety of computers, Pocket PCs, Smartphones, and other consumer and professional media devices. The encoder compresses digital media into Windows Media Format by using the technologies of Windows Media Format SDK and Microsoft DirectShow.

When the encoder converts digital media from one format to another, the input can be either a file or a live stream, and the output can be stored as a file or distributed as a live stream to a server, a player, or another encoder. After it is compressed using the appropriate profile, the media can be output to either a Windows Media file for storage or broadcast over a network to another destination. The broadcast output of the encoder can be streamed to a server for delivery to a player, or the output can go directly to a player to test the quality of a stream.

The encoder uses profiles to define the level and type of data conversion. These profiles create a unique template of numeric settings that can be tailored to your specific needs. When you choose a profile, you can specify compression settings such as the bit rate, video frame rate and size, codec, and other options. The encoder includes a collection of default profiles that you can use to achieve the different compression levels necessary for broadband, dial-up modem, or a home digital theater. The appendix discusses encoding profiles in more detail. For additional information about profiles and codecs, see the Windows Media Encoder documentation.

Additional features of the encoder include the ability to customize its operations by writing special effects plug-ins to modify audio and video content, control input devices such as video tape recorders, and provide plug-and-play support for audio and video capture devices that have been added to your computer. These features are not covered in this book, but you can find out more about them in the Windows Media Encoder documentation.

Figure 1.2 shows Windows Media Encoder compressing digital media by choosing from two source inputs and outputting the result to a file or a stream for distribution.

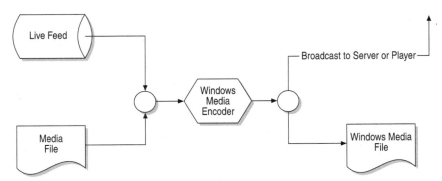

Figure 1.2   Windows Media Encoder compressing digital media with a choice of two inputs and two outputs.

Using the Encoder with Other Components

Windows Media Encoder is designed to work in conjunction with Windows Media Player or a server running Windows Media Services.

Using the Encoder with Windows Media Player

The Player can play encoded files that have been saved to disk, or it can receive audio and video streams directly from the encoder or from a server running Windows Media Services.

Playing Files

Windows Media Player can play music or video that the encoder has compressed into Windows Media files. It can also play many other file formats, such as MP3, WAV, and so on. When the user requests the file, the Player opens it and decodes the compressed media by using the same codec that the encoder used. The Player passes the decompressed digital audio and video it receives to the operating system, which routes the data to speakers and the video display. Chapter 5 shows you how to create an application that enables the Player to play files automatically after they have been encoded.

Broadcasting Streams

Windows Media Player can also receive a stream of digital media that is output from Windows Media Encoder over a network by connecting directly to the Windows Media Encoder using the HTTP protocol. When data is sent through a network, it is broken into small segments called packets. These packets stream through the network until the Player receives them. The Player then assembles the packets to recreate the original digital media. Because the encoder is designed to broadcast to no more than five users simultaneously, streaming from the encoder is recommended only for situations that involve a few users or for testing to be certain your media is encoded properly. Chapter 4 will show you how to easily create an application that makes the encoder trigger the Player whenever an input stream begins encoding. For example, you could use the Player to view the encoded stream and raise an alert if the live audio and video were interrupted.

Users can adjust the total number of connections allowed by the encoder by changing a registry key value. The default value is 5. Streaming from the encoder is also good for applications where only one or two users will connect. For example, this system could be used to monitor your home with a webcam and have the encoder broadcast the video from your home to a laptop computer at another location through the Internet.

Using Windows Media Encoder with Windows Media Services

A server running Windows Media Services can receive streams from the encoder by one of two methods: encoder push or encoder pull.

Pushing Streams from the Encoder to the Server

The encoder can send an encoded stream directly to the server. This technology is called encoder push, and it allows you to publish content directly from the encoder to a publishing point running on the server. If the server is configured to receive streams from the encoder, it can transmit the stream over the Internet or a corporate intranet.

To set up an encoder push transaction, there are several details that the encoder and server must agree upon, such as server name, address, port, and publishing point. The encoder instructs the server to publish a stream by using a specific publishing point, which is a name that references live streams or folders containing media files. The encoder then sends the stream to the server. The server accepts the stream and then delivers it to a Player that requests the stream by using the publishing-point name provided by the encoder. The server is just acting as a relay between encoder and Player, but because the server has far greater power and ability to deliver a stream, it can stream to many more users with higher efficiency.

Pushing a stream to a server from an encoder is useful when you want to have many publishing points on a server, with each publishing point providing streams from a different encoder. Individual publishing points can be started and stopped by custom encoder applications, making push distribution useful in situations where the operator at the encoding workstation controls the flow of the content. For example, encoder push would be a good choice for a video news service that publishes many video streams on different subjects that change frequently. Push distribution is helpful because it reduces the number of steps needed to broadcast content. It also enables you to distribute content to a server that is behind a firewall.

Figure 1.3 shows an encoder pushing a stream to a server.

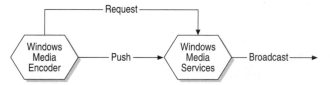

Figure 1.3   Encoder pushing a stream to a server.

Chapter 6 shows you how to create an application that automatically sets up the server to receive a stream pushed from the encoder.

Pulling Streams from the Encoder to the Server

If you want the server to request media streams from an encoder, another technology is used, called encoder pull. The digital media stream still flows from the encoder to the server, but the server determines when the content will be received from the encoder.

To set up an encoder pull transaction, the operator must first enable a publishing point on the server and specify the URL of the remote encoder. The encoder must be running and broadcasting before the publishing point can be started. The server creates a publishing point and uses a stream from the encoder. When a Player makes a request to the publishing point, the server relays the stream from the encoder to the Player.

Pulling a stream from the encoder to the server is useful when you want to have one publishing point providing different encoder streams at different times. By using playlists, the server can switch from one encoder stream to another, but publish only one stream at a time. For example, encoder pull would be a good choice for a service that broadcasts live video of different street intersections to provide viewers with up-to-date traffic information. At ten-second intervals, the playlist could switch the view to a different intersection. Because playlists can be modified at any time, an operator could use programming to force the playlist to only show the view from a particular intersection in the event of a traffic accident.

Figure 1.4 shows a server pulling a stream from an encoder.

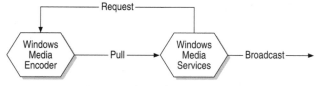

Figure 1.4   Server pulling a stream from an encoder.

Chapter 7 explains how to create an application that automatically sets up the server to receive a stream pulled from the encoder.

Adding Data to a Stream

Windows Media Encoder can be used to add text strings of attributes and script commands to a digital media stream to provide information about the stream or to control actions on a Player.

Adding Attributes to a Stream

The encoder allows you to use text strings to add attributes to a media file or stream. The attributes consist of a name-and-value pair that can give the user information about the file or stream, including the title, author, description, and so on. You can also add custom attributes to a stream for custom applications that use Windows Media Player.

Adding standard attributes to a file while encoding is recommended, so that users can see the attributes when the Player is playing, or when they are looking at the file properties in Windows Explorer. Custom attributes can be used for remote control automation of the Player by embedding text data in the stream. For example, you could have an Internet radio station contest asking listeners to answer a question by choosing an answer from a selection displayed in a user interface created for the Player. You could then write code to compare the user's answer with the custom attribute embedded in the media stream. If the answer matched the custom attribute value, a Web page could pop up to tell the user how to claim a prize.

Chapter 5 gives you an application in which Windows Media Encoder embeds standard and custom attributes in a media file, and the Player displays them. These principles can be used to provide remote control automation of a Player by using the encoder. Part IV of this book shows you many different ways to create automation code for Windows Media Player that can be used in conjunction with file attributes to control a Player remotely.

Adding Script Commands to a Stream

You can add script commands to an encoded media file or a live stream in order to remotely control Windows Media Player. The encoder can embed standard types of script commands such as TEXT, URL, FILENAME, EVENT, and OPENEVENT. Each type of script command causes the Player to take a specific action when the command is received by the Player as part of the file or stream. The Player handles these commands in different ways, depending on the type of command. For example, the TEXT command displays text in the Player's captioning area, and the URL command loads a Web page in the default browser. Custom script commands can be used to send any text information that you want to detect in an embedded Player application. For more information about standard and custom script commands, see the Windows Media Encoder SDK and the Windows Media Player SDK.

Chapter 8 provides you with an application that uses Windows Media Encoder to embed custom script commands in a file that is then received by a Player in a Web page.

It demonstrates simple automation principles by having the Player change the color of the Web page whenever it receives a custom script command containing the new color name. Part IV of this book shows you many different ways to create automation code for Windows Media Player that can be used in conjunction with script commands to control a Player remotely.

Encoding Live Audio and Video

Windows Media Encoder can encode audio and video from a live media stream. When it receives a stream from a capture device such as a microphone, video camera, or webcam, it compresses the data according to settings in an encoding profile. The encoder will then save the digital media to a file, or stream the data to another destination over a network, or do both. The destination for the stream can be either a Player or a server. Except for testing purposes, the destination is usually a server that will broadcast the stream over the Internet or a corporate network.

Chapter 9 shows you how to automate the encoding of audio and video from a simple webcam. The encoder in this application can display previews and postviews of the video being encoded, and play the video on the Player automatically.

Understanding Windows Media Services

A Windows Media server is a computer running Windows Media Services software that can distribute encoded audio and video over a network to computers, Pocket PCs, and other digital media devices. Windows Media Services is the main services component of the Windows Media platform. It is built with the technologies in the Windows Media Format SDK. Windows Media Services is a software service that is included with most versions of the Windows Server 2003 family of operating systems. (For details about the versions, see Operating System Requirements for This Book, in the Introduction.)

About Windows Media Services

A server running Windows Media Services distributes digital media by sending out a stream of encoded packets over a network to users with playback devices (such as Windows Media Player) on their computers. The Player and server communicate with each other through publishing points, which are server reference names used to identify streams from an encoder or folders that contain digital media. The server creates a publishing point, and the Player then makes a network request for the digital media by using the name of the server and the name of the publishing point. When the server receives the request, it streams the media back to the Player so the user can play it.

A Windows Media server can distribute digital media over a network in three ways: on-demand publishing, unicast broadcasting, or multicast broadcasting. On-demand publishing distributes files to each user individually whenever the user requests them. Unicast broadcasting sends a separate copy of a live stream to each user at the same time. Multicast broadcasting is similar to unicast broadcasting, but it sends a single, shared live stream to all users at the same time.

The server also has the ability to create and use server-side playlists. A server-side playlist automates the distribution of digital media by letting you choose the order of files you want to distribute. You can use XML (Extensible Markup Language) to change the order of the files or take other actions in response to events within the server. For example, you could program a server-side playlist to choose between one of two files to broadcast, depending on the identity of the user, the time of day, or the availability of a stream from the encoder.

Windows Media Services includes several additional features. Intelligent Streaming automatically picks the best video size and audio quality to stream, based on the current network conditions. Multiple language tracks allow several different audio language tracks to be included in the same stream, enabling the Player to choose the preferred audio language automatically, or the user to select or change languages during playback. Fast Streaming makes the content stream available to a computer more quickly than before, and if the network connection is broken, the stream will automatically resume when the network returns. The server's unique plug-in architecture allows developers to extend server functionality by writing custom plug-in software that modifies the way that the server does authentication, authorization, event notification, logging, and other server tasks. These additional server features are not covered in this book. For more information, see the Windows Media Services documentation.

Using the Server with Other Components

A Windows Media server can receive digital media packets from the encoder and transfer the packets over a network to users who have Windows Media Player on their computers or other hardware devices. The Player decodes the packets into an audio or video format so users can see and hear the content. These packets are encoded and decoded with Windows Media Format, which provides the transfer compatibility that makes the encoder, server, and Player work together efficiently to deliver the highest quality audio and video.

Using the Server with Windows Media Player

Windows Media Player uses the same Windows Media Format SDK technologies as a server running Windows Media Services. As a result, these two components can work together effectively because the Player already has the codecs it needs to decode the streams from the server. If Windows Media codecs change in the future, the Player can download new codecs automatically.

Using the Server with Windows Media Encoder

Windows Media Encoder and Windows Media Services are both built with the Windows Media Format SDK and are designed to work closely together. The encoder converts files or streams into Windows Media Format and the server uses the same format to distribute the encoded data. The server and encoder also work well together because they use high-speed Windows Media transfer protocols to connect to each other over a network.

The server can receive a stream from an encoder in one of two ways. It can either make a request to pull the stream from the encoder, or it can receive and broadcast a stream from the encoder when the encoder requests the server to do so. In addition to streams from the encoder, the server can use on-demand publishing to deliver files that the encoder previously compressed using Windows Media Format.

> **Note** The server can also stream digital media encoded in formats not created by the encoder, such as MP3, JPEG, and others. Because the focus of this book is on the Windows Media platform, these formats will not be covered. For information about the other file formats the server streams, see Windows Media Services Help.

Understanding the Three Types of Streaming Media

A server running Windows Media Services has the unique ability to distribute audio and video over a network by using one of three different technologies: on-demand publishing, unicast broadcast, and multicast broadcast.

Serving On Demand

The most common way to receive digital media from a server is to request it on demand, rather than to wait for a broadcast. On-demand distribution makes it possible for users to get their audio and video exactly when they want it, and also allows them to fast forward and rewind the media at their convenience. In order to set up a server to distribute media on demand, you must first create a publishing point that has a name that refers to a folder that contains the files that will be streamed. The server links the name of the publishing point to a folder on the server containing media files. The publishing point is then used by the Player to request one or more files from the server. After the server receives the request, it streams the contents of the file to the Player, and the user can listen to each file as soon as the packets of the stream begin arriving. Publishing points can also include server-side playlists, which let the server stream a series of files to the Player. The user can go back and forth between items in the playlist, as well as rewind or fast forward through each item.

As a way to prevent the unauthorized use of copyrighted material, Windows Media on-demand publishing does not allow the file or playlist contents to be saved by the user or copied to another computer. If users want to hear the file again at a later date, they must request the file from the server again. This enables the content owner to determine who receives a file and ensures that the files are not redistributed without the owner's permission.

Figure 1.5 shows how a server uses an on-demand publishing point to process requests from a Player.

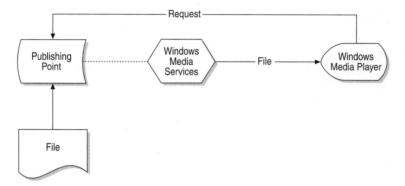

Figure 1.5 Windows Media Services serving on-demand files and streams to Windows Media Player.

Chapter 11 explains concepts that will help you automate the process of setting up a server for on-demand publishing. Chapter 19 provides you with a complete application that uses server-side playlists and on-demand publishing.

Serving Unicast Broadcasts

A unicast broadcast is a continuous stream of digital media packets that is broadcast from a server to a user when the user requests it with the Player. The request is made through a publishing point that the server creates. The publishing point is used to identify the live stream from an encoder or the folder that contains a playlist of files. The server streams the content from the publishing point to each user separately, and all streams from the same publishing point are synchronized. If a Player makes a request for a unicast broadcast after the broadcast has begun, it will not receive the stream from the beginning, but will pick up at the point where the other streams are currently playing.

The main difference between on-demand publishing and a unicast broadcast is that with a unicast broadcast, users do not request a file, they request the contents of the publishing point. When they play the stream on the Player, they cannot rewind or fast forward the stream. But unicasting is similar to on-demand publishing in that users cannot archive the stream to a file, they can only listen to it.

The important advantage of unicast broadcasting is that the server operator has complete control over the timing and content of the stream. Another advantage is that the server doesn't have to process requests from users to fast forward and rewind, reducing server load. The load is further reduced because the server needs to make a copy of the stream in progress only when a new user requests the stream. Unicast broadcasts are more appropriate for broadcasting live events or for prerecorded material that can be looped over and over again.

Figure 1.6 shows how a server processes a unicast broadcast request from a Player.

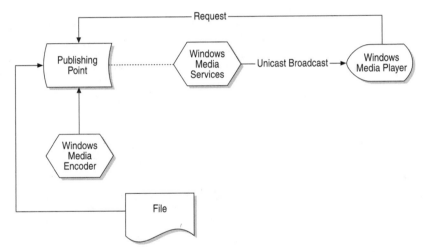

Figure 1.6 Windows Media Services serving a unicast broadcast stream to Windows Media Player.

Chapter 12 explains concepts that will help you automate the process of setting up a server to make a unicast broadcast and send it to the Player.

Serving Multicast Broadcasts

Multicast broadcasts are similar to television and radio in that they distribute the media to the entire audience simultaneously. Each user tunes into the broadcast at a specific time and they cannot rewind or fast forward the stream. Multicasting is the most efficient system for providing information to a large number of people at one time over a corporate intranet.

In order to prepare a multicast, the server must create an announcement file that is posted on a Web site or sent in an e-mail message. Instead of requesting a stream from the server, users download the announcement to the Player. This announcement file configures Windows Media Player to "listen" for the multicast broadcast. When the server sends the packets of the multicast broadcast out over the Internet or a corporate network, a Player that has been configured to receive the multicast will decode the packets and begin playing the content.

To receive a multicast, instead of sending a request to the server's network address, the user sends a request to a multicast address, which is not the address of any particular server, but is chosen from a specific range of network addresses assigned for multicasting. A multicast address is the equivalent of the channel of a TV station. The announcement file tells the Player to "listen" for packets that have a particular multicast address and to play the data from packets with that address.

Figure 1.7 shows how the Player uses server announcement files to receive a multicast.

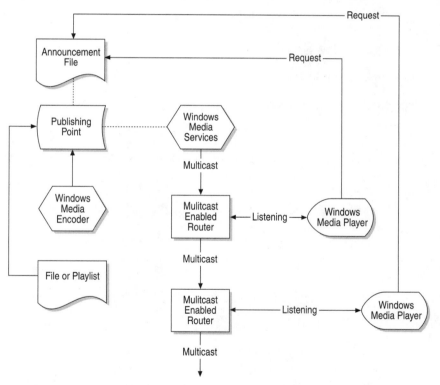

Figure 1.7   Windows Media Services serving a multicast broadcast stream to players.

The advantage of a multicast is that the server has to send out only one set of packets to all the users who want to receive the multicast. The server doesn't process individual requests and can stream a multicast with very little network load. Multicasting is appropriate for media of interest to a large audience because it is sent out to everyone at the same time.

The disadvantage of multicasting is that networks must use hardware routers that are multicast-enabled. Routers relay packets from one network to another. The newer generation of network routers can pass along multicast packets, but older routers often cannot. For this reason and others, multicast packets may not be delivered to all users over the Internet. Multicasting is ideal for a corporate network where all routers can be multicast-enabled. For example, in a large corporation, it might be difficult for a network to handle 20,000 unique simultaneous sessions of a unicast broadcast of the CEO making a speech. But using multicasting would allow every single employee to hear the speech at the same time without slowing down the network.

Chapter 13 explains concepts that will help you automate the process of setting up a server to make a multicast broadcast and notifying the Player to receive it.

Using Playlists on the Server

Playlists are used by the server to stream a series of files to the Player. When the Player requests a server-side playlist from an on-demand publishing point, the server streams the contents of the playlist to the Player. The user can rewind or fast forward from item to item in the playlist, as well as rewind or fast forward within any item. The power of server-side playlists is that they can automate the distribution of files or streams by informing the server what to play next. Playlists use XML to define the order of distribution for the media items, and, through the use of the Document Object Model (DOM), to let the developer change the contents of the playlist. For example, you can start with a sequence of songs in a playlist and, with the push of a button, insert an advertisement that will play after the next song is finished.

You can also use playlists to tailor content for individual users by having them register the genre of music they prefer. Then you can choose items from that genre to stream to an individual user. If your playlist is provided through on-demand publishing, the user can skip any items they want to in the playlist or request a new set of songs in the same or a different genre.

Figure 1.8 shows how a playlist works on the server.

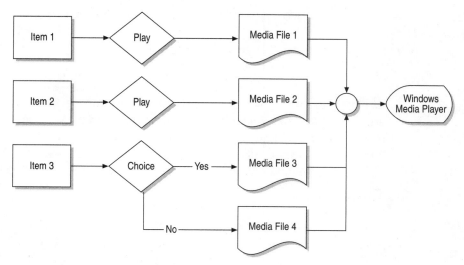

Figure 1.8   How servers use playlists.

Chapter 14 shows you how to automate the sequencing of files distributed from a server by creating a playlist with XML programming code that streams the files to a Player automatically. Chapter 19 provides you with a complete radio station application that uses automation techniques to create server-side playlists that send a stream of media files to the Player.

Understanding Windows Media Player

Windows Media Player is the main end-user component in the playback category of the Windows Media platform. The Player is a software feature of the Windows operating system that is designed to receive digital media from a file or a network stream and then play the audio and video on a user's computer. Windows Media Player is built with the technologies in the Windows Media Format SDK.

About Windows Media Player

Windows Media Player does more than play digital media. You can use it to surf the Web for music and videos, copy music from CDs, receive radio stations from around the world, copy content to a CD or portable device, and organize digital media on your computer. It can also provide visual entertainment with visualizations and skin technology.

Windows Media Player is designed to play files and streams that are encoded with the technologies in the Windows Media Format SDK. Windows Media Encoder creates these files and streams with these same technologies, and Windows Media Services uses those technologies to stream the content to the Player. Because the encoder, server, and Player use the same Windows Media technologies, all three work together faster and more efficiently than ever before.

> **Note**   The Player also can play digital media encoded in formats that are not created by Windows Media Encoder, such as MP3, WAV, and others. Because the focus of this book is on the Windows Media platform, these formats will not be covered. See Windows Media Player Help for information about other file formats that the Player will play.

One of the most powerful features of the Player is that you can add its functionality to your own applications. Instead of writing code to create a new music or video player, you can embed the Player in your own program by using just a few lines of code. In addition, you can add the Player to a Web page to let visitors to your site play digital media over the Internet.

It is also possible to customize the Player user interface. You can use the Player skin programming language to give it a different look, or you can remove parts of the user interface that you don't need and provide new controls that let you do what you want in a more efficient manner. For example, you might want to create a custom Player interface that would allow you to change the network protocol with one click instead of the several clicks it takes to do it with the Full Mode Windows Media Player interface.

If you want to modify the Player to change how it processes streams and files, you can write custom plug-ins that use COM technology to process digital signals, decode and render unique types of data, add new user interface panes to the Full Mode of the Player, and create artistic visualizations. Plug-in programming is not covered in this book; for more information about plug-ins, see the Windows Media Player SDK.

Using Windows Media Player with Other Components

The Player works with the server and encoder to enable users to access and play back digital media content.

Using the Player with Windows Media Encoder

The encoder has the ability to add custom attributes to a stream that the Player can detect and act on. You can control the functions of an individual Player by creating custom user interfaces that process file and stream attributes inserted by the encoder. Chapter 5 explains concepts that will help you to automate the Player by using custom attributes.

It is also possible to program the encoder to add script commands to a stream that will further enable automation of a remote Player by supplying lines of programming code that the Player can process. Chapter 8 provides an application that will show you how to modify the user interface of a Web page by using script commands added by the encoder.

Using the Player with Windows Media Services

The Player sends requests for files and streams to the server, which sends the files or streams to the Player over a network. The Player then plays back those files and streams for the user. Because the Player and server both use the technologies in the Windows Media Format SDK, the streaming and playback of media is of the highest quality and has the greatest efficiency available.

In addition, the server can use playlists to provide customized media streams to individual users. Playlists can be generated through programming to automate the delivery of specific content from server to Player. For example, custom content can be sent to each Player based on region, media preference, or bandwidth.

Customizing the Player

You can use automation principles to simplify the operation of the Player and its user interface. This can be done with Visual Basic, Microsoft JScript in Web pages, or the skin programming language of the Player. Other modifications can be made to enhance the features and artistic content available to the Player.

Customizing the Player with Visual Basic

Windows Media Player provides an ActiveX control that can be used by Windows programming languages, such as Visual Basic, to create custom user interfaces and automate the functions of the Player. ActiveX is a COM technology that lets the programmer include all the functions of one program inside another. This technique is called embedding and lets you design anything from a simple Player with only a few buttons and knobs, to a one with 100 or more controls. For example, you could create a program to keep track of a large collection of video clips, automatically transfer the clips to another computer when your hard disk runs out of space, and automatically show you the last ten video files you've added.

Figure 1.9 shows how Visual Basic uses ActiveX to create a custom version of Windows Media Player.

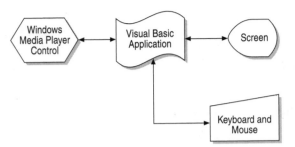

Figure 1.9 Customizing Windows Media Player by using Visual Basic.

Many of the chapters in this book use the principle of ActiveX embedding in order to use the Player as part of an automation application. For example, Chapter 5 demonstrates a way to automatically start the Player when the encoder is finished encoding a file. Chapter 15 gives you a stand-alone Windows application using Visual Basic that creates a simplified user interface for the Player. You can use the same principles to embed the Player in any Windows-based programming language, such as C# or C++, to automate Player functions or create a custom user interface.

Embedding the Player in a Web Page

You can create custom user interfaces for Windows Media Player by embedding it in a Web page. Adding the Player functionality to your Web site allows visitors to play music and video without having to start up the full version of the Player. By using automation programming techniques, you can create custom user interfaces to let visitors select content, to provide them with information on the media they are playing, and to give them links to other sites that will educate them or allow them to make purchases related to the media. Also, by providing audio and video on your Web site, you can attract more visitors and keep them entertained.

Figure 1.10 shows the concept of embedding the Player in a Web page.

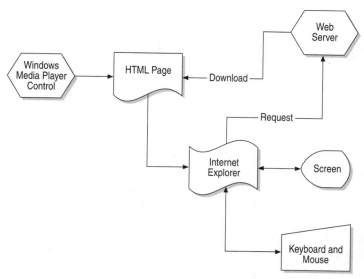

Figure 1.10   Embedding Windows Media Player in a Web page.

Chapter 16 provides an application that embeds the Player in a Web page. Chapter 8 also demonstrates how to use the Player on a Web site to change the design of the Web page by using custom script commands.

Customizing the Player with Skins

Skins are custom user interfaces that provide graphical features for changing the way Windows Media Player looks and operates. You can use skins to develop complex visual designs for the Player interface, completely replacing the original buttons and windows with new artwork. Skins can also be used to automate functions of the Player for custom programming applications. The art for skins can add useful features, not just decorative ones. For example, you could create a skin that displays slides that are synchronized to a lecture, or a skin that sorts the audio and video selections in the Windows Media Player Media Library by using custom attributes. The skin programming language uses XML, Microsoft JScript, and unique art files to make creative designs. The Player comes with several original skins, and there are hundreds of other skins that can be downloaded from the Internet. In addition, the skin technology of Windows Media Player is specifically designed to provide a high degree of security in order to prevent hackers from using a skin to attack your computer.

Figure 1.11 shows how a skin works with the Player.

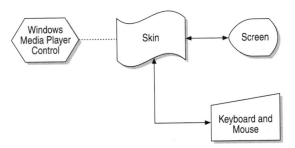

Figure 1.11   Customizing Windows Media Player with skins.

Chapter 17 explains how to use skins to customize the user interface of the Player, and it includes automation programs for modifying the operation of the Player.

Customizing the Player with Additional Techniques

Windows Media Player offers a variety of techniques for customizing and automating its user interface with Windows programming, Web technologies, and skins. You can modify the full user interface of the Player to develop further enhancement and automation possibilities. Three interesting techniques that work with the central video window of the Player, known as the Video and Visualization pane, are banners, embedded Web pages, and borders. These features are discussed in Chapter 18, where three simple applications are provided that you can expand upon.

Using Banners

The standard user interface of the Player provides a hidden pane that can be used to display narrow graphic strips. This hidden pane is called the banner bar and is displayed by a command embedded in a playlist. When the command is encountered, the graphical banner appears in the banner bar. The banner can also show a short text message to the user or provide a link to a Web page. This technique is relatively simple to program, and it can give users more information about a media item or direct them to a Web page.

Using Embedded Web Pages

One of the most interesting automation and customizing techniques for the Player involves embedding a Web page into the Video and Visualization pane. Like the skin techniques mentioned earlier, the Web page is embedded by a command that resides in a playlist. When this command is issued, the Web page is loaded in the Player, allowing the user to surf the Web while listening to music. Because the Player control is now embedded in a Web page that is displayed in the Video and Visualization pane of the Player, you can use all the automation techniques available in a Web page to program the Player control, but work within the context of the Full Mode of the Player. With this technique, it is possible to create a Web portal application that has the Player as the frame for the Web page, allowing a user to surf the Web and simultaneously play music.

Figure 1.12 shows a Player ActiveX control embedded in a Web page that is embedded in the Video and Visualization pane of the Full Mode Player.

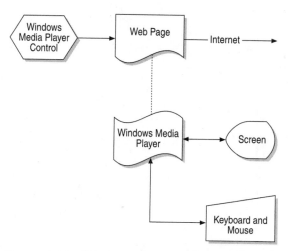

Figure 1.12   Windows Media Player control embedded in a Web page that is embedded in the Full Mode Windows Media Player.

Using Borders

Earlier in this chapter, the Player skin technology was described as a way to customize and automate the user interface of Windows Media Player. Skins can replace the interface completely, but you can also use skin technology inside the original user interface of the Player to add additional automation techniques without losing the buttons and controls that the user is familiar with. When the Video and Visualization pane is replaced with a skin, this technology is called a border. In order to insert the border in the Video and Visualization pane, you must create the artwork for the skin and load it into the Player with a command embedded in a playlist. The end result provides interactive artwork that resides inside the familiar user interface of the Player.

Part II

Encoding Windows Media

Windows Media Encoder makes it possible to convert digital media into a format that can be distributed by a server running Windows Media Services and received by Windows Media Player. This part of the book will cover the programming techniques needed to make the encoder, the server, and the Player work together efficiently. You will be shown how to develop a series of stand-alone sample applications that you can use and expand on in the future to create, distribute, and play streaming digital media. Detailed step-by-step instructions for every line of code will be provided, enabling you to: encode digital media files into Windows Media Format, play those files in the Player, and add text attributes to encoded content for easy media identification. You'll learn the differences between pushing a media stream from encoder to server, and having the server pull content from the encoder. You will also learn how to control the Player remotely by using script commands and, finally, how to set up and encode live audio and video streams for a broadcast. The sample applications in this part of the book include automation techniques that simplify the user interfaces of the Windows Media components and reduce the number of tasks needed to make the components work together.

2

Creating a Simple Encoder

This chapter will give you step-by-step directions on how to create an easy-to-use file encoder that will convert digital media files. The sample application will be called Simple Encoder and it will convert your MP3, WAV, or other digital media files to Windows Media Format.

Introduction to the Simple Encoder Application

Encoding is the process of using a mathematical formula to compress audio and video so it can be converted from one digital media format into another. This makes it possible to adapt media from a variety of sources and transfer them to an even wider variety of end users. The advantage of compressed files is that they take up less space on a hard disk and can be downloaded quickly. Uncompressed files (such as WAV) are larger, but have more faithful and accurate reproduction of sound and images.

This chapter explains how to use the Windows Media encoding process to create compressed digital media files. You'll learn how to convert MP3 files to Windows Media Format, which gives you the highest level of compression while retaining the best sound quality. Windows Media has many levels of compression. Each compression level is defined by a mathematical profile to compress media for different uses, ranging from broadband to the Pocket PC. Windows Media Encoder includes a set of default profiles for various uses. Chapter 8 will show you how to design a custom profile for encoding jobs that don't fit into one of the standard profiles.

To build the Simple Encoder application for this chapter, you will use Visual Basic to create a form, place controls on it, and add code to perform the programming tasks. When you are finished with this chapter, you should copy the Visual Basic project and form to another folder, because you will use parts of that form to create the application in Chapter 3.

After you have completed the Simple Encoder application, it will be able to perform the following tasks:

- Let the operator choose the source media file for encoding into Windows Media Format. A default file path and name will be provided. The encoder can convert files with the following extensions: .wav, .avi, and .mp3, as well as standard Windows Media formats such as .wma, .wmv, and .asf.

- Let the operator choose the path and name of the destination media file that will be created by the encoding process. A default path and file name will be provided. A standard Windows Media file name extension should be used, such as .wma for audio or .wmv for video.

- Let the operator select an encoding profile from a list. Any profile can be chosen from the profiles that are already loaded into the encoder.

- After choosing file names and a profile, let the operator click a button to start the encoding process. The data in the chosen source file will then be converted to raw data and encoded into Windows Media Format as specified by the chosen profile.

- During and after encoding, display the status of the encoding process.

Setting Up Your Programming Environment

Before you begin programming, be sure you have installed the following software and configured it properly.

Installing the Required Software

The following software must be installed on your computer before you can develop the Simple Encoder example application:

- Windows Server 2003, Standard Edition; Windows Server 2003, Enterprise Edition; or Windows Server 2003, Datacenter Edition. Windows Media Services is a component of all three versions. (The example application in this chapter does not require the server functionality, but using this operating system here enables you to use the same operating system for all example applications in this book.)

- Windows Media Encoder 9 Series. You can install the encoder from the companion CD.

- Microsoft Visual Basic 6.0.

> **Note**   You should go to the Windows Update Web site and download any updates available for the required software.

Configuring Visual Basic

To configure Visual Basic for the Simple Encoder application:

1. Start Visual Basic and create a new programming project by selecting New Project from the File menu and selecting the Standard EXE option. Click OK.

2. Add a reference to a COM object that contains the Windows Media Encoder functionality. Add the reference by selecting References from the Project menu and scrolling down to Windows Media Encoder. Select the encoder check box and click OK.

Creating a Visual Basic Form for the Simple Encoder Application

When Visual Basic loads a new project, a blank form is provided. You will need to modify the form to create the Simple Encoder example application. First, you need to add user interface controls to the form, and then add programming code for the form and each of the controls.

To create the Simple Encoder user interface, add the following five controls to the blank form:

- **ProfileComboBox**   Create a ComboBox control and name it Profile-ComboBox. It will hold all the default encoder profiles. Add a Label control nearby to identify the profile combo box.

- **MySourcePath**   Create a TextBox control and name it MySourcePath. It will hold the path to the file that is to be encoded. The operator can enter a new source path in this control. Add a Label control nearby to identify the source-path control.

- **MyDestinationPath**   Create a TextBox control and name it MyDestinationPath. It will hold the path to the new file that is created in the encoding process. The operator can enter a new destination path in this control. Add a Label control nearby to identify the destination-path control.

- **StartEncoder**   Create a CommandButton control and name it StartEncoder. Then set the caption property to "Start Encoding". This button will be used to start the encoding process.

■   **MyState**   Create a Label control and name it MyState. It will display the current status of the encoder.

Note   Add captions to the controls and add labels near the controls to help you remember what each control does. The examples in this book avoid extra labels to keep the coding simple, and they set caption and text properties in the code itself unless the values are arbitrary and can be set to any value you want.

When you have added the controls, resize the form and the controls so that the form is easy to read and understand. Figure 2.1 shows the Simple Encoder form with the new controls on it.

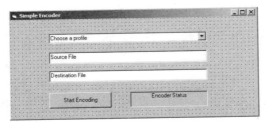

Figure 2.1   Simple Encoder form with controls.

Designing the Code for the Simple Encoder Application

The code for the Simple Encoder application needs to perform the following tasks:

1.   Let the operator select a profile.

2.   Let the operator select a file to be encoded. A default path and file name are provided.

3.   Let the operator select where the newly encoded file will be created. A default path and file name are provided.

4.   Start the encoding process. If the operator has not selected a profile, the encoding will not start, and a message will be displayed, asking the operator to select a profile first.

5.   Display the status of the encoding process.

Adding the Code

The code for the Simple Encoder application is divided into these four blocks, which are discussed in the sections that follow:

- **General declarations**   Variables that can be used in any procedure need to be declared in this block. Variables defined inside a procedure are not available in another procedure.

- **Form_Load procedure**   This is code that runs when the application starts. After this code has been executed, the application is ready for operator input.

- **StartEncoder_Click procedure**   This is code that runs when the operator clicks the Start Encoding button to start the encoding process.

- **MyEncoder_OnStateChange procedure**   This is code that runs whenever the state of Windows Media Encoder changes. This code displays the current state of the encoder so that the operator knows when encoding has begun and when it is finished.

Adding the General Declarations Code

The declarations are part of the general code object, and are accessible from any procedure in the form module. The declarations are inserted at the beginning of the form module, ahead of any procedures.

Declaring the Encoder Objects

Add the following lines to declare the necessary Windows Media Encoder objects. Each line declares a particular encoder object that will be used in a separate procedure.

```
Dim WithEvents MyEncoder As WMEncoder
Dim MyProColl As IWMEncProfileCollection
Dim MySrcGrpColl As IWMEncSourceGroupCollection
Dim MySrcGrp As IWMEncSourceGroup
Dim MyAudioSource As IWMEncSource
Dim MyFile As IWMEncFile
```

The *WMEncoder* object uses the ***WithEvents*** modifier to enable trapping encoder events. By using encoder events, the program can display the status of the encoder during the encoding process.

The following Windows Media Encoder objects are used in this program:

- **WMEncoder object**   This object, named MyEncoder in this program, is the primary encoder object. All other encoder objects are referenced through this central object.

■ **IWMEncProfileCollection object**   This object, named MyProColl, is a collection of profiles that the encoder uses to determine which codec and bit rate will be used for encoding. The operator will choose a profile from this collection.

> **Note**   This chapter and several of the following chapters use the profile collection object, which is maintained for compatibility with previous versions of Windows Media Encoder. For information on other ways to use profiles, see the appendix.

■ **IWMEncSourceGroupCollection object**   This object, named MySrcGrpColl, is a collection of source groups. A source group is a synchronized collection of sources that includes a combination of audio, video, HTML, and script sources, but no more than one of each type. (A typical source group would include one audio and one video source.) You must first create a source-group collection, then add a source group to it, and finally, add a source to a group in the collection.

■ **IWMEncSourceGroup object**   This object, named MySrcGrp, is the source group that will contain the source for your encoding. A source group must be part of a source-group collection.

■ **IWMEncSource object**   This source object, named MyAudioSource, defines where the information to be encoded is coming from. This application will use an audio file as a source. Sources must be part of a source group, and source groups must be part of a source-group collection.

■ **IWMEncFile object**   This file object, named MyFile, defines the path and file name of the output file to be created.

See the Windows Media Encoder SDK for more information about the object model of Windows Media Encoder.

> **Note**   Be sure that you have added Windows Media Encoder as a reference when you set up the project for this application. If you don't, the objects will not be defined. For more information, see the section earlier in this chapter called "Setting Up Your Programming Environment."

Declaring Other Variables

After the code lines that declare the encoder objects, add the following line to declare a variable.

```
Dim DummyText As String
```

The DummyText variable has two uses:

- It will contain the string that is used to tell the operator to select a profile.

- This string will later be used to check whether the operator has selected a profile.

Adding the Form_Load Code

The Form_Load procedure runs every time the form is loaded. The following tasks are performed in this procedure and discussed in the sections that follow this list:

1. Create a Windows Media Encoder object.

2. Create an encoder profile collection and fill a combo box with all the items in the collection. This lets the operator select a profile for encoding.

3. Create an audio source. To do this, you must first create an audio source group collection and an audio source group. The source will be a file, and the path to the file will be defined in a text box so that the operator can modify the input path before encoding.

4. Create a file path for the output. The file path will be defined in a text box so that the operator can modify the output path before encoding.

5. Create a default text message for the combo box that contains the source profiles (ProfileComboBox). This message will be stored in the global variable DummyText. Later, the program can determine whether the operator has chosen a profile by checking whether the default text has changed.

All the Form_Load code must be inserted in the following procedure, which is automatically created in the code module when you double-click the form.

```
Private Sub Form_Load()

End Sub
```

Creating the Encoder Object

To create the encoder object, add the following line of code as the first line inside the empty Form_Load procedure.

```
Set MyEncoder = New WMEncoder
```

In the declarations section, the encoder object variable was declared, but the object doesn't exist until you create it with the ***New*** command and assign the new object to the previously defined variable name. This two-step process of first declaring an object and then creating it is required in Visual Basic for using any COM objects.

Filling the ComboBox with All Profiles

Next add the following code lines to the procedure to create the encoding profiles and put them into the ProfileComboBox.

```
Dim i As Integer
Set MyProColl = MyEncoder.ProfileCollection
For i = 0 To (MyProColl.Count - 1)
  ProfileComboBox.AddItem MyProColl.Item(i).Name, i
Next i
```

As with all COM objects, you must first define the object in the declarations section with a ***Dim*** statement and then create the object when you are ready to use it. All profiles are stored in the encoder profile collection. Using a simple ***For...Next*** loop, you can go through each item in the profile collection and add its name to the combo box. The index of the first item in the profile collection is 0, making it necessary to subtract 1 from the *Count* property to be sure that the loop copies all the profiles to the combo box.

> **Note**   This code will fill the combo box with all the profiles that are installed on your computer. Some of these profiles may not be appropriate for specific media types. For example, if the operator chooses an audio profile for video media, an error will occur. For information on other ways to use profiles, see the appendix.

Creating the Audio Source

Add the following code lines to the procedure to create the audio source.

```
Set MySrcGrpColl = MyEncoder.SourceGroupCollection
Set MySrcGrp = MySrcGrpColl.Add("MY_SOURCE_GROUP")
Set MyAudioSource = MySrcGrp.AddSource(WMENC_AUDIO)
MySourcePath.Text = "C:\media\laure02.mp3"
```

Because the encoder can choose from many sources of audio and video, you must first create a source-group collection, add a source group to it, and finally add a source to the source group. In this example, the single source is an audio source (MyAudioSource), and it belongs to one source group (MySrcGrp), which in turn belongs to one source-group collection (MySrcGrpColl). The source group is defined by the WMENC_AUDIO constant to be an audio source. The name of the source group is arbitrary and is not used for anything in this simple application, but you must give the group a name.

You assign the default source-file path C:\media\laure02.mp3 to the *text* property of the MySourcePath text box. This is the location of the MP3 file that will be converted.

> **Note**   The file laure02.mp3 is on the companion CD. Copy it to your hard disk in a folder named media on the C drive. If you use any other file name or file path, be sure to change the code appropriately when defining the default path and file name for the audio source.

Adding the Output Path

Add the following lines to the Form_Load procedure to create the output path.

```
Set MyFile = MyEncoder.File
MyDestinationPath.Text = "C:\media\laure02.wma"
```

The first line creates an encoder file object from the encoder *File* property. The file name and path won't be determined until the *LocalFileName* property is used in the StartEncoder_Click procedure.

The second line puts the output file path into a text box for later use. The output file will be created as a WMA file using the encoding profile that the operator selects.

Adding a Default Text Message.

Next add the following lines to create a default text message for the profile combo box.

```
DummyText = "Choose a profile first."
ProfileComboBox.Text = DummyText
```

The DummyText variable has two uses: the first is to set the default text for the profile combo box, reminding the operator to choose a profile; the second use will be to check later whether the operator did choose a profile.

Adding the StartEncoder_Click Code

After the global variables have been declared and the Form_Load procedure has been executed, the application is ready for operator input. The operator can change the source and destination paths by typing new values in the text boxes. When ready to encode, the operator clicks the button. The following tasks are performed in the StartEncoder_Click procedure:

1. Pass the source and destination file paths to the encoder, based on the values in the source and destination text boxes.

2. Get the profile name that was chosen by the operator. If the operator did not choose a profile, display a message box asking the operator to choose a profile, and do not start encoding.

3. If the operator did choose a profile, check the profile name against the profile collection and pass the appropriate profile object to the encoder.

4. Start the encoder.

All the code for these tasks must be inserted in the following StartEncoder_Click procedure, which is automatically created in the code editor when you double-click the button on the form.

```
Private Sub StartEncoder_Click()

End Sub
```

Passing the Source and Destination Paths to the Encoder
First, add the following code lines as the first lines in the StartEncoder_Click procedure. They set up the source and destination paths.

```
MyAudioSource.SetInput (MySourcePath.Text)
MyFile.LocalFileName = MyDestinationPath.Text
```

The first line uses the *SetInput* method to obtain the path to the audio source from the MySourcePath text box. The second line sets the *LocalFileName* property to the path for the file output.

Getting the Profile Name
Next add the following lines to the procedure to get the profile name.

```
Dim MyProfileName As String
MyProfileName = ProfileComboBox.Text
If MyProfileName = DummyText Then
    MsgBox ("Please enter a profile before encoding.")
    Exit Sub
End If
```

The first two lines get the profile name from the combo box. Then the name is checked to determine whether it matches the default text that was set in the Form_Load procedure. If it does, then the operator has not chosen a profile. A message is displayed asking the operator to choose a profile, and the StartEncoder_Click procedure is exited.

Giving the Profile Name to the Encoder

Now add the following lines to the StartEncoder_Click procedure to give the profile name to the encoder.

```
Dim i As Integer
Dim MyProfile As IWMEncProfile
For i = 0 To (MyProColl.Count - 1)
    If MyProColl.Item(i).Name = MyProfileName Then
        Set MyProfile = MyProColl.Item(i)
        MySrcGrp.Profile = MyProfile
        Exit For
    End If
Next i
```

These lines set up a *For...Next* loop that will go through the profile collection looking for a match to the profile name that was chosen. The number of profiles is obtained from the *Count* property of the profile collection and 1 is subtracted because the profile-collection index is zero-based. Each time through the loop, a profile name is checked to determine whether it matches the one that was selected by the operator. If the name matches, three things happen: the profile that matches the name is assigned to a profile object, the object is passed to the source group as the working profile, and the *For...Next* loop is exited without checking any more profiles.

Starting the Encoder

Add the following line to start Windows Media Encoder.

```
MyEncoder.Start
```

Now that the encoder has the profile, source, and destination, this line will start the encoder.

Displaying the Encoder State

It is very important to give the operator feedback on the state of Windows Media Encoder. Without feedback, the operator won't know whether the encoding has started or whether it is finished. A simple label can be used to display the state of the encoder.

Add the following procedure to display the state of the encoder. You can have Visual Basic add it or you can add the lines by hand. If you want to use Visual Basic, select MyEncoder from the object list in the code editor and then select OnStateChange from the procedure list.

The following lines should now be added to the module.

```
Private Sub MyEncoder_OnStateChange(ByVal enumState As _
    WMEncoderLib.WMENC_ENCODER_STATE)


End Sub
```

Next add the following lines inside the empty procedure to display the encoder state.

```
Select Case enumState
    Case WMENC_ENCODER_RUNNING
        MyState.Caption = "Running"
    Case WMENC_ENCODER_STOPPED
        MyState.Caption = "Stopped"
End Select
```

This procedure will work only if you declared the encoder object using the ***With-Events*** keyword. This sets up a procedure that handles the encoder *StateChange* event. This procedure will be called only when the state of the encoder changes and the encoder raises a *StateChange* event.

The first line sets up the event procedure to listen for the *StateChange* event. The variable enumState is created to pass the value of the state to the procedure. The enumState variable contains a number that defines the current state of the encoder. The encoder states are defined by the WMENC_ENCODER_STATE enumeration as defined in the Windows Media Encoder SDK. The following values of the encoder state will be used by this procedure to display the two most useful encoder states for this chapter. The state names and their values are:

```
WMENC_ENCODER_RUNNING = 2
WMENC_ENCODER_STOPPED = 5
```

The event handler evaluates the enumState argument in a ***Select Case*** structure. If enumState matches one of the enumerated values, a related value is assigned to the caption of the MyState label.

Running the Simple Encoder Application

After you have entered all the code, run the project in Visual Basic. From the Run menu, select Start. If there are no errors, the user interface of your application should look like Figure 2.2. You can compare your code to the complete code listing in the next section.

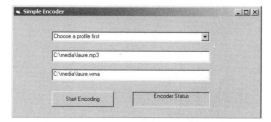

Figure 2.2   Simple Encoder user interface.

Use the following procedure to test the Simple Encoder application:

1. Choose an encoding profile.

2. Change the default paths to valid source and destination files, if desired.

3. Click the Start Encoding button when you are ready to encode. You should observe the status of the encoding process. It should display "Running" when you click the button and then display "Stopped" when the encoding process is complete.

4. After you have encoded the file, you can find out how it sounds by playing it in Windows Media Player. Open the folder you saved the file to, right-click the newly encoded file, and select Play to play it.

> **Note** To test this application, you need to copy a suitable digital media file to your hard disk and place it in a location that can be pointed to by the source file path. Suitable media files (such as MP3) are included on the companion CD.

Complete copies of the source code and digital media for the Simple Encoder application are on the companion CD.

Source Code for the Simple Encoder Application

Here is the complete source code listing for the Simple Encoder application.

```
Dim WithEvents MyEncoder As WMEncoder
Dim MyProColl As IWMEncProfileCollection
Dim MySrcGrpColl As IWMEncSourceGroupCollection
Dim MySrcGrp As IWMEncSourceGroup
Dim MyAudioSource As IWMEncSource
Dim MyFile As IWMEncFile
Dim DummyText As String

Private Sub Form_Load()
    Set MyEncoder = New WMEncoder

    Dim i As Integer
    Set MyProColl = MyEncoder.ProfileCollection
    For i = 0 To (aMyProColl.Count - 1)
      ProfileComboBox.AddItem MyProColl.Item(i).Name, i
    Next i
```

```
        Set MySrcGrpColl = MyEncoder.SourceGroupCollection
        Set MySrcGrp = MySrcGrpColl.Add("SG_1")
        Set MyAudioSource = MySrcGrp.AddSource(WMENC_AUDIO)
        MySourcePath.Text = "C:\media\laure02.mp3"

        Set MyFile = MyEncoder.File
        MyDestinationPath.Text = "C:\media\laure02.wma"

        DummyText = "Choose a profile first."
        ProfileComboBox.Text = DummyText
    End Sub

    Private Sub StartEncoder_Click()
        MyAudioSource.SetInput (MySourcePath.Text)
        MyFile.LocalFileName = MyDestinationPath.Text

        Dim MyProfileName As String
        MyProfileName = ProfileComboBox.Text
        If MyProfileName = DummyText Then
            MsgBox ("Please enter a profile before encoding.")
            Exit Sub
        End If

        Dim i As Integer
        Dim MyProfile as IWMEncProfile
        For i = 0 To (MyProColl.Count - 1)
            If MyProColl.Item(i).Name = MyProfileName Then
                Set MyProfile = MyProColl.Item(i)
                MySrcGrp.Profile = MyProfile
                Exit For
            End If
        Next i

        MyEncoder.Start

    End Sub

    Private Sub MyEncoder_OnStateChange(ByVal enumState As _
            WMEncoderLib.WMENC_ENCODER_STATE)

        Select Case enumState
            Case WMENC_ENCODER_RUNNING
                MyState.Caption = "Running"
            Case WMENC_ENCODER_STOPPED
                MyState.Caption = "Stopped"
        End Select
    End Sub
```

3

Playing an Encoded File

This chapter will show you how to add Windows Media Player to the simple file encoder you developed in Chapter 2. The new application is called File Player and it will let you encode files and play them as soon as they have been encoded.

Introduction to the File Player Application

When a file has been encoded into a digital media format, it needs special software to play the audio and video contained in the file. A player is a specific type of software that can read the data encoded in the digital media file and decode it into audio and video. After the audio and video are decoded, the player will route the data to the speakers and video display hardware on your computer.

This chapter shows how to use Windows Media Player to play the files you created with the Simple Encoder application from Chapter 2. You'll be shown how to take the simple encoding application you've already created and put Windows Media Player inside your application so that you can conveniently play a newly encoded file by clicking a single button on your application. The process of putting one program inside another is called *embedding*. By embedding the Player, you make it easier for the operator because the Player runs automatically and you save all the steps it would take to run it manually. Embedding not only can save the operator some steps, it can provide additional feedback to your program on how the embedded software is running.

To build the File Player application for this chapter, you will use a copy of the Visual Basic form you created in Chapter 2 and add new controls and code to perform the additional programming tasks required. When you have completed the File Player application, copy the Visual Basic project and form to another folder, because you will use parts of that form to create the applications in Chapters 4 and 5.

The File Player application will perform the following tasks:

■ Let the operator choose the source media file for encoding into Windows Media Format. A default file path and name will be provided. The encoder can convert files with the following extensions: .wav, .avi, and .mp3, as well as standard Windows Media formats such as .wma, .wmv, and .asf.

■ Let the operator choose the path and name for the destination media file that will be created by the encoding process. A default path and file name will be provided. Use a standard Windows Media file name extension: .wma for audio or .wmv for video.

■ Let the operator select an encoding profile from a list. Any profile can be chosen from the profiles that are already loaded into the encoder.

■ After choosing file names and a profile, the operator can click a button to start the encoding process. The data in the chosen source file will then be converted to raw data and encoded into Windows Media Format as specified by the chosen profile.

■ When the encoding is finished, let the operator click a button to play the file that was encoded.

■ After the Player starts playing the file, display the bit rate of the encoded file. The operator can check it against the bit rate of the profile that was used for encoding. One of the advantages of having the Player be part of your application is that you can encode files with profiles having different bit rates and see the results instantly.

Setting Up Your Programming Environment

Before you begin programming, be sure you have installed the following software and configured it properly.

Installing the Required Software

The following software must be installed on your computer before you can develop the File Player example application. If you created the Simple Encoder application in Chapter 2, all of these should be installed already:

■ Windows Server 2003, Standard Edition; Windows Server 2003, Enterprise Edition; or Windows Server 2003, Datacenter Edition. Windows Media Services is a component of all three versions. (The example application in this chapter does not require the server functionality, but using this operating system here enables you to use the same operating system for all example applications in this book.)

- Windows Media Encoder 9 Series. You can install the encoder from the companion CD.

- Windows Media Player 9 Series, if it is not already installed.

- Microsoft Visual Basic 6.0.

> **Note** You should go to the Windows Update Web site and download any updates available for the required software.

Configuring Visual Basic

To configure Visual Basic for the File Player application, follow these steps. The first two are the same as for the Simple Encoder application in Chapter 2.

1. Start Visual Basic and create a new programming project by selecting New Project from the File menu and selecting the Standard EXE option. Click OK.

2. Add a reference to a COM object that contains the Windows Media Encoder functionality. Add the reference by selecting References from the Project menu and scrolling down to Windows Media Encoder. Select the encoder check box and click OK.

3. Add the Windows Media Player ActiveX control to the Visual Basic toolbox. Add the Player control by selecting Components from the Project menu and then selecting the Windows Media Player check box. After you click OK in the Components dialog box, the Windows Media Player icon is displayed in the toolbox.

Creating a Visual Basic Form for the File Player Application

In this chapter, you will build on the form that was created in Chapter 2 for the Simple Encoder application.

Using the Simple Encoder Form from Chapter 2

You can start by making a copy of the form that was created in Chapter 2. That form contains the following five controls:

- **ProfileComboBox** A ComboBox control named ProfileComboBox. It holds all the default encoding profiles.

- **MySourcePath**   A TextBox control named MySourcePath. It holds the path to the file that is to be encoded. The user can enter a new source path in this control.

- **MyDestinationPath**   A TextBox control named MyDestinationPath. It holds the path to the new file that is created in the encoding process. The user can enter a new destination path in this box.

- **StartEncoder**   A CommandButton control named StartEncoder. This button is used to start the encoding process and has a caption of "Start Encoding".

- **MyState**   A Label control named MyState. It displays the current status of the encoder.

Figure 3.1 shows the Simple Encoder form created in Chapter 2.

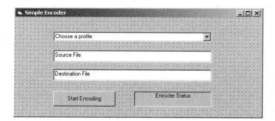

Figure 3.1   Simple Encoder form from Chapter 2.

Adding New Controls to the Form

First, resize the form to make room for the new controls. Click and drag the bottom of the form to make the form approximately twice as tall as it was before. Then add the following four controls:

- **PlayPlayer**   A CommandButton control named PlayPlayer. Give it a caption of "Play Player". It makes Windows Media Player start playing. The button-click procedure checks whether Windows Media Encoder has finished encoding; if it has not finished, the Player will not be allowed to play.

- **StopPlayer**   A CommandButton control named StopPlayer. Give it a caption of "Stop Player".

- **BitRate**   A Label control named BitRate. It displays the bit rate of the encoded file. The bit-rate data will be supplied by the Player.

■   **Player**   A WindowsMediaPlayer ActiveX control named Player. It displays the default visualization of the audio file that is playing. This will give the user a visual cue that the file is playing.

> **Note**   Add captions to the controls and add labels near the controls to help you remember what each control does. The examples in this book avoid extra labels to keep the coding simple, and they set caption and text properties in the code itself unless the values are arbitrary and can be set to any value you want.

Figure 3.2 shows the File Player form with the new controls on it.

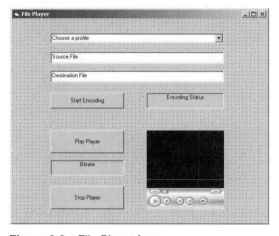

Figure 3.2   File Player form.

Designing the Code for the File Player Application

The code for the File Player application begins with the same form and code that was used by the Simple Encoder application in Chapter 2. The code for the Simple Encoder lets the user select a profile, change default paths to the source and destination files, and start the encoding process. The code also verifies that the user selected a profile, and, after the encoding starts, displays the progress of the encoding.

In the File Player application, new code must be added to perform the following additional tasks:

1. Check whether the encoding process is finished.

2. Give the URL of the newly encoded file to Windows Media Player.

3. Display the bit rate of the newly encoded file, as determined by Windows Media Player. This is a good reality check to verify that the encoding worked properly. You can also listen to the file to be sure that it sounds right.

4. Let users stop Windows Media Player if they don't want to play a whole file.

Adding the Code

The Simple Encoder application in Chapter 2 included the following four Visual Basic code blocks:

■   General declarations

■   Form_Load procedure

■   StartEncoder_Click procedure

■   MyEncoder_OnStateChange procedure

The File Player application will add the following two new procedures:

■   **PlayPlayer_Click procedure**   This is code that runs when the user clicks the play button. The code will first check to determine whether the encoding is finished. Then it will start Windows Media Player playing the newly encoded file and display the bit rate of the encoded file.

■   **StopPlayer_Click procedure**   This is code that runs when the user clicks the Stop Player button.

Reusing the Simple Encoder Application Code

Here is the code that will be reused from the Simple Encoder application in Chapter 2.

```
Dim WithEvents MyEncoder As WMEncoder
Dim MyProColl As IWMEncProfileCollection
Dim MySrcGrpColl As IWMEncSourceGroupCollection
Dim MySrcGrp As IWMEncSourceGroup
Dim MyAudioSource As IWMEncSource
Dim MyFile As IWMEncFile
Dim DummyText As String
```

```
Private Sub Form_Load()
    Set MyEncoder = New WMEncoder

    Dim i As Integer
    Set MyProColl = MyEncoder.ProfileCollection
    For i = 0 To (MyProColl.Count - 1)
      ProfileComboBox.AddItem MyProColl.Item(i).Name, i
    Next i

    Set MySrcGrpColl = MyEncoder.SourceGroupCollection
    Set MySrcGrp = MySrcGrpColl.Add("SG_1")
    Set MyAudioSource = MySrcGrp.AddSource(WMENC_AUDIO)
    MySourcePath.Text = "C:\media\laure02.mp3"

    Set MyFile = MyEncoder.File
    MyDestinationPath.Text = "C:\media\laurelaure02.wma"

    DummyText = "Choose a profile first."
    ProfileComboBox.Text = DummyText
End Sub

Private Sub StartEncoder_Click()
    MyAudioSource.SetInput (MySourcePath.Text)
    MyFile.LocalFileName = MyDestinationPath.Text

    Dim MyProfileName As String
    MyProfileName = ProfileComboBox.Text
    If MyProfileName = DummyText Then
        MsgBox ("Please enter a profile before encoding.")
        Exit Sub
    End If

    Dim i As Integer
    Dim MyProfile as IWMEncProfile
    For i = 0 To (MyProColl.Count - 1)
        If MyProColl.Item(i).Name = MyProfileName Then
            Set MyProfile = MyProColl.Item(i)
            MySrcGrp.Profile = MyProfile
            Exit For
        End If
    Next i

    MyEncoder.Start
End Sub

Private Sub MyEncoder_OnStateChange(ByVal enumState _
            As WMEncoderLib.WMENC_ENCODER_STATE)
```

(continued)

```
Select Case enumState
    Case WMENC_ENCODER_RUNNING
        MyState.Caption = "Running"
    Case WMENC_ENCODER_STOPPED
        MyState.Caption = "Stopped"
End Select
End Sub
```

Modifying the Simple Encoder Application Code

Several lines need to be added, removed, or modified to the original code to add the Player functionality to the File Player application.

Changing the Form_Load Code

Add the following line at the end of the Form_Load procedure, before the ***End Sub*** line.

```
Player.uiMode = "none"
```

This line changes the display mode of the Windows Media Player control on the form. If you do not add this line, the transport controls will be displayed below the video area, and you want to control the Player through programming, not operator input.

Next find the following two lines in the Form_Load procedure.

```
MySourcePath.Text = "C:\media\laure02.mp3"
MyDestinationPath.Text = "C:\media\laure02.wma"
```

Change them to read:

```
MySourcePath.Text = "C:\media\laure03.mp3"
MyDestinationPath.Text = "C:\media\laure03.wma"
```

Every chapter will use different media files.

> **Note**   Using a different media file for each chapter will avoid the confusion that could occur if the same file were used for different purposes in different chapters. For example, if you used the same digital media file in this chapter that you did in the last, and you had already encoded the file in the last chapter, the file would already be encoded before you ran the application from this chapter. Using different media for each chapter will be most important when working with Windows Media Services because you will want to verify that the server is streaming the correct media.

Adding the PlayPlayer_Click Code

The PlayPlayer_Click procedure must perform the following tasks:

1. Check to be sure the encoding has finished.

2. If the encoding has finished, start the Windows Media Player control by passing the file path to the Player and then displaying the bit rate by passing it from the Player to the Label control.

3. If the encoding has not finished, display a message box and do not play the file.

The code to start the Player must be inserted in the following procedure, which is automatically created in the code module when the button is double-clicked on the form.

```
Private Sub PlayPlayer_Click()

End Sub
```

Checking the Encoding Process

Add the following lines inside the PlayPlayer_Click procedure to check the status of Windows Media Encoder.

```
If MyState.Caption = "Stopped" Then

Else
    MsgBox "Please encode a file before playing it."
End If
```

The first line sets up an *If* statement to test whether the encoding process has stopped. It does this by checking the *Caption* property of the MyState label, which contains the current status of the encoder.

If the state is anything but Stopped, a message box is displayed. The remaining four lines in this procedure will be placed between the following two lines.

```
If MyState.Caption = "Stopped" Then

Else
```

Starting the Player

Add this line, just before the *Else*, to make the Player start playing.

```
Player.URL = MyDestinationPath.Text
```

This gets the path to the file that was created by the encoding process and passes it to the Player through the *URL* property.

Getting the Bit Rate

Add the following lines next, to get the bit rate of the file that is playing.

```
Dim AC As Integer
Dim MyRate As Long
AC = Player.currentMedia.getAttributeCountByType("Bitrate", "") - 1
MyRate = Player.currentMedia.getItemInfoByType("Bitrate", "", AC)
BitRate.Caption = "Bit rate = " & CStr(MyRate) & " bits/second"
```

The first line after the two declarations gets the number of attributes that are named *Bitrate*. The best way to get attribute information is to first find out how many attributes have the same name as the one that you want to find. This is the purpose of the *getAttributeCountByType* method. For some kinds of attributes, the answer may be more than 1, and you have to pick the attribute you want. In this case, the answer is 1 because there should be only one *Bitrate* attribute. Note that 1 is subtracted at the end of the line to prepare the answer for the next line.

The next line gets the actual bit rate by using the *getItemInfoByType* method. Using the variable you created in the first line, you can finally obtain the correct bit rate. While this might seem complicated, this procedure allows you to deal with media that may have very complex kinds of attributes.

The last line assigns the bit rate to the caption of the BitRate label by taking the results of the first two lines and adding some extra text before and after to clarify that the rate is in bits instead of kilobits. For more information about using attributes in the Player, see the Windows Media Player SDK.

Adding the StopPlayer_Click Code

This code stops the playing of a file. The code must be inserted in the following procedure, which is automatically created in the code module when the button is double-clicked on the form.

```
Private Sub StopPlayer_Click()

End Sub
```

Add the following line inside the procedure to stop the Player when this procedure is called.

```
Player.Controls.Stop
```

The complete procedure should look like the following three lines.

```
Private Sub StopPlayer_Click()
    Player.Controls.Stop
End Sub
```

Running the File Player Application

After you have entered all the code, run the project in Visual Basic. From the Run menu, select Start. If there are no errors, the user interface of your application should look like Figure 3.3. You can compare your code to the complete code listing in the next section.

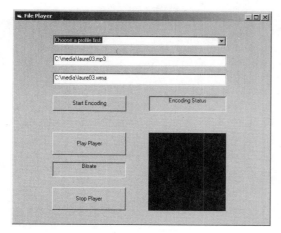

Figure 3.3   File Player user interface.

Use the following procedure to test the File Player application:

1.   Choose an encoding profile.

2.   Change the default paths to valid source and destination files, if desired.

3.   Click the Start Encoding button when you are ready to encode.

4.   When the encoding is finished and the status label is "Stopped", click the play button. You know the Player is playing because:

   ❏   You can hear the sound of the newly created file.

   ❏   You can see the visualization generated by playing the file.

   ❏   You can see the bit rate of the file as determined by the Player.

Note   To test this application, you need to copy a suitable digital media file to your hard disk and place it in a location that can be pointed to by the source file path. Suitable media files (such as MP3) are included on the companion CD.

Complete copies of the source code and digital media for the File Player application are on the companion CD.

Source Code for the File Player Application

Here is the complete source code listing for the File Player application.

```
Dim WithEvents MyEncoder As WMEncoder
Dim MyProColl As IWMEncProfileCollection
Dim MySrcGrpColl As IWMEncSourceGroupCollection
Dim MySrcGrp As IWMEncSourceGroup
Dim MyAudioSource As IWMEncSource
Dim MyFile As IWMEncFile

Dim DummyText As String

Private Sub Form_Load()
    Set MyEncoder = New WMEncoder

    Dim i As Integer
    Set MyProColl = MyEncoder.ProfileCollection
    For i = 0 To (MyProColl.Count - 1)
      ProfileComboBox.AddItem MyProColl.Item(i).Name, i
    Next i

    Set MySrcGrpColl = MyEncoder.SourceGroupCollection
    Set MySrcGrp = MySrcGrpColl.Add("SG_1")
    Set MyAudioSource = MySrcGrp.AddSource(WMENC_AUDIO)
    MySourcePath.Text = "C:\media\laure03.mp3"

    Set MyFile = MyEncoder.File
    MyDestinationPath.Text = "C:\media\laure03.wma"

    DummyText = "Choose a profile first."
    ProfileComboBox.Text = DummyText

    Player.uiMode = "none"
End Sub

Private Sub StartEncoder_Click()
    MyAudioSource.SetInput (MySourcePath.Text)
    MyFile.LocalFileName = MyDestinationPath.Text

    Dim MyProfileName As String
    MyProfileName = ProfileComboBox.Text
    If MyProfileName = DummyText Then
        MsgBox ("Please enter a profile before encoding.")
```

```
            Exit Sub
        End If

        Dim i As Integer
        Dim MyProfile As IWMEncProfile
        For i = 0 To (MyProColl.Count - 1)
            If MyProColl.Item(i).Name = MyProfileName Then
                Set MyProfile = MyProColl.Item(i)
                MySrcGrp.Profile = MyProfile
                Exit For
            End If
        Next i

        MyEncoder.Start
    End Sub

    Private Sub MyEncoder_OnStateChange(ByVal enumState _
                    As WMEncoderLib.WMENC_ENCODER_STATE)
        Select Case enumState
            Case WMENC_ENCODER_RUNNING
                MyState.Caption = "Running"
            Case WMENC_ENCODER_STOPPED
                MyState.Caption = "Stopped"
        End Select
    End Sub

    Private Sub PlayPlayer_Click()
        If MyState.Caption = "Stopped" Then
            Player.URL = MyDestinationPath.Text

            Dim AC As Integer
            Dim MyRate As Long
            AC = Player.currentMedia.getAttributeCountByType _
                            ("Bitrate", "") - 1
            MyRate = Player.currentMedia.getItemInfoByType _
                            ("Bitrate", "", AC)
            BitRate.Caption = "Bitrate = " & CStr(MyRate) & _
                            " bits/second"
        Else
            MsgBox "Please encode a file before playing it."
        End If
    End Sub

    Private Sub StopPlayer_Click()
        Player.Controls.Stop
    End Sub
```

4

Broadcasting to the Player

This chapter will demonstrate how to make Windows Media Encoder broadcast a media stream directly to Windows Media Player. The new application is called Encoder Broadcast and it will enable you to stream encoded media data from the encoder to the Player without creating a file.

Introduction to the Encoder Broadcast Application

When Windows Media Encoder converts and encodes digital media, it can save the newly encoded data to a file, as was shown in Chapters 2 and 3. However, the encoder can also broadcast the encoded data directly to Windows Media Player by using a network connection. Broadcasting directly, without using a file, is called streaming. Using a network to stream encoded media directly to the Player avoids filling up your hard disk with extra files. Plus, it lets you play the media as it is being broadcast. You don't have to wait until the complete file is read into the encoder and is finished being encoded. Another advantage of streaming is that the Player doesn't need the name of the file it is receiving, all it needs is the name of the encoder and the network port that the encoder is using to stream the encoded data.

This chapter will explain how to use Windows Media Encoder to broadcast a digital media file directly to the Player. You'll be shown how to connect the encoder and Player by using standard network technology instead of creating a new file and having the Player read it. In order to do this, the encoder and Player must agree on the networking protocols and addressing. After the networking protocols are set up properly, the Player can send a network request to the encoder to broadcast the encoded media stream.

> **Note**   By default, up to five different players can connect to one encoder and receive a broadcast using an HTTP port. If you want to broadcast to more than five users, it is recommended that you use a server running Windows Media Services to take advantage of the server's greater power and efficiency.

To create the Encoder Broadcast application for this chapter, you will use a copy of the Visual Basic form you created in Chapter 3 and add new controls and code to perform the new programming tasks required. When you are finished, copy the Visual Basic project and form to another folder, because you will need them to create the applications in chapters 6, 8, and 9.

The Encoder Broadcast application will perform the following tasks:

- Let the operator choose the source media file for encoding. A default file path and name will be provided. The encoder can convert files with the following extensions: .wav, .avi, and .mp3, as well as .asf and the standard Windows Media formats, .wma and .wmv.

- Let the operator select an encoding profile from a list. Any profile can be chosen from the profiles that are already loaded into the encoder.

- After choosing a file and profile, let the operator click a button to start the encoding process. The data in the chosen file will then be converted to raw data and encoded into Windows Media Format, as specified by the chosen profile.

- As soon as the encoding process begins, let the operator click a button that tells the Player to request a media stream from the encoder, using the agreed-upon port number.

- After the Player starts playing the file, display the bit rate of the encoded file.

Setting Up Your Programming Environment

Before you begin programming, be sure you have installed the following software and configured it properly.

Installing the Required Software

The following software must be installed on your computer before you can develop the Encoder Broadcast example application. If you created the File Player application in Chapter 3, all of these are installed already:

- Windows Server 2003, Standard Edition; Windows Server 2003, Enterprise Edition; or Windows Server 2003, Datacenter Edition. Windows Media Services is a component of all three versions. (The example application in this chapter does not require the server functionality, but using this operating system here enables you to use the same operating system for all example applications in this book.)

- Windows Media Encoder 9 Series. You can install the encoder from the companion CD.

- Windows Media Player 9 Series, if it is not already installed.

- Microsoft Visual Basic 6.0.

> **Note**   You should go to the Windows Update Web site and download any updates available for the required software.

Configuring Visual Basic

To configure Visual Basic for the Encoder Broadcast application, follow these steps. All three are the same as for the File Player application in Chapter 3.

1. Start Visual Basic and create a new programming project by selecting New Project from the File menu and selecting the Standard EXE option. Click OK.

2. Add a reference to a COM object that contains the Windows Media Encoder functionality. Add the reference by selecting References from the Project menu and scrolling down to Windows Media Encoder. Select the encoder check box and click OK.

3. Add the Windows Media Player ActiveX control to the Visual Basic toolbox. Add the Player control by selecting Components from the Project menu and then selecting the Windows Media Player check box. After you click OK in the Components dialog box, the Windows Media Player icon is displayed in the toolbox.

Creating a Visual Basic Form for the Encoder Broadcast Application

In this chapter, you will build on the form that was created in Chapter 3 for the File Player application. The File Player application uses the encoder to encode a file and play it on Windows Media Player. This chapter uses most of the same form, but modifies it to broadcast the digital media over a network instead of creating a new file.

Using the File Player Form from Chapter 3

You can start by making a copy of the form that was created in Chapter 3. That form contains the following nine controls:

- **ProfileComboBox**   A ComboBox control named ProfileComboBox. It holds all the default encoder profiles.

- **MySourcePath**   A TextBox control named MySourcePath. It holds the path to the file that is to be encoded. The user can enter a new source path in this control.

- **MyDestinationPath**   A TextBox control named MyDestinationPath. It holds the path to the new file that is created in the encoding process. The user can enter a new destination path in this control.

- **StartEncoder**   A CommandButton control named StartEncoder. This button is used to start the encoding process and has a caption of "Start Encoding".

- **MyState**   A Label control named MyState. It displays the current status of the encoder.

- **PlayPlayer**   A CommandButton control named PlayPlayer. It starts Windows Media Player playing and has a caption of "Play Player". The button-click procedure checks whether Windows Media Encoder has finished encoding; if it has not finished, the Player will not play.

- **StopPlayer**   A CommandButton control named StopPlayer. It has a caption of "Stop Player".

- **BitRate**   A Label control named BitRate. It displays the bit rate of the encoded file. The bit-rate data will be supplied by the Player.

- **Player**   A Windows Media Player ActiveX control named Player. It displays the default visualization of the audio file that is playing. This will give the user a visual cue that the file is playing.

Figure 4.1 shows the File Player form created in Chapter 3.

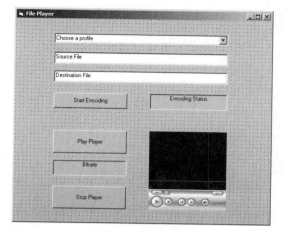

Figure 4.1   File Player form from Chapter 3.

Modifying the Form

Before you can add new controls to the form, you must make room for them. Do the following tasks:

1. Remove the text box named MyDestinationPath. A destination file is not needed because the encoder will not be creating a file, it will be broadcasting the digital media through a network.

2. Move the button that starts the encoding process, StartEncoder, up to where the MyDestinationPath text box was.

3. Move the MyState label to where the StartEncoder button was.

Now you are ready to add the following two new controls to the form:

- **StopEncoder**   A CommandButton control named StopEncoder. It stops Windows Media Encoder. The encoder is broadcasting continuously, and the user may want to stop the broadcast at any point. Give this button a caption of "Stop Encoding" and place it to the right of the StartEncoder button.

- **Address**   A TextBox control named Address. It displays the default network port that the broadcast will use. The user can change this to another port if needed. Place this control below the StopEncoder button.

Figure 4.2 shows the Encoder Broadcast form with the new controls on it.

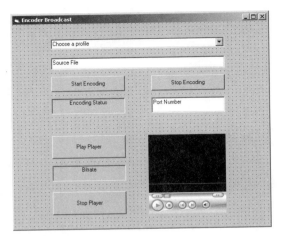

Figure 4.2   Encoder Broadcast form.

Designing the Code for the Encoder Broadcast Application

The code in the Encoder Broadcast application begins with the same form and code that was used by the File Player application in Chapter 3. The File Player code lets the user select a profile, change default paths to the source and destination files, start the encoding process, and then test the newly created file by playing it in Windows Media Player.

In the Encoder Broadcast application, new code must be added to perform the following additional tasks:

1. Broadcast the digital media over a network instead of creating a new file.

2. Let the user choose the HTTP network port that the broadcast will use.

3. Stop the encoding broadcast at any time.

4. Prevent the Player from playing until after the encoding begins. In Chapter 3, the File Player code prevented the Player from playing until the encoding was finished, but the encoding will not finish in this application until the user stops it with a button click. And you don't want the Player trying to play the broadcast before the encoder begins broadcasting.

Adding the Code

The File Player application in Chapter 3 included the following six Visual Basic code blocks:

- General declarations
- Form_Load procedure
- StartEncoder_Click procedure
- MyEncoder_OnStateChange procedure
- PlayPlayer_Click procedure
- StopPlayer_Click procedure

The Encoder Broadcast application will add the following two new code blocks:

- **StopEncoder_Click procedure**   This is code that runs when the user clicks the Stop Encoding button.
- **Player_PlayStateChange procedure**   This is code that is called when the state of the Player changes.

Reusing the File Player Application Code

Here is the code that will be reused from the File Player application in Chapter 3.

```
Dim WithEvents MyEncoder As WMEncoder
Dim MyProColl As IWMEncProfileCollection
Dim MySrcGrpColl As IWMEncSourceGroupCollection
Dim MySrcGrp As IWMEncSourceGroup
Dim MyAudioSource As IWMEncSource
Dim MyFile As IWMEncFile

Dim DummyText As String

Private Sub Form_Load()
    Set MyEncoder = New WMEncoder

    Dim i As Integer
    Set MyProColl = MyEncoder.ProfileCollection
    For i = 0 To (MyProColl.Count - 1)
      ProfileComboBox.AddItem MyProColl.Item(i).Name, i
    Next i

    Set MySrcGrpColl = MyEncoder.SourceGroupCollection
    Set MySrcGrp = MySrcGrpColl.Add("SG_1")
    Set MyAudioSource = MySrcGrp.AddSource(WMENC_AUDIO)
    MySourcePath.Text = "C:\media\laure03.mp3"

    Set MyFile = MyEncoder.File
    MyDestinationPath.Text = "C:\media\laure03.wma"
```

(continued)

```
        DummyText = "Choose a profile first."
        ProfileComboBox.Text = DummyText

        Player.uiMode = "none"
End Sub

Private Sub StartEncoder_Click()
    MyAudioSource.SetInput (MySourcePath.Text)
    MyFile.LocalFileName = MyDestinationPath.Text

    Dim MyProfileName As String
    MyProfileName = ProfileComboBox.Text
    If MyProfileName = DummyText Then
        MsgBox ("Please enter a profile before encoding.")
        Exit Sub
    End If

    Dim i As Integer
    Dim MyProfile As IWMEncProfile
    For i = 0 To (MyProColl.Count - 1)
        If MyProColl.Item(i).Name = MyProfileName Then
            Set MyProfile = MyProColl.Item(i)
            MySrcGrp.Profile = MyProfile
            Exit For
        End If
    Next i

    MyEncoder.Start
End Sub

Private Sub MyEncoder_OnStateChange(ByVal enumState As _
                    WMEncoderLib.WMENC_ENCODER_STATE)
    Select Case enumState
        Case WMENC_ENCODER_RUNNING
            MyState.Caption = "Running"
        Case WMENC_ENCODER_STOPPED
            MyState.Caption = "Stopped"
    End Select
End Sub

Private Sub PlayPlayer_Click()
    If MyState.Caption = "Stopped" Then
        Player.URL = MyDestinationPath.Text

        Dim AC As Integer
        Dim MyRate As Long
        AC = Player.currentMedia.getAttributeCountByType _
                        ("Bitrate", "") - 1
```

```
        MyRate = Player.currentMedia.getItemInfoByType _
                             ("Bitrate", "", AC)
        BitRate.Caption = "Bitrate = " & CStr(MyRate) & _
                             " bits/second"
    Else
        MsgBox "Please encode a file before playing it."
    End If
End Sub


Private Sub StopPlayer_Click()
    Player.Controls.Stop
End Sub
```

Modifying the File Player Application Code

A few lines need to be changed in the original procedures of the File Player code so that the encoder will broadcast to the Player instead of creating a file. Look at the code that was copied from the File Player application when you copied the File Player form.

The following code blocks from the Encoder Broadcast application must be modified:

- General declarations

- Form_Load procedure

- StartEncoder_Click procedure

- PlayPlayer_Click procedure

Changing the Declarations Code

Remove the following line from the declarations section of the code.

```
Dim MyFile As IWMEncFile
```

This line is not needed because the Encoder Broadcast application will create only a broadcast, so you do not need to create an output file object.

Replace the previous line with the following one.

```
Dim MyBroadcast As IWMEncBroadcast
```

This line declares a broadcast object that will be created later.

Changing the Form_Load Code

Remove the following two lines from the Form_Load procedure.

```
Set MyFile = MyEncoder.File
MyDestinationPath.Text = "C:\media\laure03.wma"
```

These two lines are not needed because the encoder does not need to create a file object or define its path if it is only broadcasting.

Add the following line at the end of the Form_Load code, just before the **End Sub** line.

```
Address.Text = "8080"
```

This line puts a default port number into the Address text box, allowing the user to change the network port number if desired. By storing the port number in a text box, you can be sure that the Player is receiving on the same port that Windows Media Encoder is sending on.

Any port number can be used; the important thing is to be sure that the Player and encoder are using the same number. Port numbers can be any number from 0 to 65535. Individual port numbers are reserved for specific kinds of network protocols and applications. If you are broadcasting through a firewall, certain port numbers may be blocked. For encoder broadcasts through a firewall, port 8080 is recommended. The Internet Assigned Numbers Authority (*www.iana.org*) provides a list of commonly used port numbers.

Find the following line in the Form_Load procedure.

```
MySourcePath.Text = "C:\media\laure03.mp3"
```

Change it to read:

```
MySourcePath.Text = "C:\media\laure04.mp3"
```

Every chapter will use different media files.

Changing the StartEncoder_Click Code

Remove the following line from the StartEncoder_Click procedure.

```
MyFile.LocalFileName = MyDestinationPath.Text
```

This line isn't needed because the Encoder Broadcast application is only sending out a broadcast. There is no need to create a destination file.

Replace the previous line with the following one.

```
MyAudioSource.Repeat = True
```

This line will make the audio source file repeat indefinitely. This allows the broadcast to continue until the user stops the encoder, regardless of the length of the file.

Next find the following line.

```
MyEncoder.Start
```

Add the following two lines immediately *before* it.

```
Set MyBroadcast = MyEncoder.Broadcast
MyBroadcast.PortNumber(WMENC_PROTOCOL_HTTP) = Address.Text
```

The first line creates a new broadcast object for the encoder.

The second line sets up the protocol and port number for the broadcast. The port number is obtained from the Address text box, where the user may have modified the port number before the broadcast.

Changing the PlayPlayer_Click Code

Find the following line in the PlayPlayer_Click procedure.

```
If MyState.Caption = "Stopped" Then
```

Replace it with the following line.

```
If MyState.Caption = "Running" Then
```

Unlike the File Player application, where you wanted to wait until the encoder was finished creating a new file before you tried to play it, the Encoder Broadcast application needs to prevent the user from starting the Player before the encoder has started. If the encoder is in any other state except "Running", the Player will not play.

Remove the following line.

```
Player.URL = MyDestinationPath.Text
```

This line is not needed because the Player will not be reading a file.

Replace the previous line with the following one.

```
Player.URL = "http://" & Environ("COMPUTERNAME") & ":" & Address.Text
```

This line uses the HTTP protocol with the network port that was defined in the Address text box. Because it is assumed that the application is on the same computer as the encoder and Player, the COMPUTERNAME environment variable is used to create the encoder address name, but you could put in the network name of the computer instead.

Remove the following lines.

```
Dim i As Integer
Dim MyRate As Long
AC = Player.currentMedia.getAttributeCountByType("Bitrate", "") - 1
MyRate = Player.currentMedia.getItemInfoByType("Bitrate", "", AC)
BitRate.Caption = "Bitrate = " & CStr(MyRate) & " bits/second"
```

The lines you just removed will be used in the new procedure named Player_Play-StateChange discussed later in the chapter.

Next remove the following line.

```
MsgBox "Please encode a file before playing it."
```

Replace it with the following one.

```
MsgBox "Please start the encoding process."
```

This line changes the message that is displayed if the user clicks the Play Player button too soon.

Adding New Procedures for the Encoder Broadcast Application

Two new code procedures are needed to complete the Encoder Broadcast application. The first procedure lets the user stop the encoding process, and the second procedure changes the way that the bit-rate data is obtained from Windows Media Player.

Adding Code to Stop the Encoding Process

Because the encoding is set to repeat indefinitely, it is a good idea to provide a way for the user to stop the encoding process.

The code to stop the encoding goes in the following procedure, which is created automatically in the code module when you double-click the button on the form.

```
Private Sub StopEncoder_Click()

End Sub
```

Add the following line of code inside the StopEncoder_Click procedure.

```
MyEncoder.Stop
```

This stops Windows Media Encoder from encoding. After a few moments, the encoder status display will change to "Stopped" and the Player will automatically stop playing.

Adding a Player Event Handler to Display the Bit Rate

In the File Player application, the Player was able to supply the bit rate of the newly encoded file as soon as it started playing. But, if you try the same code procedure as last time, the Player may not be able to supply the information if you click the Play Player button immediately after you click the Start Encoding button.

This is because it takes the Player a few seconds to begin receiving the broadcast. The only way to be sure that the Player can supply you with up-to-date information is to create an event handler. This is a code procedure that runs every time a specific event occurs in the Player. In this case, the event you are interested in is the *PlayStateChange* event.

The Player has several possible play states. The only one that matters in this application is the state that signifies that the Player is playing.

In order to respond to the changes in the play state of the Player, add the following complete procedure to your code. Be sure it is not inside any other procedure.

```
Private Sub Player_PlayStateChange(ByVal NewState As Long)
    If NewState = 3 Then
        Dim AC As Integer
        Dim MyRate As Long
        AC = Player.currentMedia.getAttributeCountByType _
                        ("Bitrate", "") - 1
        MyRate = Player.currentMedia.getItemInfoByType _
                        ("Bitrate", "", AC)
```

```
        BitRate.Caption = "Bitrate = " & CStr(MyRate) & _
                            " bits/second"
    End If
End Sub
```

Whenever this code is called, the current state of the Player is assigned to the New-State variable.

The first line inside the procedure checks to determine whether NewState is equal to 3, which is the enumeration value that corresponds with the playing state of the Player. For a table of values, see the *Player.playState* topic in the Windows Media Player SDK.

The next five lines are the ones that you removed from the PlayPlayer_Click procedure. They obtain the bit rate of the currently playing digital media.

The *If* statement is ended with an ***End If***.

This procedure will run every time the *PlayStateChange* event occurs in the Player.

Running the Encoder Broadcast Application

After you have entered all the code, run the project in Visual Basic. From the Run menu, select Start. If there are no errors, the user interface of your application should look like Figure 4.3. You can compare your code to the complete code listing in the next section.

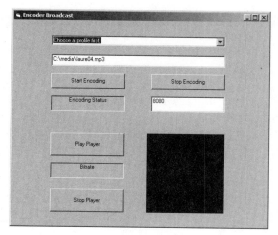

Figure 4.3   Encoder Broadcast application ready to broadcast to the Player.

Use the following procedure to test the Encoder Broadcast application:

1.   Choose an audio encoding profile.

2.   Change the path to the file you want encoded, if different from the default.

3. Change the network port number, if desired.

4. Click the Start Encoding button. The encoder status label should read "Running".

5. Click the Play Player button. The following events occur:

    ❑ You should hear the audio track playing.

    ❑ You should see the visualization.

    ❑ The bit rate should be displayed in the bit-rate label control. It should approximately match the bit rate in the profile you chose.

6. Click the Stop Player button. The Player stops, but the encoder is still encoding. Start the Player again by clicking the Play Player button.

7. Click the Stop Encoding button. The encoder status label control should display the message "Stopped". After a moment, the visualization and audio track will stop.

Complete copies of the source code and digital media for this application are on the companion CD.

Source Code for the Encoder Broadcast Application

Here is the complete source code listing for the Encoder Broadcast application.

```
Dim WithEvents MyEncoder As WMEncoder
Dim MyProColl As IWMEncProfileCollection
Dim MySrcGrpColl As IWMEncSourceGroupCollection
Dim MySrcGrp As IWMEncSourceGroup
Dim MyAudioSource As IWMEncSource
Dim MyBroadcast As IWMEncBroadcast

Dim DummyText As String

Private Sub Form_Load()
    Set MyEncoder = New WMEncoder

    Dim i As Integer
    Set MyProColl = MyEncoder.ProfileCollection
    For i = 0 To (MyProColl.Count - 1)
      ProfileComboBox.AddItem MyProColl.Item(i).Name, i
    Next i
```

```
        Set MySrcGrpColl = MyEncoder.SourceGroupCollection
        Set MySrcGrp = MySrcGrpColl.Add("SG_1")
        Set MyAudioSource = MySrcGrp.AddSource(WMENC_AUDIO)
        MySourcePath.Text = "C:\media\laure04.mp3"

        DummyText = "Choose a profile first."
        ProfileComboBox.Text = DummyText

        Player.uiMode = "none"

        Address.Text = "8080"
End Sub

Private Sub StartEncoder_Click()
        MyAudioSource.SetInput (MySourcePath.Text)
        MyAudioSource.Repeat = True

        Dim MyProfileName As String
        MyProfileName = ProfileComboBox.Text
        If MyProfileName = DummyText Then
            MsgBox ("Please enter a profile before encoding.")
            Exit Sub
        End If

        Dim i As Integer
        Dim MyProfile As IWMEncProfile
        For i = 0 To (MyProColl.Count - 1)
            If MyProColl.Item(i).Name = MyProfileName Then
                Set MyProfile = MyProColl.Item(i)
                MySrcGrp.Profile = MyProfile
                Exit For
            End If
        Next i

        Set MyBroadcast = MyEncoder.Broadcast
        MyBroadcast.PortNumber(WMENC_PROTOCOL_HTTP) = Address.Text

        MyEncoder.Start
End Sub

Private Sub MyEncoder_OnStateChange(ByVal enumState As _
                          WMEncoderLib.WMENC_ENCODER_STATE)
        Select Case enumState
            Case WMENC_ENCODER_RUNNING
                MyState.Caption = "Running"
            Case WMENC_ENCODER_STOPPED
                MyState.Caption = "Stopped"
        End Select
End Sub
```

(continued)

```
Private Sub PlayPlayer_Click()
    If MyState.Caption = "Running" Then
        Player.URL = "http://" & Environ("COMPUTERNAME") & ":" _
                     & Address.Text
    Else
        MsgBox "Please start the encoding process."
    End If
End Sub

Private Sub StopEncoder_Click()
    MyEncoder.Stop
End Sub

Private Sub StopPlayer_Click()
    Player.Controls.Stop
End Sub

Private Sub Player_PlayStateChange(ByVal NewState As Long)
    If NewState = 3 Then
        Dim AC As Integer
        Dim MyRate As Long
        AC = Player.currentMedia.getAttributeCountByType _
                        ("Bitrate", "") - 1
        MyRate = Player.currentMedia.getItemInfoByType _
                        ("Bitrate", "", AC)
        BitRate.Caption = "Bitrate = " & CStr(MyRate) & _
                        " bits/second"
    End If
End Sub
```

5

Adding Attributes to a Digital Media File

This chapter will explain how to expand the simple file player you created in Chapter 3 so that you can add attributes to a file. The sample application is called Adding Attributes and it will let you add standard and custom text attributes to a file when it is encoded.

Introduction to the Adding Attributes Application

Attributes are text strings that can be added to a digital media file to provide the user with useful information about the file. Some attributes, such as title and author, are standard file properties that can be displayed in a Windows file browser or by Windows Media Player. Attributes are helpful to users because they allow them to easily sort their audio and video collections by artist, album, or year.

Windows Media Encoder lets you add custom attributes to a file that can be read by Windows Media Player. For example, a custom attribute embedded in the content could provide additional information about the content, and the Player could display that information. All attributes consist of a name and a value. Both the name and value of an attribute are stored as text in the media file.

This chapter will show you how to use Windows Media Encoder to add standard and custom attributes to a file while it is being encoded. You'll be shown how to take the File Player application you created in Chapter 3 and modify it to add four standard attributes to the encoded file: Title, Author, Copyright, and Description. You'll also see how to add a custom attribute named Favorite Color. After the file is encoded with the new attributes, Windows Media Player will display the standard and custom attributes that you added. Attributes can be encoded in a file or a stream, but this chapter shows only how to encode attributes in a file.

To create the Adding Attributes application for this chapter, you will use the Visual Basic form you created in Chapter 3 and add new controls and code to perform the new programming tasks required. Note that the Adding Attributes application is not built on the form used in Chapter 4. No new applications in this book will build on the Adding Attributes application, but you may want to save it for further use, modification, and study.

The Adding Attributes application will perform the following tasks:

■ Let the operator choose the source media file for encoding into Windows Media Format. A default file path and name will be provided. The encoder can convert files with the following extensions: .wav, .avi, and .mp3, as well as .asf and the standard Windows Media formats .wma and .wmv.

■ Let the operator choose the path and name of the destination media file that will be created by the encoding process. A default file name and path will be provided. Use a standard Windows Media file extension: .wma for audio or .wmv for video.

■ Let the operator select an encoding profile from a list. Any appropriate profile can be chosen from the profiles that are already loaded into the encoder.

■ Let the operator select text for four standard attributes. Default values will be provided. Any appropriate text values can be used.

■ Let the operator select text for the name and value of the custom attribute to be encoded. Default values will be provided. Any appropriate text values can be used.

■ After choosing source and destination files, a profile, and text for the standard and custom attributes, let the operator click a button to start the encoding process. The data in the chosen source file will then be converted to raw data and encoded into Windows Media Format, as specified by the chosen profile, and the attribute names and related values will be added to the encoded file.

■ When the encoding is finished, play the encoded file. The standard and custom attributes in the file will be displayed by the Player.

Setting Up Your Programming Environment

Before you begin programming, be sure you have installed the following software and configured it properly.

> **Note**   The Adding Attributes application developed in this chapter is built on the File Player application from Chapter 3, not on the Encoder Broadcast application from Chapter 4.

Installing the Required Software

The following software must be installed on your computer before you can develop the Adding Attributes example application. If you created the File Player application in Chapter 3, all of these are installed already:

- Windows Server 2003, Standard Edition; Windows Server 2003, Enterprise Edition; or Windows Server 2003, Datacenter Edition. Windows Media Services is a component of all three versions. (The example application in this chapter does not require the server functionality, but using this operating system here enables you to use the same operating system for all example applications in this book.)

- Windows Media Encoder 9 Series. You can install the encoder from the companion CD.

- Windows Media Player 9 Series, if it is not already installed.

- Microsoft Visual Basic 6.0.

> **Note**   You should go to the Windows Update Web site and download any updates available for the required software.

Configuring Visual Basic

To configure Visual Basic for the Adding Attributes application, follow these steps. All three are the same as for the File Player application in Chapter 3.

1.   Start Visual Basic and create a new programming project by selecting New Project from the File menu and selecting the Standard EXE option. Click OK.

2.   Add a reference to a COM object that contains the Windows Media Encoder functionality. Add the reference by selecting References from the Project menu and scrolling down to Windows Media Encoder. Select the encoder check box and click OK.

3. Add the Windows Media Player ActiveX control to the Visual Basic toolbox. Add the Player control by selecting Components from the Project menu and then selecting the Windows Media Player check box. After you click OK in the Components dialog box, the Windows Media Player icon is displayed in the toolbox.

Creating a Visual Basic Form for the Adding Attributes Application

In this chapter, you will create the Adding Attributes application by building on the File Player form that was created in Chapter 3—not the Encoder Broadcast form from Chapter 4. The File Player application uses the encoder to encode a file and play it on Windows Media Player. This chapter uses most of the same form, but modifies it to let Windows Media Encoder add some common attributes to the file, such as author and title, as well as custom attributes. The Player will play the newly encoded file and display the values of the new attributes.

Using the File Player Form from Chapter 3

You can start by making a copy of the form that was created in Chapter 3. That form contains the following nine controls:

- **ProfileComboBox**   A ComboBox control named ProfileComboBox. It holds all the default encoder profiles.

- **MySourcePath**   A TextBox control named MySourcePath. It holds the path to the file that is to be encoded. The user can enter a new source path in this control.

- **MyDestinationPath**   A TextBox control named MyDestinationPath. It holds the path to the new file that is created in the encoding process. The user can enter a new destination path in this control.

- **StartEncoder**   A CommandButton control named StartEncoder. This button is used to start the encoding process and has a caption of "Start Encoding".

- **MyState**   A Label control named MyState. It displays the current status of the encoder.

- **PlayPlayer**   A CommandButton control named PlayPlayer. It has a caption of "Play Player" and makes Windows Media Player start playing. The button-click procedure checks whether Windows Media Encoder has finished encoding; if it has not finished, the Player will not play.

- **StopPlayer**   A CommandButton control named StopPlayer. It has a caption of "Stop Player".

- **BitRate**   A Label control named BitRate. It displays the bit rate of the encoded file. The bit-rate data will be supplied by the Player.

- **Player**   A WindowsMediaPlayer ActiveX control that displays the default visualization of the audio file that is playing. This will give the user a visual cue that the file is playing.

Figure 5.1 shows the File Player form created in Chapter 3.

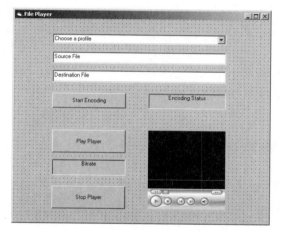

Figure 5.1   File Player form from Chapter 3.

Modifying the Form

Several of the user interface controls on the Adding Attributes form will be the same as on the File Player form. Three old controls will be removed from the form and 17 new controls will be added.

Removing Old Controls

Begin modifying the File Player form by removing the following three controls. They are no longer needed.

- **PlayPlayer**   The Adding Attributes application doesn't need to manually start Windows Media Player. When the file is finished encoding, the Player will be started by Windows Media Encoder instead of the Play Player button.

- **StopPlayer**   This button isn't needed because you can stop the Player by right-clicking the embedded Player window and clicking Stop on the shortcut menu.

■   **BitRate**   This label isn't needed because the Player event handler will not be displaying the bit rate of the current media in this application.

Adding New Controls

Next add the following 17 controls to the form to provide the new functionality needed to add attributes to a file by using the encoder:

■   **PlayerStatus**   A Label control that displays the status of the Player.

■   **Label1**   A Label control to identify the encoder status label, MyState. Put this label to the left of the encoder status label and give it a caption of "Encoder".

■   **Label2**   A Label control to identify the Player status label, PlayerStatus. Put this label to the left of the Player status label and give it a caption of "Player".

■   **Label3**   A Label control to identify a column of text boxes that specify the descriptions and attributes that will be encoded with the file. Give it a caption of "Encoder".

■   **Label4**   A Label control to identify the column of text boxes that will specify the descriptions and attributes seen by the Player. Give it a caption of "Player".

■   **MyTitle**   A TextBox control that lets the user supply a title for the digital media.

■   **MyAuthor**   A TextBox control that lets the user supply an author name.

■   **MyCopyright**   A TextBox control that lets the user supply a copyright description.

■   **MyDescription**   A TextBox control that lets the user supply a description of the digital media.

■   **MyCustomName**   A TextBox control that lets the user supply a custom attribute name.

■   **MyCustomValue**   A TextBox control that lets the user supply a custom value that will be paired with the custom name to create a custom attribute.

■   **Title**   A Label control that displays the *Title* attribute that the Player reads from the newly encoded file.

■   **Author**   A Label control that displays the *Author* attribute that the Player reads from the newly encoded file.

■   **Copyright**   A Label control that displays the *Copyright* attribute that the Player reads from the newly encoded file.

- **Description**   A Label control that displays the *Description* attribute that the Player reads from the newly encoded file.

- **CustomName**   A Label control that displays the name of the custom attribute that the Player reads from the newly encoded file.

- **CustomValue**   A Label control that displays the value of the custom attribute that the Player reads from the newly encoded file.

Figure 5.2 shows the Adding Attributes form with the new controls on it.

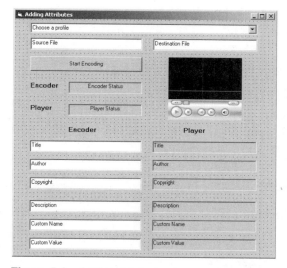

Figure 5.2   Adding Attributes form.

Designing the Code for the Adding Attributes Application

The code for the Adding Attributes application begins with the same code that was used by the File Player application in Chapter 3. The File Player code lets the user select a profile, change default paths to the source and destination files, and start the encoding process. The File Player code also verifies that the user selected a profile, and, after the encoding starts, displays the progress of the encoding. After the file is encoded, the user can test the newly created file by playing it in Windows Media Player. A button is provided for stopping the Player, and a label displays the bit rate of the file being played.

In the Adding Attributes application, new code must be added to perform the following tasks:

1.   Get the values of the description attributes from the user and supply default values.

2.   Get the name-and-value pair for a custom attribute from the user and supply default values.

3.   Make the Player start playing automatically when the encoding is completed.

4.   Display the status of the Player after it begins playing.

Adding the Code

The File Player application in Chapter 3 included the following six Visual Basic code blocks:

■   General declarations

■   Form_Load procedure

■   StartEncoder_Click procedure

■   MyEncoder_OnStateChange procedure

■   PlayPlayer_Click procedure

■   StopPlayer_Click procedure

The Adding Attributes application will add the following new procedure.

■   **Player_PlayStateChange procedure**   This is code that is called when the play state of the Player changes.

Reusing the File Player Application Code

Here is the code that will be reused from the File Player application in Chapter 3.

```
Dim WithEvents MyEncoder As WMEncoder
Dim MyProColl As IWMEncProfileCollection
Dim MySrcGrpColl As IWMEncSourceGroupCollection
Dim MySrcGrp As IWMEncSourceGroup
Dim MyAudioSource As IWMEncSource
Dim MyFile As IWMEncFile

Dim DummyText As String

Private Sub Form_Load()
    Set MyEncoder = New WMEncoder

    Dim i As Integer
    Set MyProColl = MyEncoder.ProfileCollection
    For i = 0 To (MyProColl.Count - 1)
      ProfileComboBox.AddItem MyProColl.Item(i).Name, i
    Next i
```

```
        Set MySrcGrpColl = MyEncoder.SourceGroupCollection
        Set MySrcGrp = MySrcGrpColl.Add("SG_1")
        Set MyAudioSource = MySrcGrp.AddSource(WMENC_AUDIO)
        MySourcePath.Text = "C:\media\laure03.mp3"

        Set MyFile = MyEncoder.File
        MyDestinationPath.Text = "C:\media\laure03.wma"

        DummyText = "Choose a profile first"
        ProfileComboBox.Text = DummyText

        Player.uiMode = "none"
End Sub

Private Sub StartEncoder_Click()
        MyAudioSource.SetInput (MySourcePath.Text)
        MyFile.LocalFileName = MyDestinationPath.Text

        Dim MyProfileName As String
        MyProfileName = ProfileComboBox.Text
        If MyProfileName = DummyText Then
            MsgBox ("Please enter a profile before encoding.")
            Exit Sub
        End If

        Dim i As Integer
        Dim MyProfile As IWMEncProfile
        For i = 0 To (MyProColl.Count - 1)
            If MyProColl.Item(i).Name = MyProfileName Then
                Set MyProfile = MyProColl.Item(i)
                MySrcGrp.Profile = MyProfile          .
                Exit For
            End If
        Next i

        MyEncoder.Start
End Sub

Private Sub MyEncoder_OnStateChange(ByVal enumState As _
                        WMEncoderLib.WMENC_ENCODER_STATE)
        Select Case enumState
            Case WMENC_ENCODER_RUNNING
                MyState.Caption = "Running"
            Case WMENC_ENCODER_STOPPED
                MyState.Caption = "Stopped"
        End Select
End Sub
```

(continued)

```
Private Sub PlayPlayer_Click()
    If MyState.Caption = "Stopped" Then
        Player.URL = MyDestinationPath.Text

        Dim AC As Integer
        Dim MyRate As Long
        AC = Player.currentMedia.getAttributeCountByType _
                            ("Bitrate", "") - 1
        MyRate = Player.currentMedia.getItemInfoByType _
                            ("Bitrate", "", AC)
        BitRate.Caption = "Bitrate = " & CStr(MyRate) & _
                            " bits/second"
    Else
        MsgBox "Please encode a file before playing it."
    End If
End Sub

Private Sub StopPlayer_Click()
    Player.Controls.Stop
End Sub
```

Modifying the File Player Application Code

Several lines need to be added, removed, or modified in the original procedures so that common and custom attributes can be encoded into a digital media file and displayed by Windows Media Player.

The following code blocks from the File Player application must be modified:

■   General declarations

■   Form_Load procedure

■   StartEncoder_Click procedure

Adding New Declarations

Two lines need to be added to the declarations to define the objects needed for descriptions and custom attributes. Add the following lines.

```
Dim Descr As IWMEncDisplayInfo
Dim Attr As IWMEncAttributes
```

The first line defines the description object that will be used to add the standard attributes such as author, title, and so on.

The second line defines the custom attribute object that will be used to create unique attributes; for example, you could create an attribute such as favorite color for a radio contest. Then, you could write code to run on the Player that would let the user pick a favorite color. When the digital media was broadcast, code on the Player could detect the value of the custom attribute and compare it with the color chosen by the user. If the user had picked the matching color, they would win the contest.

Adding New Lines to the Form_Load Code

You must add several lines to the Form_Load procedure to create attribute and description objects and to define defaults for the descriptions and custom attribute pairs. Add the following new lines at the end of the Form_Load procedure, before the ***End Sub*** line.

Creating Description and Custom-Attribute Objects

Add the following two lines to create the description and custom-attribute objects.

```
Set Descr = MyEncoder.DisplayInfo
Set Attr = MyEncoder.Attributes
```

The first line creates the description object by using the *DisplayInfo* object of the encoder. This line allows common attributes such as author and title to be embedded in the encoded file.

The second line creates the custom-attributes object by using the *Attributes* object of the encoder. This allows you to create custom name-and-value pairs for attributes that you want to embed in the file that are not one of the standard description types.

These objects were defined in the declarations module of the code, but the objects must be created before they can be used.

Creating Default Descriptions

Add the following lines to create default values for the description attributes.

```
MyTitle.Text = "Laure"
MyAuthor.Text = "Triode48"
MyCopyright.Text = "Copyright (c) Microsoft Corporation"
MyDescription.Text = "Song for the Windows Media Player SDK"
```

These lines create defaults for the title, author, copyright, and description values of the standard description attributes.

> **Note**   There are actually five standard attributes. The fifth standard attribute is called *Rating*. However, because Windows Media Player 9 Series uses a new system of rating content, if you use the encoder to assign a value to the *Rating* attribute, the value will not be displayed when you use the *getItemInfo* method of the Player and use the parameter value of "Rating".

Creating Default Custom Attributes

Add the following lines to create default values for a custom-attribute name-and-value pair.

```
MyCustomName.Text = "Favorite Color"
MyCustomValue.Text = "Alizarin Crimson"
```

Custom attributes require a paired name and value. These lines define one custom attribute named "Favorite Color", with the value of "Alizarin Crimson".

Changing the Media File Names

Find the following lines.

```
MySourcePath.Text = "C:\media\laure03.mp3"
MyDestinationPath.Text = "C:\media\laure03.wma"
```

Change them to read:

```
MySourcePath.Text = "C:\media\laure05.mp3"
MyDestinationPath.Text = "C:\media\laure05.wma"
```

Changing the StartEncoder_Click Code

You must add a few lines to the StartEncoder_Click procedure to tell Windows Media Encoder what values to use for descriptions and custom attributes. The description and custom attribute lines should be inserted immediately *before* the following line.

```
Encoder.Start
```

Adding the Description Details

Add the following lines to tell the encoder what values to use for the descriptions.

```
Descr.Title = MyTitle.Text
Descr.Author = MyAuthor.Text
Descr.Copyright = MyCopyright.Text
Descr.Description = MyDescription.Text
```

These lines get the values for the standard descriptions from the appropriate text boxes. Default values are used unless the user has supplied new information.

Adding the Custom Name and Value Attributes

Add the following line, immediately after the lines you just added, to tell the encoder what name and value to use for the custom attribute pair.

```
Attr.Add MyCustomName.Text, MyCustomValue.Text
```

Adding to the Encoder-StateChange Code

You need to add one line to the MyEncoder_OnStateChange procedure to make the Player start playing. Find this line in the procedure.

```
MyState.Caption = "Stopped"
```

Add the following line immediately after that line to make the Player start playing when the encoder finishes encoding.

```
Player.URL = MyDestinationPath.Text
```

In the File Player application, the user had to click a button to start the Player, and the Player would not start playing unless the encoder had finished encoding. In the Adding Attributes application, it is more convenient to start the Player automatically.

The new line is added to the WMENC_ENCODER_STOPPED case that is executed when the encoder stops encoding. The file that was encoded is assigned to the *URL* property of the Player, which will cause the Player to start playing the file.

Adding the Player-StateChange Code

You need to create a new procedure that will be called whenever the Player changes its state. The purpose of this code is to display the attributes that are embedded in the file.

Adding the Event Procedure

Add the following lines to the end of the module after all other procedures.

```
Private Sub Player_PlayStateChange(ByVal NewState As Long)

End Sub
```

This procedure will be called every time the state of the Player changes. The new state will be stored in the NewState variable.

Looking for the Playing State

Add the following lines inside the Player_PlayStateChange procedure.

```
If NewState = 3 Then

End If
```

These lines check whether the state of the Player is 3, which means the Player is playing. If the Player is playing, the code inside the *If* statement will run. For more information about the *PlayStateChange* event procedure, see the Windows Media Player SDK.

Displaying the Player Status

Add the following line inside the *If...End If* statement.

```
PlayerStatus.Caption = "Playing"
```

This will display the status of the Player as "Playing".

Displaying the Attributes

Add the following lines immediately after the line you just added.

```
Title.Caption = _
    Player.currentMedia.getItemInfo("Title")
Author.Caption = _
    Player.currentMedia.getItemInfo("Author")
```

(continued)

```
        Copyright.Caption = _
            Player.currentMedia.getItemInfo("Copyright")
        Description.Caption = _
            Player.currentMedia.getItemInfo("Description")

        CustomName.Caption = MyCustomName.Text
        CustomValue.Caption = _
            Player.currentMedia.getItemInfo(MyCustomName.Text)
```

The first four lines get the standard attributes from Windows Media Player by using the *getItemInfo* method and display them in the appropriate Label control.

The next line displays the name of the custom attribute that was stored in the MyCustomName TextBox control.

The line after that obtains the value of the custom attribute from the Player by using *getItemInfo* and the custom attribute name stored in the MyCustomName TextBox control.

The complete Player_PlayStateChange event procedure looks like this.

```
Private Sub Player_PlayStateChange(ByVal NewState As Long)
    If NewState = 3 Then
        PlayerStatus.Caption = "Playing"

        Title.Caption = _
            Player.currentMedia.getItemInfo("Title")
        Author.Caption = _
            Player.currentMedia.getItemInfo("Author")
        Copyright.Caption = _
            Player.currentMedia.getItemInfo("Copyright")
        Description.Caption = _
            Player.currentMedia.getItemInfo("Description")

        CustomName.Caption = MyCustomName.Text
        CustomValue.Caption = _
            Player.currentMedia.getItemInfo(MyCustomName.Text)
    End If
End Sub
```

Removing Unneeded Procedures

The following two procedures in the File Player application are not needed by the Adding Attributes application.

- **PlayPlayer_Click procedure**   This procedure is not needed because the Player will be started automatically in the MyEncoder_OnStateChange procedure. Remove the entire PlayPlayer_Click procedure from the code.

- **StopPlayer_Click procedure**   This procedure is not needed because the user can stop the Player by quitting the Adding Attributes application. Remove this entire procedure.

Running the Adding Attributes Application

After you have entered all the code, run the project in Visual Basic. From the Run menu, select Start. If there are no errors, the user interface of your application should look like Figure 5.3. You can compare your code to the complete code listing in the next section.

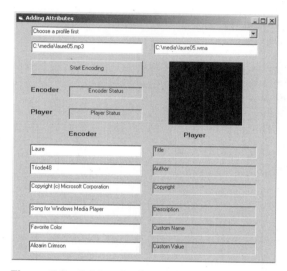

Figure 5.3   Adding Attributes user interface.

Use the following procedure to test the Adding Attributes application:

1.   Choose an encoding profile.

2.   Change the default paths to valid source and destination files, if desired.

3.   Change the default values of the standard attributes and the name and value of the custom attribute.

4.   Click the StartEncoder button when you are ready to encode.

5.   When the encoding is finished and the status label is "Stopped", the Player will start playing. You know the Player is playing because:

❑   You can hear the sound of the newly created file.

❑   You can see the visualization generated by playing the file.

❑   You can see the status of the Player.

6.   After Windows Media Player starts playing, the new values you chose for descriptions and attributes appear in the right column of the Player display.

Complete copies of the source code and digital media for the Adding Attributes application are on the companion CD.

Source Code for the Adding Attributes Application

Here is the complete source code listing for the Adding Attributes application.

```
Dim WithEvents MyEncoder As WMEncoder
Dim MyProColl As IWMEncProfileCollection
Dim MySrcGrpColl As IWMEncSourceGroupCollection
Dim MySrcGrp As IWMEncSourceGroup
Dim MyAudioSource As IWMEncSource
Dim MyFile As IWMEncFile

Dim Descr As IWMEncDisplayInfo
Dim Attr As IWMEncAttributes

Dim DummyText As String

Private Sub Form_Load()
    Set MyEncoder = New WMEncoder

    Dim i As Integer
    Set MyProColl = MyEncoder.ProfileCollection
    For i = 0 To (MyProColl.Count - 1)
      ProfileComboBox.AddItem MyProColl.Item(i).Name, i
    Next i

    Set MySrcGrpColl = MyEncoder.SourceGroupCollection
    Set MySrcGrp = MySrcGrpColl.Add("SG_1")
    Set MyAudioSource = MySrcGrp.AddSource(WMENC_AUDIO)
    MySourcePath.Text = "C:\media\laure05.mp3"

    Set MyFile = MyEncoder.File
    MyDestinationPath.Text = "C:\media\laure05.wma"

    DummyText = "Choose a profile first"
    ProfileComboBox.Text = DummyText

    Player.uiMode = "none"

    Set Descr = MyEncoder.DisplayInfo
    Set Attr = MyEncoder.Attributes

    MyTitle.Text = "Laure"
    MyAuthor.Text = "Triode48"
    MyCopyright.Text = "Copyright (c) Microsoft Corporation"
```

```
        MyDescription.Text = "Song for Windows Media Player"
        MyCustomName = "Favorite Color"
        MyCustomValue = "Alizarin Crimson"
    End Sub


Private Sub StartEncoder_Click()
    MyAudioSource.SetInput (MySourcePath.Text)
    MyFile.LocalFileName = MyDestinationPath.Text

    Dim MyProfileName As String
    MyProfileName = ProfileComboBox.Text
    If MyProfileName = DummyText Then
        MsgBox ("Please enter a profile before encoding.")
        Exit Sub
    End If

    Dim i As Integer
    Dim MyProfile As IWMEncProfile
    For i = 0 To (MyProColl.Count - 1)
        If MyProColl.Item(i).Name = MyProfileName Then
            Set MyProfile = MyProColl.Item(i)
            MySrcGrp.Profile = MyProfile
            Exit For
        End If
    Next i

    Descr.Title = MyTitle.Text
    Descr.Author = MyAuthor.Text
    Descr.Copyright = MyCopyright.Text
    Descr.Description = MyDescription.Text

    Attr.Add MyCustomName.Text, MyCustomValue.Text

    MyEncoder.Start
End Sub


Private Sub MyEncoder_OnStateChange(ByVal enumState As _
        WMEncoderLib.WMENC_ENCODER_STATE)
    Select Case enumState
        Case WMENC_ENCODER_RUNNING
            MyState.Caption = "Running"
        Case WMENC_ENCODER_STOPPED
            MyState.Caption - "Stopped"
            Player.URL = MyDestinationPath.Text
    End Select
End Sub
```

(continued)

```
Private Sub Player_PlayStateChange(ByVal NewState As Long)
    If NewState = 3 Then
        PlayerStatus.Caption = "Playing"

        Title.Caption = _
            Player.currentMedia.getItemInfo("Title")
        Author.Caption = _
            Player.currentMedia.getItemInfo("Author")
        Copyright.Caption = _
            Player.currentMedia.getItemInfo("Copyright")
        Description.Caption = _
            Player.currentMedia.getItemInfo("Description")

        CustomName.Caption = MyCustomName.Text
        CustomValue.Caption = _
            Player.currentMedia.getItemInfo(MyCustomName.Text)
    End If
End Sub
```

6

Pushing Content to the Server

This chapter will show you how to make Windows Media Encoder broadcast a media stream directly to a server running Windows Media Services. The new application is called Encoder Push and it will stream encoded media data from the encoder to the server without creating a file.

Introduction to the Encoder Push Application

As was shown in Chapter 4, Windows Media Encoder can broadcast encoded media directly to Windows Media Player. However, the encoder is not designed to stream media to more than a few players at a time. Fortunately, the encoder can also broadcast the encoded data to a Windows Media server, which is designed to stream media to large numbers of users simultaneously. The encoder can send a media stream directly to the server, and in turn, the server can send that stream to many players at the same time. Sending a stream from the encoder to the server is called *pushing* the data, because the encoder is in control of the process. The encoder instructs the server to receive the stream on a specific network port and publish the stream on a specific publishing point. The server then sends the data stream to users who request it.

This chapter will show you how to use Windows Media Encoder to broadcast a media stream directly to the server. You'll be shown how to modify the Encoder Broadcast application you created in Chapter 4 to broadcast to the server instead of the Player, so that the server can broadcast to users who request the stream. The encoder will encode a file and then send it to the server. But before the encoder sends the file, it will notify the server to set up a publishing point and to be ready to receive a media stream on a specific network port. After the encoding starts, the server will be notified to begin receiving the stream, and at the same time, the Player will request the stream from the server and start playing it. The Player will display the bit rate of the received file and the server will display the amount of computer resources that it is using.

> **Note**   The example code in this chapter assumes that the encoder and the server are on the same computer. In many cases, you will have the encoder on one computer and the server on another, and they may be separated by firewall. For example, you may have an encoder running inside a corporate intranet that can be used to broadcast executive news reports through a firewall to a server on the Internet, making the reports available to everyone both inside and outside the corporate intranet. For more information on how to work with remote servers and encoders using networks and firewalls, see the Windows Media Services SDK and the Windows Media Encoder SDK.

To create the Encoder Push application for this chapter, you will use the Visual Basic form you created in Chapter 4 and add new controls and code to perform the new programming tasks required. When you are finished, copy the Visual Basic project and form to another folder, because you will use them to create the Encoder Pull application in Chapter 7.

The Encoder Push application will perform the following tasks:

- Let the operator choose the source media file for encoding. A default file path and name will be provided. The encoder can convert files with the following extensions: .wav, .avi, and .mp3, as well as .asf and the standard Windows Media formats, .wma and .wmv.

- Let the operator select an encoding profile from a list. Any appropriate profile can be chosen from the profiles that are already loaded into the encoder.

- Let the operator select a server name to send the encoded media stream to. A default will be provided. Any valid server name can be used. The operator must have permissions to publish to the specified server.

- Let the operator select a publishing-point name that the server will use to publish the stream from the encoder. A default will be provided. Any valid publishing-point name can be used.

- Let the operator select a network port that will be used to send the stream from the encoder to the server and from the server to the Player. A default will be provided. Any valid network port number can be used.

- When the operator has chosen a file name, profile, server name, publishing-point name, and network port, let the operator click a button to start the encoding process. The data in the chosen source file will then be converted to raw data and encoded into Windows Media Format, as specified by the chosen profile.

- When the encoding process begins, instruct the server to set up a publishing point and receive data on a specific network port.

- When the encoding process begins, instruct the Player to send a request to the server for whatever stream is available on the publishing point. This stream will be the stream from the encoder.

- After the Player starts playing the file, display the bit rate of the encoded file.

- Display the percent of CPU utilization, which indicates how well your computer handles the server's need for resources.

> **Note**   Because this chapter focuses on Windows Media Encoder, some of the details about the server are covered only lightly. For more detailed discussion about Windows Media Services, see Chapters 10 through 14.

Setting Up Your Programming Environment

Before you begin programming, be sure you have installed the following software and configured it properly.

Installing the Required Software

The following software must be installed on your computer before you can develop the Encoder Push example application. If you created the Encoder Broadcast application in Chapter 4, all of these are installed already:

- Windows Server 2003, Standard Edition; Windows Server 2003, Enterprise Edition; or Windows Server 2003, Datacenter Edition. Windows Media Services is a component of all three versions.

- Windows Media Encoder 9 Series. You can install the encoder from the companion CD.

- Windows Media Player 9 Series, if it is not already installed.

- Microsoft Visual Basic 6.0.

> **Note**   You should go to the Windows Update Web site and download any updates available for the required software.

Configuring Visual Basic

To configure Visual Basic for the Encoder Push application, follow these steps:

1. Start Visual Basic and create a new programming project by selecting New Project from the File menu and selecting the Standard EXE option. Click OK.

2. Add a reference to a COM object that contains the Windows Media Services functionality. Add the reference by selecting References from the Project menu and scrolling down to Windows Media Services. Select the services check box and click OK.

3. Add a reference to a COM object that contains the Windows Media Encoder functionality. Add the reference by selecting References from the Project menu and scrolling down to Windows Media Encoder. Select the encoder check box and click OK.

4. Add the Windows Media Player ActiveX control to the Visual Basic toolbox. Add the Player control by selecting Components from the Project menu and then selecting the Windows Media Player check box. After you click OK in the Components dialog box, the Windows Media Player icon is displayed in the toolbox.

Creating a Visual Basic Form for the Encoder Push Application

In this chapter, you will build on the Encoder Broadcast form that was created in Chapter 4. The Encoder Broadcast application lets the operator choose an encoding format and a file to encode, and then broadcast the encoded file directly to Windows Media Player without using a server. This chapter uses most of the same form, but modifies it to make Windows Media Encoder push the file to a server running Windows Media Services, and then make the server broadcast the file to the Player.

Using the Encoder Broadcast Form from Chapter 4

You can start by making a copy of the form that was created in Chapter 4. That form contains the following 10 controls:

- **ProfileComboBox**   A ComboBox control to hold all the default encoder profiles.

- **MySourcePath**   A TextBox control to hold the path to the file that is to be encoded. The operator can enter a new source path in this control.

- **StartEncoder**   A CommandButton control to start the encoding process. It has a caption of "Start Encoding".

- **StopEncoder**   A CommandButton control to stop the encoding process. It has a caption of "Stop Encoding".

- **MyState**   A Label control to display the current status of the encoder.

- **Address**   A TextBox control to display the default network port that the broadcast will use. The operator can change this to another port if needed.

- **PlayPlayer**   A CommandButton control to make Windows Media Player start playing. The button-click procedure checks whether Windows Media Encoder has finished encoding; if it has not finished, the Player will not play.

- **StopPlayer**   A CommandButton control to stop the Player.

- **BitRate**   A Label control to display the bit rate of the encoded file. The bit-rate data will be supplied by the Player.

- **Player**   A WindowsMediaPlayer ActiveX control to display the default visualization of the audio file that is playing. This will give the operator a visual cue that the file is playing.

Figure 6.1 shows the Encoder Broadcast form created in Chapter 4.

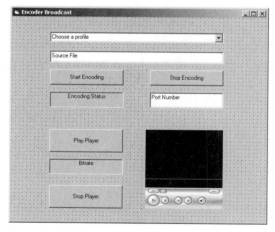

Figure 6.1   Encoder Broadcast form from Chapter 4.

Modifying the Form

Most of the user interface controls on the Encoder Push form will be the same as on the Encoder Broadcast form in Chapter 4. Two old controls will be removed from the form and three new ones will be added.

Removing Old Controls

Begin modifying the form by removing the following two controls. They are no longer needed.

- **PlayPlayer**   This button isn't needed because, in the new application, the Player will start automatically when the encoder starts encoding.

- **StopPlayer**   This button isn't needed because you can stop the Player by right-clicking the embedded Player window and clicking Stop on the shortcut menu.

Adding New Controls

Next add the following four controls to the form to provide the new functionality needed to push the digital media to the server and have the server create a broadcast that can be received by the Player:

- **PubPoint**   A TextBox control named PubPoint to hold the name of the publishing point that the encoder will create on the server.

- **ServerName**   A TextBox control to hold the name of the server that the encoder will push digital media to.

- **ServerStatus**   A Label control that displays the percentage of CPU utilization.

- **Timer1**   A Timer control that lets the server update the ServerStatus caption every second to display the CPU utilization value. The Timer control will not be visible when the Encoder Push application is running, so place it anywhere on the form.

Figure 6.2 shows the Encoder Push form with the new controls on it.

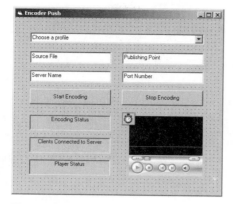

Figure 6.2   Encoder Push form.

Designing the Code for the Encoder Push Application

The code in the Encoder Push application begins with the same code that was used by the Encoder Broadcast application in Chapter 4. The Encoder Broadcast code lets the operator select a profile, change the default path to the source file for the encoding, and specify a port number for the broadcast. After Windows Media Encoder begins encoding the file, the operator can start Windows Media Player and begin receiving the broadcast.

In the Encoder Push application, new code must be added to perform the following tasks:

1.   Set up the encoder to push media to the server for a broadcast.

2.   Get a server name, publishing point, and network port number for the push from the encoder to the server and supply default values.

3.   Set up the server to allow the encoder to use the HTTP protocol and use an agreed-upon port number.

4.   Instruct the Player to send a request to the server for a broadcast.

5.   Request that the server display the CPU utilization percentage at one-second intervals.

Adding the Code

The Encoder Broadcast application in Chapter 4 included the following eight Visual Basic code blocks:

■   General declarations

■   Form_Load procedure

- StartEncoder_Click procedure

- StopEncoder_Click procedure

- MyEncoder_OnStateChange procedure

- PlayPlayer_Click procedure

- StopPlayer_Click procedure

- Player_PlayStateChange procedure

The following two of those code procedures will be deleted for the Encoder Push application:

- PlayPlayer_Click procedure

- StopPlayer_Click procedure

The Encoder Push application will add one new procedure.

- **Timer1_Timer**   This is a procedure that will be called by the Visual Basic Timer object to display CPU information from the server at regular intervals.

Reusing the Encoder Broadcast Application Code

Here is the code that will be reused from the Encoder Broadcast application in Chapter 4.

```
Dim WithEvents MyEncoder As WMEncoder
Dim MyProColl As IWMEncProfileCollection
Dim MySrcGrpColl As IWMEncSourceGroupCollection
Dim MySrcGrp As IWMEncSourceGroup
Dim MyAudioSource As IWMEncSource
Dim MyBroadcast As IWMEncBroadcast

Dim DummyText As String

Private Sub Form_Load()
    Set MyEncoder = New WMEncoder

    Dim i As Integer
    Set MyProColl = MyEncoder.ProfileCollection
    For i = 0 To (MyProColl.Count - 1)
      ProfileComboBox.AddItem MyProColl.Item(i).Name, i
    Next i

    Set MySrcGrpColl = MyEncoder.SourceGroupCollection
    Set MySrcGrp = MySrcGrpColl.Add("SG_1")
    Set MyAudioSource = MySrcGrp.AddSource(WMENC_AUDIO)
    MySourcePath.Text = "C:\media\laure04.mp3"
    DummyText = "Choose a profile first."
```

```
        ProfileComboBox.Text = DummyText
        Player.uiMode = "none"

        Address.Text = "8080"
    End Sub

  Private Sub StartEncoder_Click()
        MyAudioSource.SetInput (MySourcePath.Text)
        MyAudioSource.Repeat = True

        Dim MyProfileName As String
        MyProfileName = ProfileComboBox.Text
        If MyProfileName = DummyText Then
            MsgBox ("Please enter a profile before encoding.")
            Exit Sub
        End If

        Dim i As Integer
        Dim MyProfile As IWMEncProfile
        For i = 0 To (MyProColl.Count - 1)
            If MyProColl.Item(i).Name = MyProfileName Then
                Set MyProfile = MyProColl.Item(i)
                MySrcGrp.Profile = MyProfile
                Exit For
            End If
        Next i

        Set MyBroadcast = MyEncoder.Broadcast
        MyBroadcast.PortNumber(WMENC_PROTOCOL_HTTP) = Address.Text

        MyEncoder.Start
    End Sub

  Private Sub MyEncoder_OnStateChange(ByVal enumState As _
                WMEncoderLib.WMENC_ENCODER_STATE)
        Select Case enumState
            Case WMENC_ENCODER_RUNNING
                MyState.Caption = "Running"
            Case WMENC_ENCODER_STOPPED
                MyState.Caption = "Stopped"
        End Select
    End Sub

  Private Sub PlayPlayer_Click()
        If MyState.Caption = "Running" Then
            Player.URL = "http://" & Environ("COMPUTERNAME")
                        & ":" & Address.Text
```

(continued)

```
        Else
            MsgBox "Please start the encoding process."
        End If
End Sub

Private Sub StopEncoder_Click()
    MyEncoder.Stop
End Sub

Private Sub StopPlayer_Click()
    Player.Controls.Stop
End Sub

Private Sub Player_PlayStateChange(ByVal NewState As Long)
    If NewState = 3 Then
        Dim AC As Integer
        Dim MyRate As Long
        AC = Player.currentMedia.getAttributeCountByType _
                        ("Bitrate", "") - 1
        MyRate = Player.currentMedia.getItemInfoByType _
                        ("Bitrate", "", AC)
        BitRate.Caption = "Bitrate = " & CStr(MyRate) & _
                        " bits/second"
    End If
End Sub
```

Modifying the Encoder Broadcast Application Code

Several lines need to be added, removed, or modified to change the Encoder Broadcast code so that the new application can push encoded media to a Windows Media server and have that media received by Windows Media Player as a broadcast. Look at the code that was copied from the Encoder Broadcast application when you copied the Encoder Broadcast form. The following code blocks from the Encoder Broadcast application must be modified:

- General declarations

- Form_Load procedure

- StartEncoder_Click procedure

- MyEncoder_OnStateChange procedure

Changing the Declarations Code

The declaration for the type of encoder broadcast needs to be changed, and new declarations must be added for the server to allow the encoder to make a push distribution to it.

Changing the Type of Broadcast from the Encoder

The Encoder Broadcast application used this line to define a regular broadcast.

```
Dim MyBroadcast As IWMEncBroadcast
```

Replace it with the following line to change the broadcast type.

```
Dim PushDist As IWMEncPushDistribution
```

This changes the broadcast to a push distribution. The encoder can encode media and push it to the server for rebroadcast. The type of broadcast that the Encoder Broadcast application uses is limited to a set number of clients. Pushing the encoded content to the server lets the server do the work of broadcasting.

Adding Server Declarations

Add the following lines to the declarations block to define server objects for the Encoder Push application.

```
Dim Server As WMSServer
Dim Plugin As IWMSPlugin
Dim CPAdmin As IWMSCPPluginAdmin
Dim BoundIPAddr As IWMSBoundIPAddresses
```

These lines define the server object, the server plug-in, and the predefined system plug-in administration objects. An object for the collection of bound IP addresses is defined so that Windows Media Services can store the addresses of allowed connections.

Changing the Form_Load Code

In the Form_Load procedure, you must add new defaults for the publishing-point name and the server name. You must also set up the server to receive the pushed broadcast from the encoder and set the interval for the timer.

Adding a Default Publishing Point

Add the following line to set up a default name for the server publishing point to which the encoder will push the broadcast.

```
PubPoint.Text = "PubPoint06"
```

Any name can be used. This sets up a publishing point on the server to which clients can connect to receive the broadcast. See the Windows Media Services documentation for more information about publishing points.

Adding a Default Server Name

Add the following line to set up a default name for the server that the encoder push will be sent to.

```
ServerName.Text = Environ("COMPUTERNAME")
```

You can specify the name of any server. Because this application is written to run on the same computer as the encoder, the server, and the Player, the environment string COMPUTERNAME can be used to get the name of the server.

Changing the Media Name

Find the following line.

```
MySourcePath.Text = "C:\media\laure04.mp3"
```

Change it to this line.

```
MySourcePath.Text = "C:\media\laure06.mp3"
```

Each chapter will use different media.

Setting Up the Server

Add the following lines to the Form_Load procedure to set up the server so it can accept the push from the encoder.

```
Set Server = New WMSServer
Set Plugin = _
    Server.ControlProtocols("WMS HTTP Server Control Protocol")
Set CPAdmin = Plugin.CustomInterface()
Set BoundIPAddr = CPAdmin.BoundIPAddresses
```

When Windows Media Services is originally installed, it is set up so that the HTTP Server Control protocol is disabled. It also is set up not to accept pushed data from any encoders. So you must enable the HTTP Control Protocol on the server and notify the server to allow push connections on a specific port.

The preceding code performs the following tasks:

1. Creates a new server object.

2. Creates a predefined system plug-in object of the WMS HTTP Server Control Protocol type.

3. Enables the control protocol plug-in.

4. Creates a custom administrative interface for the control protocol plug-in.

5. Creates a collection of bound IP port addresses for the control protocol plug-in so that the server can allow the encoder to connect on a specific port.

Note   Any valid port number can be used, as long as that port is not being used by another application on your computer. For example, if you use port 80, you will get the error shown in Figure 6.3. This error occurs because port 80 is used by Microsoft Internet Information Services (IIS) and other HTTP servers for HTTP page requests. Whatever number you choose, be sure that the encoder and server are using the same port number.

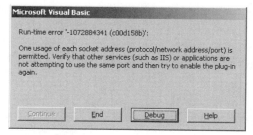

Figure 6.3   Error generated if you attempt to perform an encoder push using port 80.

Setting the Timer Interval

Add the following line to set the interval of the timer.

```
Timer1.Interval = 1000
```

This sets the interval of the timer to 1000 milliseconds (one second). This timer is used to poll the server every second to get the CPU utilization percentage.

Changing the StartEncoder_Click Code

You must change the type of broadcast from a regular broadcast that goes directly to a Player, to a broadcast that pushes digital media to a server. Because you are going to push media to a server, the encoder must be given the server name and the publishing-point name on that server. The server must also be notified which port the encoder will use.

Changing the Type of Broadcast

To change the type of broadcast, find the following line in the StartEncoder_Click procedure and remove it.

```
Set MyBroadcast = MyEncoder.Broadcast
```

Replace it with the following line.

```
Set PushDist = MyEncoder.Broadcast
```

This creates a push distribution object that will be used instead of the normal method of encoder broadcasting.

Changing the Information About the Broadcast

To change the information needed by the encoder for the broadcast, find the following line and remove it.

```
MyBroadcast.PortNumber(WMENC_PROTOCOL_HTTP) = Address.Text
```

Replace it with the following lines.

```
PushDist.ServerName = ServerName.Text & ":" & Address.Text
PushDist.PublishingPoint = PubPoint.Text
```

The first line gets the server name from the ServerName TextBox and combines it with the network port number from the Address TextBox (using a semicolon to separate the two parts of the address).

The second line gets the publishing-point name from the PubPoint TextBox.

Giving the Port Number to the Server

Add the following line to the StartEncoder_Click procedure to notify the server on which port to allow a push from the encoder.

```
CPAdmin.Port = Address.Text
```

The server must have the port number before it can accept the push. The port number is obtained from the Address TextBox and given to the server administration plug-in.

Enabling the Plug-in

Add the following line to enable the plug-in.

```
Plugin.Enabled = True
```

The plug-in is disabled by default and needs to be enabled for the interface to work properly.

Preparing the Encoder

Add the following line to prepare the encoder.

```
MyEncoder.PrepareToEncode True
```

This will begin a new encoding session and make sure that everything is ready for the encoded push.

Changing the Encoder State-Change Code

You must add one line to make the Player start playing when the encoder starts encoding. Find the following line in the MyEncoder_OnStateChange procedure.

```
MyState.Caption = "Encoder Running"
```

Add the following line immediately after it.

```
Player.URL = _
    "mms://" & ServerName.Text & ":" & _
    Address.Text & "/" & PubPoint.Text
```

This line uses the MMS protocol to make a request from the Player to the server to play whatever digital media has been assigned to the publishing point on the specified server and port. For example, if you had a publishing point named LaurePublishingPoint on a computer named LaureServer with a port of 40754, the URL would resolve to this:

mms://LaureServer:40754/LaurePublishingPoint

Adding Timer Code to Get Data from the Server

Create a Timer1_Timer procedure by double-clicking the Timer control on the form. Then add the following code inside the procedure.

```
ServerStatus.Caption = "CPU Utilization: " & _
    CStr(Server.CPUUtilization) & "%"
```

This line will be called every 1000 milliseconds (one second) to display the CPU utilization percentage in the ServerStatus label.

The complete timer code procedure will look like this.

```
Private Sub Timer1_Timer()
    ServerStatus.Caption = "CPU Utilization: " & _
                        CStr(Server.CPUUtilization) & "%"
End Sub
```

Removing Unneeded Procedures

The following two procedures from the Encoder Broadcast application are not needed by the Encoder Push application:

- **PlayPlayer_Click procedure**   This procedure is not needed because the Player will be started automatically when the encoder starts encoding. Remove the entire PlayPlayer_Click procedure from the code.

- **StopPlayer_Click procedure**   This procedure is not needed because the operator can stop playing by quitting the Player. Remove this procedure entirely.

Running the Encoder Push Application

After you have entered all the code, run the project in Visual Basic. From the Run menu, select Start. If there are no errors, the user interface of your application should look like Figure 6.4. You can compare your code to the complete code listing in the next section.

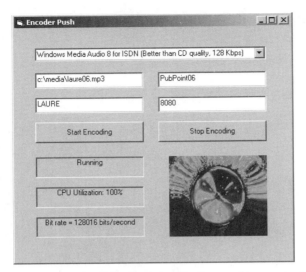

Figure 6.4 Encoder Push application pushing content to the server.

Use the following procedure to test your application:

1. Choose an audio encoding profile.

2. Change the path to the file you want encoded, if different from the default.

3. Change the publishing-point name, if desired.

4. Change the server name, if desired.

5. Change the network port number, if desired.

6. Click the Start Encoding button. The encoder status label (MyState) should read "Running". After a moment, the ServerStatus label should show the CPU utilization percentage. The initial percentage will probably be low. After a second or two, the Player should start playing and the bit rate will be displayed. By then, the CPU utilization percentage should be significantly higher unless you have a very fast computer.

7. Click the Stop Encoding button. The encoder status label should display the message "Stopped". After a moment, the visualization and audio track will stop. The CPU utilization percentage should drop significantly unless you have a very fast computer.

Complete copies of the source code and digital media for this application are on the companion CD.

Source Code for the Encoder Push Application

Here is the complete source code for the Encoder Push application.

```
Dim WithEvents MyEncoder As WMEncoder
Dim MyProColl As IWMEncProfileCollection
Dim MySrcGrpColl As IWMEncSourceGroupCollection
Dim MySrcGrp As IWMEncSourceGroup
Dim MyAudioSource As IWMEncSource
Dim PushDist As IWMEncPushDistribution

Dim Server As WMSServer
Dim Plugin As IWMSPlugin
Dim CPAdmin As IWMSCPPluginAdmin
Dim BoundIPAddr As IWMSBoundIPAddresses

Dim DummyText As String

Private Sub Form_Load()
    Set MyEncoder = New WMEncoder

    Dim i As Integer
    Set MyProColl = MyEncoder.ProfileCollection
    For i = 0 To (MyProColl.Count - 1)
      ProfileComboBox.AddItem MyProColl.Item(i).Name, i
    Next i

    Set MySrcGrpColl = MyEncoder.SourceGroupCollection
    Set MySrcGrp = MySrcGrpColl.Add("SG_1")
    Set MyAudioSource = MySrcGrp.AddSource(WMENC_AUDIO)
    MySourcePath.Text = "c:\media\laure06.mp3"

    DummyText = "Choose a profile first"
    ProfileComboBox.Text = DummyText
    Player.uiMode = "none"

    PubPoint.Text = "PubPoint06"
    ServerName.Text = Environ("COMPUTERNAME")
    Address.Text = "8080"

    Set Server = New WMSServer
    Set Plugin = Server.ControlProtocols("WMS HTTP Server Control Protocol")
    Set CPAdmin = Plugin.CustomInterface()
    Set BoundIPAddr = CPAdmin.BoundIPAddresses

    Timer1.Interval = 1000
End Sub
```

(continued)

```
Private Sub StartEncoder_Click()
    MyAudioSource.SetInput (MySourcePath.Text)
    MyAudioSource.Repeat = True

    Dim MyProfileName As String
    MyProfileName = ProfileComboBox.Text
    If MyProfileName = DummyText Then
        MsgBox ("Please enter a profile before encoding.")
        Exit Sub
    End If

    Dim i As Integer
    Dim MyProfile As IWMEncProfile
    For i = 0 To (MyProColl.Count - 1)
        If MyProColl.Item(i).Name = MyProfileName Then
            Set MyProfile = MyProColl.Item(i)
            MySrcGrp.Profile = MyProfile
            Exit For
        End If
    Next i

    Set PushDist = MyEncoder.Broadcast

    PushDist.ServerName = ServerName.Text & ":" & Address.Text
    PushDist.PublishingPoint = PubPoint.Text

    CPAdmin.Port = Address.Text

    Plugin.Enabled = True

    MyEncoder.PrepareToEncode True
    MyEncoder.Start
End Sub

Private Sub MyEncoder_OnStateChange(ByVal enumState As _
                      WMEncoderLib.WMENC_ENCODER_STATE)
    Select Case enumState
        Case WMENC_ENCODER_RUNNING
            MyState.Caption = "Running"
            Player.URL = "mms://" & ServerName.Text & ":" & _
                         Address.Text & "/" & PubPoint.Text
        Case WMENC_ENCODER_STOPPED
            MyState.Caption = "Stopped"
    End Select
End Sub

Private Sub StopEncoder_Click()
    MyEncoder.Stop
End Sub
```

```
Private Sub Timer1_Timer()
    ServerStatus.Caption = "CPU Utilization: " & _
                        CStr(Server.CPUUtilization) & "%"
End Sub

Private Sub Player_PlayStateChange(ByVal NewState As Long)
    If NewState = 3 Then
        Dim AC As Integer
        Dim MyRate As Long
        AC = Player.currentMedia.getAttributeCountByType _
                        ("Bitrate", "") - 1
        MyRate = Player.currentMedia.getItemInfoByType _
                        ("Bitrate", "", AC)
        BitRate.Caption = "Bitrate = " & CStr(MyRate) & _
                        " bits/second"
    End If
End Sub
```

7

Pulling Content from the Encoder

The previous chapter explained how to broadcast a media stream directly from Windows Media Encoder to a server running Windows Media Services. This chapter will demonstrate the same concept, but with one major difference: the server will be controlling the encoder, instead of the encoder controlling the server. The new application is called Encoder Pull and it will let you control the data stream from the server instead of the encoder.

Introduction to the Encoder Pull Application

Windows Media Encoder and Windows Media Services are designed to work together. First the encoder prepares the data for streaming and sends it to a server running Windows Media Services, and then the server sends it out to many players simultaneously. There are two ways to control the flow of data between the encoder and server. The encoder can push or the server can pull. For example, in Chapter 6, the encoder pushes the stream to the server and the server sends it out to players when they request it. Pushing a stream from encoder to server is most useful when you have only one stream to encode. However, if you want to deliver many different streams to different players using a schedule, it makes more sense to have the server request a stream from the encoder when it fits in with the overall timetable that the server is following. This is called *pulling* a stream. Pulling a stream from the encoder makes it easy for the server to juggle a complicated mix of different types of streams at different times.

This chapter will show you how to use Windows Media Services to pull a stream from the encoder. You'll be shown how to modify the Encoder Push application you created in Chapter 6 so that the operator can control all operations through the server. The operator can start the encoder and see the encoded stream by using Windows Media Player. When satisfied that the encoded stream is working properly, the operator can start the server. The server will then request the stream from the encoder and begin receiving it. A second Player will automatically start, so that the operator can verify that the server is able to broadcast the stream.

To create the Encoder Pull application for this chapter, you will use the Visual Basic form you created in Chapter 6 and add new controls and code to perform the new programming tasks required. No later applications in this book will build on the Encoder Pull application, but you may want to save it for further use, modification, and study.

The Encoder Pull application will perform the following tasks:

■   Let the operator choose the source media file for encoding. A default file path and name will be provided. The encoder can convert files with the following extensions: .wav, .avi, and .mp3, as well as .asf and the standard Windows Media formats, .wma and .wmv.

■   Let the operator select an encoding profile from a list. Any appropriate profile can be chosen from the profiles that are already loaded into the encoder.

■   Let the operator select a publishing-point name that the server will use to publish the stream that it receives from the encoder. A default will be provided. Any valid publishing-point name can be used.

■   Let the operator select a port number to be used for the broadcast. A default will be provided. Any valid port number can be used.

■   When the operator has chosen a file name, profile, port number, and publishing-point name, let the operator click a button to start the encoding process. The data in the chosen source file will then be converted to raw data and encoded into Windows Media Format, as specified by the chosen profile.

■   After the encoding process begins, the Player will start playing the encoded stream. This can be useful to verify that you are encoding properly.

■   When the operator is ready to start the server, let the operator click a button to create the publishing point and instruct the server to request the stream from the encoder. A second Player will start playing the stream that is served by the server.

■   At any point after the encoder has started, let the operator stop the encoding process by clicking a button. This will cut off the stream from the encoder to the server.

■   At any point after the server has started, let the operator stop the server publishing point. This will stop any new players from connecting to the stream.

> **Note**   Because this chapter focuses on Windows Media Encoder, some of the details about the server are covered only lightly. For more detailed discussion about Windows Media Services, see Chapters 10 through 14.

Setting Up Your Programming Environment

Before you begin programming, be sure you have installed the following software and configured it properly.

Installing the Required Software

The following software must be installed on your computer before you can develop the Encoder Pull example application. If you created the Encoder Push application in Chapter 6, all of these are installed already.

- Windows Server 2003, Standard Edition; Windows Server 2003, Enterprise Edition; or Windows Server 2003, Datacenter Edition. Windows Media Services is a component of all three versions.

- Windows Media Encoder 9 Series. You can install the encoder from the companion CD.

- Windows Media Player 9 Series, if it is not already installed.

- Microsoft Visual Basic 6.0.

> **Note**   You should go to the Windows Update Web site and download any updates available for the required software.

Configuring Visual Basic

To configure Visual Basic for the Encoder Pull application, follow these steps. All four are the same as for the Encoder Push application in Chapter 6.

1. Start Visual Basic and create a new programming project by selecting New Project from the File menu and selecting the Standard EXE option. Click OK.

2.   Add a reference to a COM object that contains the Windows Media Services functionality. Add the reference by selecting References from the Project menu and scrolling down to Windows Media Services. Select the services check box and click OK.

3.   Add a reference to a COM object that contains the Windows Media Encoder functionality. Add the reference by selecting References from the Project menu and scrolling down to Windows Media Encoder. Select the encoder check box and click OK.

4.   Add the Windows Media Player ActiveX control to the Visual Basic toolbox. Add the Player control by selecting Components from the Project menu and then selecting the Windows Media Player check box. After you click OK in the Components dialog box, the Windows Media Player icon is displayed in the toolbox.

Creating a Visual Basic Form for the Encoder Pull Application

In this chapter, you will build on the Encoder Push form that was created in Chapter 6. The Encoder Push application enables Windows Media Encoder to push streaming media to a server running Windows Media services and then use the server to deliver a unicast broadcast. The process is entirely controlled by the encoder. This chapter uses some of the same form, but makes several changes. The most important change is that the operator will be able to start and stop both the encoder and the server, all from a single user interface. The Encoder Pull application also shows how to use two instances of Windows Media Player to provide feedback. One Player will provide feedback to show when and what the encoder is encoding, and the other Player will show the output of the server.

Using the Encoder Push Form from Chapter 6

To begin creating the Encoder Pull application, make a copy of the Encoder Push form that was created in Chapter 6. That form contains the following 12 controls:

■ **ProfileComboBox**   A ComboBox control to hold all the default encoder profiles.

■ **MySourcePath**   A TextBox control to hold the path to the file that is to be encoded. The operator can enter a new source path in this control.

■ **PubPoint**   A TextBox control to hold the name of the publishing point that the encoder will use to broadcast from.

■ **ServerName**   A TextBox control to hold the name of the server that the encoder will push digital media to.

- **Address**   A TextBox control to display the default network port that the encoder will use to connect to the server. The operator can change this to another port if needed.

- **StartEncoder**   A CommandButton control to start the encoding process. It has a caption of "Start Encoding".

- **StopEncoder**   A CommandButton control to stop the encoding process. It has a caption of "Stop Encoding".

- **MyState**   A Label control to display the current status of the encoder.

- **ServerStatus**   A Label control to display the CPU utilization.

- **BitRate**   A Label control to display the bit rate of the encoded file. The bit-rate data will be supplied by the Player.

- **Timer1**   A Visual Basic Timer object to display CPU information from the server at regular intervals.

- **Player**   A WindowsMediaPlayer ActiveX control that displays the default visualization of the audio file that is playing. This will give the operator a visual cue that the file is playing.

Figure 7.1 shows the Encoder Push form created in Chapter 6.

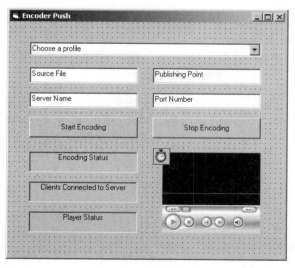

Figure 7.1   Encoder Push form from Chapter 6.

Modifying the Form

Some of the user interface controls on the Encoder Pull form will be the same as on the Encoder Push form used in Chapter 6. Five old controls will be removed from the form and three new ones will be added.

Removing Old Controls

Begin modifying the form by removing the following five controls:

- **ServerName**   The ServerName TextBox is no longer needed because the server will be sending a request to the encoder instead of the encoder sending a request to the server. There is only one encoder on a computer, and the encoder name is the same as the computer name.

- **MyState**   The MyState Label control should be removed. The status of the encoder will now be shown by the Player when the encoder starts. Instead of reading the text description of the encoder status, the operator can instantly see the status of the encoder by watching the visualization in the Player.

- **ServerStatus**   The ServerStatus Label control should be removed. The status of the server will be shown by using a second instance of the Player to show whether the server is capable of sending a unicast broadcast.

- **BitRate**   The BitRate Label control is no longer needed because the status of the Player is demonstrated by a visualization.

- **Timer1**   The Timer control is no longer needed because the status of the server is shown by starting the Player and displaying a visualization.

Adding New Controls

Next add the following three controls to the form to provide the new functionality needed to pull the digital media to the server and have the server make a unicast broadcast that can be received by a Player:

- **StartServer**   A CommandButton control named StartServer. Give it a caption of "Start Server".

- **StopServer**   A CommandButton control named StopServer. Give it a caption of "Stop Server".

- **Player2**   A WindowsMediaPlayer ActiveX control named Player2. It will display the default visualization of the audio file that is playing. This will give a visual cue to the operator that the server is capable of a unicast broadcast. The other Player control will be used to show the status of the encoder.

Figure 7.2 shows the Encoder Pull form with the new controls on it.

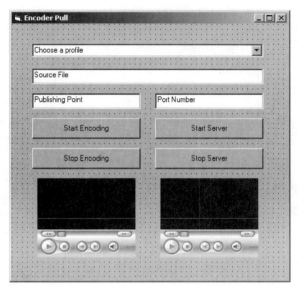

Figure 7.2   Encoder Pull form.

Designing the Code for the Encoder Pull Application

The code in the Encoder Pull application begins with the same code that was used by the Encoder Push application in Chapter 6. The Encoder Push code lets the operator select the following:

■   The path and file name of the source file.

■   The publishing-point name.

■   The server name.

■   The port number.

The operator can then start the encoder and see the status of the encoder, server, and Player. The broadcast is played by the Player.

In the Encoder Pull application, new code must be added to perform the following tasks:

1.   Provide a default file name and publishing point for the operator.

2.   Start the encoder and monitor its status by playing the stream directly from the encoder to a Player.

3.   Start the server and pull a stream from the encoder.

4.   Start a second instance of the Player to show the broadcast from the server when the publishing point starts. When the publishing point starts, the server will request a stream from the encoder and broadcast it to the Player.

Adding the Code

The Encoder Push application in Chapter 6 included the following seven Visual Basic code blocks:

- General declarations
- Form_Load procedure
- StartEncoder_Click procedure
- StopEncoder_Click procedure
- MyEncoder_OnStateChange procedure
- Timer1_Timer procedure
- Player_PlayStateChange procedure

The Encoder Pull application will keep five of those code procedures but will delete the last two.

The new application will add the following two new procedures:

- **StartServer_Click procedure**   This is code that runs when the operator clicks the Start Server button.

- **StopServer_Click procedure**   This is code that runs when the operator clicks the Stop Server button.

Reusing the Encoder Push Application Code

Here is the code that will be reused from the Encoder Push application in Chapter 6.

```
Dim WithEvents MyEncoder As WMEncoder
Dim MyProColl As IWMEncProfileCollection
Dim MySrcGrpColl As IWMEncSourceGroupCollection
Dim MySrcGrp As IWMEncSourceGroup
Dim MyAudioSource As IWMEncSource
Dim PushDist As IWMEncPushDistribution

Dim Server As WMSServer
Dim Plugin As IWMSPlugin
```

```
Dim CPAdmin As IWMSCPPluginAdmin
Dim BoundIPAddr As IWMSBoundIPAddresses

Dim DummyText As String
Private Sub Form_Load()
    Set MyEncoder = New WMEncoder

    Dim i As Integer
    Set MyProColl = MyEncoder.ProfileCollection
    For i = 0 To (MyProColl.Count - 1)
       ProfileComboBox.AddItem MyProColl.Item(i).Name, i
    Next i

    Set MySrcGrpColl = MyEncoder.SourceGroupCollection
    Set MySrcGrp = MySrcGrpColl.Add("SG_1")
    Set MyAudioSource = MySrcGrp.AddSource(WMENC_AUDIO)
    MySourcePath.Text = "c:\media\laure06.mp3"

    DummyText = "Choose a profile first."
    ProfileComboBox.Text = DummyText

    Player.uiMode = "none"

    PubPoint.Text = "PubPoint06"
    ServerName.Text = Environ("COMPUTERNAME")
    Address.Text = "8080"

    Set Server = New WMSServer
    Set Plugin = _
        Server.ControlProtocols("WMS HTTP Server Control Protocol")
    Set CPAdmin = Plugin.CustomInterface()
    Set BoundIPAddr = CPAdmin.BoundIPAddresses

    Timer1.Interval = 1000
End Sub

Private Sub StartEncoder_Click()
    MyAudioSource.SetInput (MySourcePath.Text)
    MyAudioSource.Repeat = True

    Dim MyProfileName As String
    MyProfileName = ProfileComboBox.Text
    If MyProfileName = DummyText Then
        MsgBox ("Please enter a profile before encoding.")
        Exit Sub
    End If
```

(continued)

```
        Dim i As Integer
        Dim MyProfile As IWMEncProfile
        For i = 0 To (MyProCOll.Count - 1)
            If MyProColl.Item(i).Name = MyProfileName Then
                Set MyProfile = MyProColl.Item(i)
                MySrcGrp.Profile = MyProfile
                Exit For
            End If
        Next i

        Set PushDist = MyEncoder.Broadcast

        PushDist.ServerName = ServerName.Text & ":" & Address.Text
        PushDist.PublishingPoint = PubPoint.Text

        CPAdmin.Port = Address.Text

        Plugin.Enabled = True

        MyEncoder.PrepareToEncode True
        MyEncoder.Start
    End Sub

    Private Sub MyEncoder_OnStateChange(ByVal enumState As _
                WMEncoderLib.WMENC_ENCODER_STATE)
        Select Case enumState
            Case WMENC_ENCODER_RUNNING
                MyState.Caption = "Running"
                Player.URL = "mms://" & ServerName.Text & ":" & _
                            Address.Text & "/" & PubPoint.Text
            Case WMENC_ENCODER_STOPPED
                MyState.Caption = "Stopped"
        End Select
    End Sub

    Private Sub StopEncoder_Click()
        MyEncoder.Stop
    End Sub

    Private Sub Timer1_Timer()
        ServerStatus.Caption = "CPU Utilization: " & _
                            CStr(Server.CPUUtilization) & "%"
    End Sub

    Private Sub Player_PlayStateChange(ByVal NewState As Long)
        If NewState = 3 Then

        Dim AC As Integer
        Dim MyRate As Long
```

```
AC = Player.currentMedia.getAttributeCountByType _
                    ("Bitrate", "") - 1
MyRate = Player.currentMedia.getItemInfoByType _
                    ("Bitrate", "", AC)
PlayerState.Caption = "Bitrate = " & CStr(MyRate) & _
                    " bits/second"
    End If
End Sub
```

Modifying the Encoder Push Application Code

Several lines need to be added, removed, or modified to change the Encoder Push code so that the Encoder Pull application can pull encoded media to a server and have that media received by the Player as a unicast broadcast.

The following code blocks from the Encoder Push application must be modified:

- General declarations

- Form_Load procedure

- StartEncoder_Click procedure

- MyEncoder_OnStateChange procedure

Changing the Declarations Code

The declaration for the type of encoder broadcast needs to be changed, and so do some declarations for server plug-ins and server publishing points. A separate declaration for the Player is no longer needed.

Changing the Type of Broadcast from the Encoder

The Encoder Push application used the following line to define a push broadcast.

```
Dim PushDist As IWMEncPushDistribution
```

Replace that line with the following line to change the broadcast type to a standard encoder broadcast.

```
Dim MyBroadcast As IWMEncBroadcast
```

For more information about standard encoder broadcasts, see Chapter 6.

Changing Server Declarations

Remove the following lines from the declarations block to remove the predefined system plug-in objects of the server that were used in the Encoder Push application.

```
Dim Plugin As IWMSPlugin
Dim CPAdmin As IWMSCPPluginAdmin
Dim BoundIPAddr As IWMSBoundIPAddresses
```

These lines are not needed, because this is no longer an Encoder Push application. Substitute the following lines instead.

```
Dim MyPubPoint As IWMSBroadcastPublishingPoint
Dim MyPubPoints As IWMSPublishingPoints
```

These lines are used to set up a publishing point and a publishing points collection. For more information about publishing points, see Chapter 1.

Changing the Form-Load Code

In the Form_Load procedure, you must change the source file name and the publishing point name, set the *uiMode* for the second Player, and delete several lines of code that are no longer needed for the Server Name, Port Number, and Timer defaults. The push plug-in code for the server must also be removed because this is now a pull application.

Changing the Source File Name

Find the following line.

```
MySourcePath.Text = "c:\media\laure06.mp3"
```

Change it to this line.

```
MySourcePath.Text = "c:\media\laure07.mp3"
```

Every chapter will use different media files.

Adding the uiMode for the Second Player

To define the *uiMode* for the second Player, find the following line.

```
Player.uiMode = "none"
```

Add the following line immediately after it.

```
Player2.uiMode = "none"
```

This makes sure that the second Player will not display any UI controls.

Changing the Publishing-Point Name

Find the following line in the Form_Load procedure.

```
PubPoint.Text = "PubPoint06"
```

Change it to this line.

```
PubPoint.Text = "PubPoint07"
```

You should create a different publishing-point name for every chapter to avoid duplicate publishing-point names.

Removing the Server Name Code

Find the following line.

```
ServerName.Text = Environ("COMPUTERNAME")
```

Remove it. The encoder does not need to know the server name because the server will be calling the encoder in this chapter.

Removing the Plug-in Code

The server plug-in code is not needed for this application. Remove the following lines.

```
Set Plugin = _
  Server.ControlProtocols("WMS HTTP Server Control Protocol")
Set CPAdmin = Plugin.CustomInterface()
Set BoundIPAddr = CPAdmin.BoundIPAddresses
```

Removing the Timer Default

The timer is not used in this application. Remove the following line.

```
Timer1.Interval = 1000
```

Changing the StartEncoder_Click Code

You must change the type of broadcast from push to pull. Instead of pushing media to a server, the Encoder Pull application uses the standard encoder broadcast that allows the server to pull media from an encoder that is already running.

To change the type of broadcast, find the following lines in the StartEncoder_Click procedure and remove them.

```
Set PushDist = MyEncoder.Broadcast
PushDist.ServerName = ServerName.Text & ":" & Address.Text
PushDist.PublishingPoint = PubPoint.Text
```

Add these lines instead.

```
Set MyBroadcast = MyEncoder.Broadcast
MyBroadcast.PortNumber(WMENC_PROTOCOL_HTTP) = Address.Text
```

This sets up Windows Media Encoder for a broadcast using the HTTP protocol on port 8080.

Remove the following two lines as well.

```
CPAdmin.Port = Address.Text
Plugin.Enabled = True
```

The first line instructs Windows Media Server to use a specific port for receiving the broadcast from the encoder, but it is no longer needed. The second line enables the plug-in, but is not needed because the plug-in is not used in this application.

Also remove the following line.

```
MyEncoder.PrepareToEncode True
```

The Encoder Push application needed to use the *PrepareToEncode* method to be sure that the server name and publishing points were valid. Because the Encoder Pull application needs to verify only the port number, the *PrepareToEncode* method is not necessary.

Changing the Encoder State-Change Code

To simplify the form and allow the removal of the encoder status label, the code in the MyEncoder_OnStateChange procedure should be removed. Start by removing the following lines.

```
Select Case enumState
    Case WMENC_ENCODER_RUNNING
        MyState.Caption = "Running"
        Player.URL = "mms://" & ServerName.Text & ":" & _
                     Address.Text & "/" & PubPoint.Text
    Case WMENC_ENCODER_STOPPED
        MyState.Caption = "Stopped"
End Select
```

Because you are interested in testing for only one state of the encoder and will not be displaying the states, you can use a simple *If* statement to test for the running state. Add the following lines to the now-empty procedure.

```
If enumState = WMENC_ENCODER_RUNNING Then
    Player.URL = "http://" & Environ("COMPUTERNAME") & ":" & _
                 Address.Text
End If
```

These lines will test whether the encoder is running. If it is, then a URL will be created for the Player and the Player will start playing.

The complete encoder event procedure will look like this.

```
Private Sub MyEncoder_OnStateChange(ByVal enumState As _
                    WMEncoderLib.WMENC_ENCODER_STATE)
    If enumState = WMENC_ENCODER_RUNNING Then
        Player.URL = "http://" & Environ("COMPUTERNAME") & ":" & _
                     Address.Text
    End If
End Sub
```

The URL instructs the first Player to start receiving a stream from the encoder as soon as the encoder is running. This allows the operator to see that the encoder is encoding and broadcasting a stream directly to a Player. This is a good test that the encoder is working properly and will help with troubleshooting if there are any problems between the encoder and the server.

Adding Code to Start the Server

To let the operator start the server manually, you must create a StartServer_Click procedure for the Start Server button. To create the procedure, double-click the Start Server button on the form.

The StartServer_Click procedure must perform three tasks:

1.   Check whether the name of the publishing point has already been used for some other publishing point. If it has, the old publishing point is deleted. (Instead of deleting it, you could also provide the option to quit the application or ask the operator for a different name.)

2.   Define the type of publishing point and start the server.

3.   Start the second Player by sending a request to the server for a unicast broadcast from the supplied publishing point.

Checking for Duplicate Publishing-Point Names

Add the following code inside the StartServer_Click procedure to check for duplicate publishing-point names.

```
Set MyPubPoints = Server.PublishingPoints
Dim i As Integer
Dim CheckName As String
For i = 0 To (MyPubPoints.Count - 1)
    CheckName = MyPubPoints.Item(i).Name
    If (CheckName = PubPoint.Text) Then
        MyPubPoints.Remove (PubPoint.Text)
        MsgBox ("Deleting previous " & PubPoint.Text)
    End If
Next i
```

This code gets the collection of current publishing points from the server and uses a *For...Next* loop to check whether any of the publishing-point names matches the name supplied by the operator. If there is a match, the old publishing point is removed, and a message is displayed to the operator.

Starting the Server

Add the following lines, immediately after the lines you just entered, to define and start the server.

```
Set MyPubPoint = Server.PublishingPoints.Add(PubPoint.Text, _
    WMS_PUBLISHING_POINT_BROADCAST, _
    "http://" & Environ("COMPUTERNAME") & ":" & Address.Text)
MyPubPoint.Start
```

The first line defines the type of publishing point by using three parameters:

1.   The name of the publishing point shown in the PubPoint TextBox, which the operator was free to modify.

2.   The type of publishing point, a simple unicast broadcast.

3.   The source for the publishing point. This parameter is what sets this publishing point for an encoder pull; the source of the publishing point is not a file,

it is the encoder. The stream is pulled from the encoder to the server by using the name of the encoder (which is the same as the computer name) and the port number 8080, which was defined earlier.

The second line starts the publishing point.

Starting the Second Player

Next add the following line to start the second Player.

```
Player2.URL = "mms://" & Environ("COMPUTERNAME") & "/" _
              & PubPoint.Text
```

This line starts the second Player by making a request to the publishing point of the server. The complete StartServer_Click procedure code looks like this.

```
Private Sub StartServer_Click()
    Set MyPubPoints = Server.PublishingPoints
    Dim i As Integer
    Dim CheckName As String
    For i = 0 To MyPubPoints.Count - 1
        CheckName = MyPubPoints.Item(i).Name
        If (CheckName = PubPoint.Text) Then
            MyPubPoints.Remove (PubPoint.Text)
            MsgBox ("Deleting previous " & PubPoint.Text)
        End If
    Next i

    Set MyPubPoint = Server.PublishingPoints.Add(PubPoint.Text, _
        WMS_PUBLISHING_POINT_BROADCAST, _
        "http://" & Environ("COMPUTERNAME") & ":" & Address.Text)
    MyPubPoint.Start

    Player2.URL = "mms://" & Environ("COMPUTERNAME") & "/" _
                  & PubPoint.Text
End Sub
```

Adding Code to Stop the Server

Next create a StopServer_Click procedure by double-clicking the Stop Server button on the form. The code that goes into the procedure is contained in one line.

```
MyPubPoint.Stop.
```

This line stops the publishing point. The complete StopServer_Click code procedure looks like the following.

```
Private Sub StopServer_Click()
    MyPubPoint.Stop
End Sub
```

Removing Unneeded Procedures

The following two procedures from the Encoder Push application are not needed by the Encoder Pull application:

- **Timer1_Timer procedure** This procedure is not needed because the server will not be displaying the status of the server load on the computer. Remove the Timer1_Timer procedure from the code.

- **Player_PlayStateChange procedure** This procedure is not needed because the Player will not be displaying the bit rate of the Player. Remove this procedure.

Running the Encoder Pull Application

After you have entered all the code, run the project in Visual Basic. From the Run menu, select Start. If there are no errors, the user interface of your application should look like Figure 7.3. You can compare your code to the complete code listing in the next section.

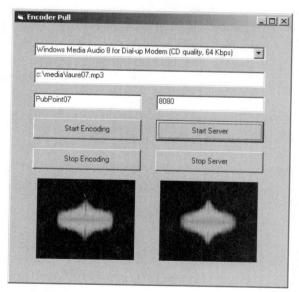

Figure 7.3 Encoder Pull application pulling content from the encoder.

Use the following procedure to test your application:

1. Choose an audio encoding profile.

2. Change the path to the file you want encoded, if different from the default.

3. Change the publishing-point name and port number, if desired.

4. Click the Start Encoding button. After a moment, the window below the Start Encoding button will display a visualization from the Player. This shows that the encoder is broadcasting and that the Player is able to receive this broadcast.

5. Click the Start Server button. After a few moments, a visualization from the Player appears below the server buttons. There will be a slight reverberation effect because you are hearing one stream directly from the encoder and the other stream after it has passed through the server.

6. Click the Stop Encoding button. After a moment, the Player below the encoder buttons will stop. A few moments later, the Player below the server buttons also stops.

7. Start the encoder again. After a moment, the Player under the encoder buttons will start playing, and a few moments later the Player below the server buttons will start playing again.

8. You can start and stop the server and see that, when the server starts again, it doesn't start at the beginning of the song, but starts at whatever point in the stream the encoder is currently broadcasting.

Complete copies of the source code and digital media for this application are on the companion CD.

Source Code for the Encoder Pull Application

Here is the complete source code listing for the Encoder Pull application.

```
Dim WithEvents MyEncoder As WMEncoder
Dim MyProColl As IWMEncProfileCollection
Dim MySrcGrpColl As IWMEncSourceGroupCollection
Dim MySrcGrp As IWMEncSourceGroup
Dim MyAudioSource As IWMEncSource
Dim MyBroadcast As IWMEncBroadcast

Dim Server As WMSServer
Dim MyPubPoint As IWMSBroadcastPublishingPoint
Dim MyPubPoints As IWMSPublishingPoints
```

```
Dim DummyText As String

Private Sub Form_Load()
    Set MyEncoder = New WMEncoder

    Dim i As Integer
    Set MyProColl = MyEncoder.ProfileCollection
    For i = 0 To (MyProColl.Count - 1)
      ProfileComboBox.AddItem MyProColl.Item(i).Name, i
    Next i

    Set MySrcGrpColl = MyEncoder.SourceGroupCollection
    Set MySrcGrp = MySrcGrpColl.Add("SG_1")
    Set MyAudioSource = MySrcGrp.AddSource(WMENC_AUDIO)
    MySourcePath.Text = "c:\media\laure07.mp3"

    DummyText = "Choose a profile first."
    ProfileComboBox.Text = DummyText

    Player.uiMode = "none"
    Player2.uiMode = "none"

    PubPoint.Text = "PubPoint07"
    Address.Text = "8080"

    Set Server = New WMSServer
End Sub

Private Sub StartEncoder_Click()
    MyAudioSource.SetInput (MySourcePath.Text)
    MyAudioSource.Repeat = True

    Dim MyProfileName As String
    MyProfileName = ProfileComboBox.Text
    If MyProfileName = DummyText Then
        MsgBox ("Please enter a profile before encoding.")
        Exit Sub
    End If

    Dim i As Integer
    Dim MyProfile As IWMEncProfile
    For i = 0 To (MyProColl.Count - 1)
        If MyProColl.Item(i).Name = MyProfileName Then
            Set MyProfile = MyProColl.Item(i)
            MySrcGrp.Profile = MyProfile
            Exit For
        End If
    Next i
```

(continued)

```
        Set MyBroadcast = MyEncoder.Broadcast
        MyBroadcast.PortNumber(WMENC_PROTOCOL_HTTP) = Address.Text

        MyEncoder.Start
    End Sub

    Private Sub MyEncoder_OnStateChange(ByVal enumState As _
                        WMEncoderLib.WMENC_ENCODER_STATE)
        If enumState = WMENC_ENCODER_RUNNING Then
            Player.URL = "http://" & Environ("COMPUTERNAME") & ":" _
                    & Address.Text
        End If
    End Sub

    Private Sub StartServer_Click()
        Set MyPubPoints = Server.PublishingPoints
        Dim i As Integer
        Dim CheckName As String
        For i = 0 To MyPubPoints.Count - 1
            CheckName = MyPubPoints.Item(i).Name
            If (CheckName = PubPoint.Text) Then
                MyPubPoints.Remove (PubPoint.Text)
                MsgBox ("Deleting previous " & PubPoint.Text)
            End If
        Next i

        Set MyPubPoint = Server.PublishingPoints.Add(PubPoint.Text, _
            WMS_PUBLISHING_POINT_BROADCAST, _
            "http://" & Environ("COMPUTERNAME") & ":" & Address.Text)
        MyPubPoint.Start

        Player2.URL = "mms://" & Environ("COMPUTERNAME") & "/" _
                    & PubPoint.Text
    End Sub

    Private Sub StopEncoder_Click()
        MyEncoder.Stop
    End Sub

    Private Sub StopServer_Click()
        MyPubPoint.Stop
    End Sub
```

8

Sending Script Commands

This chapter will show you how to use Windows Media Encoder to send script commands to Windows Media Player. The new application will be called Script Commands and it will let you insert script commands into a media stream to remotely control the Player's actions on a user's computer.

Introduction to the Script Commands Application

In addition to encoding digital media, Windows Media Encoder has the capability to add script commands to a media stream. Script commands are text strings that can launch Web pages, display captions, or provide custom commands for applications that Windows Media Player is embedded in. Because the script commands can be embedded at any point in the media stream, you can use script commands to trigger various actions through the Player. For example, you can use script commands to control a slide show so that the slides are synchronized to changes in music. When the Player is embedded in an application and receives a script command that is part of a media stream, it can take action immediately or it can pass the script to the application for further processing.

This chapter will explain how to use Windows Media Encoder to add script commands to a file while it is being encoded. A Web page will be embedded in the Script Commands application by using a Web page control. Windows Media Player will then be embedded in the Web page that is embedded in your application. When the embedded Player receives a script command, it will pass the information to the embedded Web page. For this example, the script commands will be color names and the script commands will change the background color of the embedded Web page to the color named in the script command.

To create the Script Commands application for this chapter, you will use the Visual Basic form you created in Chapter 4 and add new controls and code to perform the new programming tasks required. You will also need to create a custom encoding profile that provides the encoder with the information it needs before it can include script commands in the encoding process. In addition, you will need to create a Web page by using a Web page editor, and you must also be able to host that Web page on a Web server. No later applications in this book will build on the Script Commands application, but you may want to save it for further use, modification, and study.

> **Note** When you encode material for immediate broadcast, the process occurs in real time, and you can insert script commands to enhance the live material. For example, you could insert script commands to display the names of speakers at a conference, as they begin speaking. If you have a file that has already been encoded into Windows Media Format, you can use Windows Media File Editor to add script commands to it.

The Script Commands application will perform the following tasks:

- Let the operator choose the source media file for encoding. A default file path and name will be provided. The encoder can convert files with the following extensions: .wav, .avi, and .mp3, as well as .asf and the standard Windows Media formats, .wma and .wmv.

- Let the operator choose a file that contains the profile information for the encoding process. A default file path and name will be provided. Any appropriate profile file can be used, but it must be able to specify the simultaneous encoding of media and script commands.

- When the operator has chosen the source media file and the profile file, let the operator click a button to start the encoding process. The data in the chosen source file will then be converted to raw data and encoded into Windows Media Format, as specified by the chosen profile.

- After the encoding process has begun, stream the media to the Player embedded inside the Web page that is embedded inside the Script Commands application. The Player will start playing the file.

- At any point after the encoding has started, let the operator click one of the three color buttons (RED, GREEN, or BLUE), and change the background of the embedded Web page to the same color as the name of the button.

Setting Up Your Programming Environment

Before you begin programming, be sure you have installed the following software and configured it properly.

Installing the Required Software

The following software must be installed on your computer before you can develop the Script Commands example application. If you created the Encoder Broadcast application in Chapter 4, all but the last one are installed already:

- Windows Server 2003, Standard Edition; Windows Server 2003, Enterprise Edition; or Windows Server 2003, Datacenter Edition. Windows Media Services is a component of all three versions.

- Windows Media Encoder 9 Series. You can install the encoder from the companion CD.

- Windows Media Profile Editor. When you install Windows Media Encoder, the profile editor is also installed.

- Windows Media Player 9 Series, if it is not already installed.

- Microsoft Visual Basic 6.0.

- A text editor to create a sample Web page. For more information about creating Web pages for the Player, see Chapter 16.

> **Note**   You should go to the Windows Update Web site and download any updates available for the required software.

Configuring Visual Basic

To configure Visual Basic for the Script Commands application:

1. Start Visual Basic and create a new programming project by selecting New Project from the File menu and selecting the Standard EXE option. Click OK.

2. Add a reference to a COM object that contains the Windows Media Encoder functionality. Add the reference by selecting References from the Project menu and scrolling down to Windows Media Encoder. Select the encoder check box and click OK.

3.   Add the Microsoft Internet ActiveX control to the Visual Basic toolbox by selecting Components from the Project menu and then selecting the check box next to Microsoft Internet Controls. After you click OK in the Components dialog box, the icon of the control is displayed in the toolbox. The component name will be WebBrowser.

> **Note**   You do not need to add the Windows Media Player ActiveX control to Visual Basic for this application. The Player will be added by using the OBJECT element in the Web page that will be embedded in the application through the Web browser control.

Creating a Visual Basic Form for the Script Commands Application

In this chapter, you will build on the Encoder Broadcast form that was created in Chapter 4. The Encoder Broadcast application lets the operator choose an encoding format and a file to encode. The encoded file is then repeatedly broadcast directly to a Player. This chapter uses most of the same form, but modifies it so the application can send out script commands through the media stream to the Player.

Using the Encoder Broadcast Form from Chapter 4

Begin by making a copy of the form that was created in Chapter 4. That form contains the following 10 controls:

■   **ProfileComboBox**   A ComboBox control to hold all the default encoder profiles.

■   **MySourcePath**   A TextBox control to hold the path to the file that is to be encoded. The user can enter a new source path in this control.

■   **StartEncoder**   A CommandButton control to start the encoding process. It has a caption of "Start Encoding".

■   **StopEncoder**   A CommandButton control to stop the encoding process. It has a caption of "Stop Encoding".

■   **MyState**   A Label control to display the current status of the encoder.

■   **Address**   A TextBox control to display the default network port that the broadcast will use. The user can change this to another port if needed.

- **PlayPlayer**   A CommandButton control to make Windows Media Player start playing. It has a caption of "Play Player". The button-click procedure checks whether Windows Media Encoder has finished encoding; if it has not finished, the Player will not play.

- **StopPlayer**   A CommandButton control to stop the Player. It has a caption of "Stop Player".

- **BitRate**   A Label control to display the bit rate of the encoded file. The bit-rate data will be supplied by the Player.

- **Player**   A WindowsMediaPlayer ActiveX control to display the default visualization of the audio file that is playing. This will give the user a visual cue that the file is playing.

Figure 8.1 shows the Encoder Broadcast form created in Chapter 4.

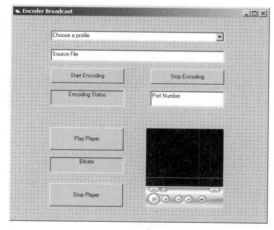

Figure 8.1   Encoder Broadcast form from Chapter 4.

Modifying the Form

Six controls will be removed from the Encoder Broadcast form and six new controls will be added to create the Script Commands application.

Removing Old Controls

Begin modifying the form by removing the following six controls:

- **ProfileComboBox**   The ProfileComboBox control is no longer needed because the profile will be generated by reading a custom profile from a file instead of by choosing a profile from the ComboBox.

- **Address**   The Address TextBox that holds the port number should be removed. The new application sets the port number to the default of 8080 in the code, and the user cannot change it.

- **PlayPlayer**   The PlayPlayer button isn't needed because the Player will now start automatically when the encoder starts encoding.

- **StopPlayer**   This button isn't needed because you can stop the Player by right-clicking the embedded Player window and clicking Stop on the shortcut menu.

- **BitRate**   The BitRate label should be removed. The user can see that the Player has started by observing the Player embedded in the Web browser control.

- **Player**   The Player control should be removed. Instead of embedding the Player directly in the Visual Basic application, the Player will be embedded in a Web page, and the Web page will be embedded in the Visual Basic application by using the Web browser control.

Adding New Controls

Next add the following six controls to the form to provide the new functionality needed to send script commands to the Player:

- **ProfilePath**   A TextBox control named ProfilePath. It holds the path and file name for the profile that is to be loaded.

- **ProfileName**   A Label control to display the name of the profile that is loaded from a file.

- **RedButton**   A CommandButton control that will change the background color of the embedded Web page to red. Name this control RedButton and give it a caption of "RED".

- **GreenButton**   A CommandButton that will change the background color of the embedded Web page to green. Name this control GreenButton and give it a caption of "GREEN".

- **BlueButton**   A CommandButton that will change the background color of the embedded Web page to blue. Name this control BlueButton and give it a caption of "BLUE".

- **WebBrowser1**   A WebBrowser control that will display an embedded Web page. This control is also known as Microsoft Internet Controls and provides the core functionality of Microsoft Internet Explorer.

Figure 8.2 shows the Script Commands form with the new controls.

Figure 8.2   Script Commands form.

Designing the Code for the Script Commands Application

The code in the Script Commands application begins with the same code that was used by the Encoder Broadcast application in Chapter 4. The Encoder Broadcast code lets the user select a profile, change the default path to the source file for the encoding, specify a port number for the broadcast, and start the encoding process. After Windows Media Encoder begins encoding the file, the user can start Windows Media Player and receive the broadcast.

To create the Script Commands application, new code must be added to perform the following tasks:

1.   Load a custom profile from a file. A default path to the file is provided.

2.   Encode a digital media file and broadcast it. A default path to the source file is provided.

3.   After the encoder is running, load a Web page into the WebBrowser control. This Web page has the Player embedded in it. As soon as the embedded Player is loaded, it starts playing the stream from the encoder.

4.   After the Player starts playing, let the user click one of three buttons labeled RED, BLUE, and GREEN. These buttons send script commands in the stream, but only if the encoder is already running.

5. Enable the embedded Player to listen for the script commands. When a script command is received, the Player changes the background color of the embedded Web page to the same color as the name of the button that was clicked.

Preparing the Profile

In previous chapters, the user picked a profile from the list of default profiles that are included with Windows Media Encoder 9 Series. However, you must use a custom profile to enable the encoder to send out script commands.

To work with script commands, you must create a custom encoding profile by using Windows Media Profile Editor. The reason for creating a custom profile is that you need to add a script profile to whatever audio and video profile you want to use for encoding. Windows Media Encoder 9 Series does not currently install a default profile that can use script commands.

When you start Windows Media Profile Editor, it opens to the General tab. In the Name box, type a name for the profile you are creating, such as Script Commands. Then on the General tab under Media types, select Audio or Video, and Script. Next enter at least one bit rate to create a complete profile. For more information about creating custom profiles, see the Help that comes with the Windows Media Profile Editor.

Figure 8.3 shows the General tab of Windows Media Profile Editor with some typical values chosen for using script commands with an audio constant bit rate (CBR) of 58 kilobits per second (Kbps). Video is not selected because this example uses only audio.

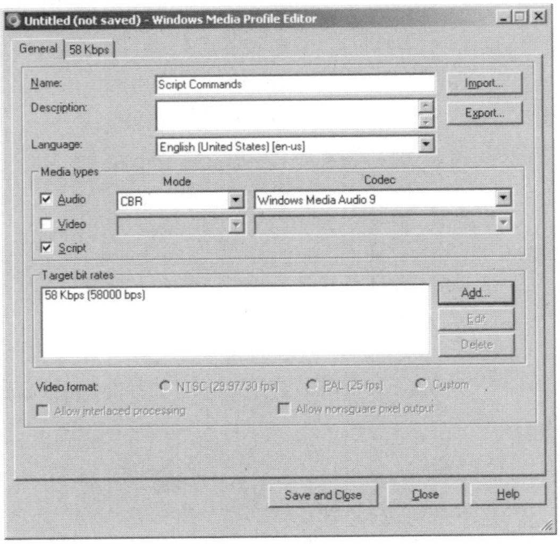

Figure 8.3   General tab of Windows Media Profile Editor.

When you have chosen an encoding profile that includes script and at least one audio or video bit rate, click Save And Close, name the file chapter08.prx, and save the file to the location you want to use (the default in this example is c:\media\chapter08.prx). Later, you will load this file in the Script Commands application. Encoding profiles are stored with the .prx file name extension. Any file name can be used, as long as you load the file with that name when you use the Script Commands application.

> **Note**   If you are encoding audio files only, do not choose a video profile. If you do, the encoder will broadcast video with no picture, and you will not be able to see a visualization to verify that the Player is playing. (This would be equivalent to running a video camera with the lens cap on. The encoder would encode video but the result would be a continuous black picture.) Visualizations are useful for monitoring the output of an audio stream in environments that are noisy or where you may not have a monitor speaker available.

Creating a Web Page

In the Script Commands example application, Windows Media Encoder will send script commands to the Player that is embedded in a Web page, but the Web browser will process the script commands. This section explains how to create a Web page for script commands and embed the Player control in the Web page.

Using Script Commands

The Script Commands application is designed to send script commands to Windows Media Player. Script commands can be processed by the Player in several ways:

- If the Player is embedded in a stand-alone Web page, a Player event handler can be created to process the script and take action. Because you have all the programming power of Internet Explorer, the possibilities for using script commands are unlimited. For more information about using the Player in a Web page, see Chapter 16.

- If the Player has a Web page embedded in the Video and Visualization pane, script commands can be processed by using an event handler. The same features available in a stand-alone Web page are also available in a Web page that is embedded in the Player.

■   Script commands can be processed by a playlist. When a script command is received, the playlist can play another item in the playlist. For example, if a script command with the value of "play ad" was sent every hour, the playlist would play an hourly advertisement. For more information about using script commands with a playlist, see the Windows Media Player SDK.

Creating a Web Page for the Script Commands Application

First you will create a Web page by using the Web-page editor of your choice. The Web page will consist of the following parts:

1.   The skeleton HTML elements of any Web page.

2.   The embedded Windows Media Player ActiveX control.

3.   A text box to display the script commands that are received.

4.   A Player event handler to listen for script commands and process them.

Creating the HTML Form

Using the editor of your choice, create the following HTML code.

```
<HTML>
<HEAD>
</HEAD>
<BODY ID="idBody">


</BODY>
</HTML>
```

This is the standard HTML code required for a Web page. The ID attribute of the BODY element will be assigned a value of idBody, which will be used for a reference later in the Web page code. All subsequent code for this example will be inserted between the two BODY tags.

Adding the Player Control

Add the following code after the first BODY element.

```
<OBJECT ID="Player1" height="110" width="110"
    CLASSID="CLSID:6BF52A52-394A-11D3-B153-00C04F79FAA6">
    <PARAM NAME="autoStart" VALUE="true">
    <PARAM NAME="URL" VALUE="http://%computername%:8080">
    <PARAM NAME="uiMode" VALUE="none">
</OBJECT>
```

This uses the HTML OBJECT element to embed the Player control in the Web page. The name of the Player is Player1. The PARAM elements are used to set up default values for the Player when it loads.

Setting the *uiMode* attribute to "none" hides the controls of the Player and displays only a video or visualization. Setting the *autoStart* attribute to "true" makes the Player start playing as soon as it receives a value for the *URL* attribute.

The *URL* attribute is set to "http://%computername%:8080" so that the Player can start receiving a broadcast from Windows Media Encoder. You may need to replace %computername% with the network name of your computer.

Adding a Text Box

Add the following code after the closing OBJECT tag in the Web page.

```
<INPUT NAME="MyText1" VALUE="" size="14">
```

This uses an INPUT element to display the script command when the Player receives it.

Adding the Player Event Handler

Add the following code to process the script command.

```
<SCRIPT for="Player1" event="scriptCommand(Type, Param)">
    if (Type == "script")
    {
    idBody.style.backgroundColor = Param;
    MyText1.value = Param;
    }
</SCRIPT>
```

The first line and the last line set up the script event handler. Whenever the Player receives a script command, it assigns the type of script command to the *Type* variable and the value of the script command to the *Param* variable.

After a script command is received by the Player, the code in the event handler is run. The code uses an *If* statement to determine whether the type of command is "script". There are several different types of script commands, and the type is defined by the code used by the encoder to send the script command. The value of the script command will be a color name ("red" or "green" or "blue"). The color name is assigned to the *backgroundColor* attribute of the document body style and is also displayed in the text INPUT box.

> **Note** Any valid color name can be used as well as any six-digit hexadecimal number. For example, you can use the color names "papayawhip" or "mintcream" or the hexadecimal numbers "FFEFDS" or "F5FFFA" which are the equivalents. For details on valid color names and values, see the Color Reference topic in the Windows Media Player SDK.

The complete Web page code looks like this.

```
<HTML>
<HEAD>
</HEAD>
<BODY ID="idBody">

<OBJECT ID="Player1" height="110" width="110"
  CLASSID="CLSID:6BF52A52-394A-11D3-B153-00C04F79FAA6">
  <PARAM NAME="autoStart" VALUE="true">
  <PARAM NAME="URL" VALUE="http://%computername%:8080">
  <PARAM NAME="uiMode" VALUE="none">
</OBJECT>
<INPUT NAME="MyText1" VALUE="" size="14">

<SCRIPT for="Player1" event="scriptCommand(Type, Param)">
    if (Type == "script")
    {
    idBody.style.backgroundColor = Param;
    MyText1.value = Param;
    }
</SCRIPT>

</BODY>
</HTML>
```

Running the Script Commands Web Page

Name the Web-page file chapter08.htm and save it to a location that can be accessed by your Web server. For example, on a default installation of IIS, the location might be C:\inetpub\wwwroot\chapter08.htm. The URL to display the Web page will be *http://%computername%/chapter08.htm*.

This page is not meant to run as a stand-alone Web page. If you load it in a browser, nothing will happen. You must load it into the Script Commands application and have the encoder running, or the Player will not play. The rest of this chapter explains how to set up Windows Media Encoder to broadcast to the Player in the Web page.

Adding the Code

To create the Script Commands application, you must modify the code from the Encoder Broadcast application in Chapter 4. That application included the following eight Visual Basic code blocks:

- General declarations
- Form_Load procedure
- StartEncoder_Click procedure
- StopEncoder_Click procedure
- MyEncoder_OnStateChange procedure
- PlayPlayer_Click procedure
- StopPlayer_Click procedure
- Player_PlayStateChange procedure

The Script Commands application will keep the first five code blocks but will delete the last three.

Then the new application will add the following three new procedures:

- **RedButton_Click procedure** This is code that will be called when the RED button is clicked.

- **GreenButton_Click procedure** This is code that will be called when the GREEN button is clicked.

- **BlueButton_Click procedure** This is code that will be called when the BLUE button is clicked.

Reusing the Encoder Broadcast Application Code

Here is the code that will be reused from the Encoder Broadcast application in Chapter 4.

```
Dim WithEvents MyEncoder As WMEncoder
Dim MyProColl As IWMEncProfileCollection
Dim MySrcGrpColl As IWMEncSourceGroupCollection
Dim MySrcGrp As IWMEncSourceGroup
Dim MyAudioSource As IWMEncSource
Dim MyBroadcast As IWMEncBroadcast

Dim DummyText As String
```

(continued)

```
Private Sub Form_Load()
    Set MyEncoder = New WMEncoder

    Dim i As Integer
    Set MyProColl = MyEncoder.ProfileCollection
    For i = 0 To (MyProColl.Count - 1)
      ProfileComboBox.AddItem MyProColl.Item(i).Name, i
    Next i

    Set MySrcGrpColl = MyEncoder.SourceGroupCollection
    Set MySrcGrp = MySrcGrpColl.Add("SG_1")
    Set MyAudioSource = MySrcGrp.AddSource(WMENC_AUDIO)
    MySourcePath.Text = "C:\media\laure04.mp3"

    DummyText = "Choose a profile first"
    ProfileComboBox.Text = DummyText

    Player.uiMode = "none"

    Address.Text = "8080"
End Sub
Private Sub StartEncoder_Click()
    MyAudioSource.SetInput (MySourcePath.Text)
    MyAudioSource.Repeat = True

    Dim MyProfileName As String
    MyProfileName = ProfileComboBox.Text
    If MyProfileName = DummyText Then
        MsgBox ("Please enter a profile before encoding.")
        Exit Sub
    End If

    Dim i As Integer
    Dim MyProfile As IWMEncProfile
    For i = 0 To (MyProColl.Count - 1)
        If MyProColl.Item(i).Name = MyProfileName Then
            Set MyProfile = MyProColl.Item(i)
            MySrcGrp.Profile = MyProfile
            Exit For
        End If
    Next i

    Set MyBroadcast = MyEncoder.Broadcast
    MyBroadcast.PortNumber(WMENC_PROTOCOL_HTTP) = Address.Text

    MyEncoder.Start
End Sub
```

```
Private Sub MyEncoder_OnStateChange(ByVal enumState As _
                    WMEncoderLib.WMENC_ENCODER_STATE)
    Select Case enumState
        Case WMENC_ENCODER_RUNNING
            MyState.Caption = "Running"
        Case WMENC_ENCODER_STOPPED
            MyState.Caption = "Stopped"
    End Select
End Sub


Private Sub PlayPlayer_Click()
    If MyState.Caption = "Running" Then
        Player.URL = "http://" & Environ("COMPUTERNAME") & ":" _
                    & Address.Text
    Else
        MsgBox "Please start the encoding process."
    End If
End Sub


Private Sub StopEncoder_Click()
    MyEncoder.Stop
End Sub
Private Sub StopPlayer_Click()
    Player.Controls.Stop
End Sub


Private Sub Player_PlayStateChange(ByVal NewState As Long)
    If NewState = 3 Then
        Dim AC As Integer
        Dim MyRate As Long
        AC = Player.currentMedia.getAttributeCountByType _
                    ("Bitrate", "") - 1
        MyRate = Player.currentMedia.getItemInfoByType _
                    ("Bitrate", "", AC)
        BitRate.Caption = "Bitrate = " & CStr(MyRate) & _
                    " bits/second"
    End If
End Sub
```

Modifying the Encoder Broadcast Application Code

Several lines need to be added, removed, or modified to change the Encoder Broadcast code so that the Script Commands application can broadcast scripts to the Player.

The following code blocks from the Encoder Broadcast application must be modified:

■   General declarations

■   Form_Load procedure

- StartEncoder_Click procedure

- MyEncoder_OnStateChange procedure

Changing the Declarations Code

One declaration needs to be deleted and a new one must be added.

Removing the Profile Flag

The *DummyText* variable was used as a way to be sure that the user chose an encoding profile from the list of available profiles. This flag is no longer needed. Delete the following line.

```
Dim DummyText As String
```

Defining the Script-Source Object

Add the following line to define the script-source object.

```
Dim MyScriptSource As IWMEncSource
```

The encoder has three main types of sources for input: audio, video, and script. The application already has an audio source, and no video is being used in this application. By adding a script source, you are defining an object that makes it possible to embed text in the encoded stream.

Changing the Form_Load Code

In the Form_Load procedure, you must remove old code that is no longer needed, create a script source object, and set up defaults for the encoder profile file and for the blank Web page to be displayed by the Web browser.

Changing the Media File Name

Find the following line.

```
MySourcePath.Text = "C:\media\laure04.mp3"
```

Change it to this line.

```
MySourcePath.Text = "C:\media\laure08.mp3"
```

Every chapter will use a different media file.

Removing the Code That Filled the Combo Box

The Encoder Broadcast application filled a ComboBox with all the items that were in the default encoder profile collection. Delete the following lines.

```
Dim i As Integer
For i = 0 To (MyProColl.Count - 1)
  ProfileComboBox.AddItem MyProColl.Item(i).Name, i
Next i
```

Instead of choosing from a list of profiles, the user will load an encoding profile from a file.

Be sure you do *not* remove the following line which is inside the ***For...Next*** statement you are removing.

```
Set MyProColl = MyEncoder.ProfileCollection
```

You will need this line for this application.

Creating the Script Source

Find the following line in the old Form_Load procedure.

```
Set MyAudioSource = MySrcGrp.AddSource(WMENC_AUDIO)
```

Add this line immediately after it.

```
Set MyScriptSource = MySrcGrp.AddSource(WMENC_SCRIPT)
```

This creates the script source object and adds it to the source group object.

Deleting Unnecessary ComboBox and Player Code

Delete the following lines that are not needed by the Script Commands application.

```
DummyText = "Choose a profile first."
ProfileComboBox.Text = DummyText

Player.uiMode = "none"
```

The first two lines were used by the Encoder Broadcast application to set up the variable and the initial value for the profile-collection ComboBox. Because the Script Commands application loads the profile from a file, the ComboBox has been removed from the form.

The final line set the *uiMode* property of the Player to "none". It can be deleted, because the Player control is not used in the Script Commands application.

Deleting the Default Port Number

The port number for the Script Commands application will always be set to 8080. Delete the following line.

```
Address.Text = "8080"
```

The Address control is no longer used to let the user change the port number.

Defining a Default Profile Path

Add the following line in place of the lines you just deleted.

```
ProfilePath.Text = "C:\media\chapter08.prx"
```

This line defines a default path to the encoding profile that is needed by the Script Commands application. The user can define a different path before encoding begins. This file should be the same file that you created by using Windows Media Profile Editor.

Loading a Blank Web Page

Next add the following line to the Form_Load procedure to load a blank page into the Web browser control.

```
WebBrowser1.Navigate2 "about:blank"
```

As soon as the encoder starts encoding, the chapter08.htm Web page will be loaded, but until then, it will look better to display a blank Web page.

Changing the StartEncoder_Click Code

In the StartEncoder_Click procedure, you must add an input for the script source, load the encoding profile from a file, hard-code the port number, and remove code that is no longer needed.

Setting the Script Source Input

Start by defining the input for the script command object. Find the following line.

```
MyAudioSource.Repeat = True
```

Add the following line immediately after it.

```
MyScriptSource.SetInput "UserScript://"
```

This line sets up the input for the script source object and uses the "UserScript" scheme. The "UserScript" scheme tells the encoder to use the script commands plug-in.

Removing the Profile-Checking Code

The Script Commands application does not need to check whether the operator chose a profile from a list. Remove the following lines.

```
Dim MyProfileName As String
MyProfileName = ProfileComboBox.Text
If MyProfileName = DummyText Then
    MsgBox ("Please enter a profile before encoding.")
    Exit Sub
End If
```

Loading the New Profile

Replace the lines you just removed with the following two lines that load the new profile.

```
MySrcGrp.Profile = ProfilePath.Text
ProfileName.Caption = MySrcGrp.Profile.Name
```

The first line gets, from a text box, the path and file name of the profile to be loaded, and allows the operator to change the default. This profile is then assigned to the source group.

The second line gets the name of the profile and displays it in the ProfileName label. This helps operators to be sure that they have loaded the correct profile.

Next find the following line.

```
If MyProColl.Item(i).Name = MyProfileName Then
```

Change it to look like this.

```
If MyProColl.Item(i).Name = ProfileName.Caption Then
```

The profile name is stored and displayed in the ProfileName label.

Inserting the Port Number

The Encoder Broadcast application obtained the port number from a text box. The Script Commands application just uses the default port of 8080. Find the following line.

```
MyBroadcast.PortNumber(WMENC_PROTOCOL_HTTP) = Address.Text
```

Change it to this.

```
MyBroadcast.PortNumber(WMENC_PROTOCOL_HTTP) = "8080"
```

Changing the Encoder State-Change Code

You must add one line to the MyEncoder_OnStateChange procedure to make the Player start playing when the encoder starts encoding.

Find the following line.

```
MyState.Caption = "Encoder Running"
```

Add this line immediately after it.

```
WebBrowser1.Navigate2 "http://%computername%/chapter08.htm"
```

This line will cause the Web browser control to load the Web page that you created earlier in this chapter. Be sure that the URL you use is accessible from your application. You may need to replace %computername% with the network name of your computer.

The Web page that is loaded has the Player embedded in it. As soon as the Web page is loaded, the Player in the Web page will start playing the stream being sent from the encoder.

Adding New Procedures for the Script Commands Application

There are three buttons on the form that will be used to send different script commands to the Player embedded in the Web page. This section shows how to add the code for those buttons.

For more information on sending and receiving script commands, see the Windows Media Encoder SDK and Windows Media Player SDK.

Adding the RED Button Code

Double-click the RED button on the form to generate the RedButton_Click procedure. Add the following lines inside the procedure.

```
If MyEncoder.RunState = WMENC_ENCODER_RUNNING Then
    MyEncoder.SendScript 0, "script", "red"
End If
```

This code checks whether the encoder is running. If it is, the *SendScript* method sends a script of type "script" with the value of "red".

The following lines show the complete code for the RedButton_Click procedure.

```
Private Sub RedButton_Click()
    If MyEncoder.RunState = WMENC_ENCODER_RUNNING Then
        MyEncoder.SendScript 0, "script", "red"
    End If
End Sub
```

Adding the GREEN Button Code

Double-click the GREEN button on the form to generate the GreenButton_Click procedure. Add the following lines inside the procedure.

```
If MyEncoder.RunState = WMENC_ENCODER_RUNNING Then
    MyEncoder.SendScript 0, "script", "green"
End If
```

This code also checks whether the encoder is running, and if it is, sends a script of type "script" with the value of "green".

The following lines show the complete code for the GreenButton_Click procedure.

```
Private Sub GreenButton_Click()
    If MyEncoder.RunState = WMENC_ENCODER_RUNNING Then
        MyEncoder.SendScript 0, "script", "green"
    End If
End Sub
```

Adding the BLUE Button Code

Double-click the BLUE button on the form to generate the BlueButton_Click procedure. Add the following lines inside the procedure.

```
If MyEncoder.RunState = WMENC_ENCODER_RUNNING Then
    MyEncoder.SendScript 0, "script", "blue"
End If
```

This code works the same way, but sends a value of "blue". The following lines show the complete code for the BlueButton_Click procedure.

```
Private Sub BlueButton_Click()
    If MyEncoder.RunState = WMENC_ENCODER_RUNNING Then
        MyEncoder.SendScript 0, "script", "blue"
    End If
End Sub
```

> **Note**   The word "script" is a custom script command type, and has no special meaning to Windows Media Player. The code in the Web page checks for the word "script" and processes any values when it finds that type.

Removing Unneeded Procedures

The following three procedures from the Encoder Broadcast application are not needed by the Script Commands application:

- **PlayPlayer_Click procedure**   This procedure is not needed because the Player will be started automatically when the encoder starts encoding. Remove the entire PlayPlayer_Click procedure from the code.

- **StopPlayer_Click procedure**   This procedure is not needed because the operator can stop playing by quitting the Player. Remove this procedure.

- **Player_PlayStateChange procedure**   This procedure is not needed because the Player will not be displaying bit rate information. Remove this procedure.

Running the Script Commands Application

After you have entered all the code, run the project in Visual Basic. From the Run menu, select Start. If there are no errors, the user interface of your application should look like Figure 8.4. You can compare your code to the complete code listing in the next section.

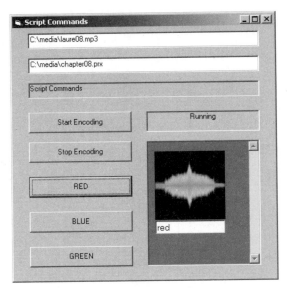

Figure 8.4 Script Commands application with the "red" script command
sent to the embedded Player.

Use the following procedure to test your application:

1.   Choose a different encoding profile if you created one. Be sure it can simultaneously encode audio and script commands. You can add video encoding if you want.

2.   Choose a different path to the file you want to encode, if you have one.

3.   Start the encoder.

4.   After a few seconds, you will see a visualization appear in the embedded Web page and hear the audio playing.

5.   Click the RED, GREEN, or BLUE buttons. After a few seconds, the background of the embedded Web page will change color. This demonstrates that the script command was sent from the encoder and processed by the Player in a Web page.

Complete copies of the source code and digital media for this application are on the companion CD.

Source Code for the Script Commands Application

Here is the complete source code listing for the Script Commands application.

```
Dim WithEvents MyEncoder As WMEncoder
Dim MyProColl As IWMEncProfileCollection
Dim MySrcGrpColl As IWMEncSourceGroupCollection
Dim MySrcGrp As IWMEncSourceGroup
Dim MyAudioSource As IWMEncSource
Dim MyBroadcast As IWMEncBroadcast

Dim MyScriptSource As IWMEncSource

Private Sub Form_Load()
    Set MyEncoder = New WMEncoder

    Set MyProColl = MyEncoder.ProfileCollection

    Set MySrcGrpColl = MyEncoder.SourceGroupCollection
    Set MySrcGrp = MySrcGrpColl.Add("SG_1")
    Set MyAudioSource = MySrcGrp.AddSource(WMENC_AUDIO)
    Set MyScriptSource = MySrcGrp.AddSource(WMENC_SCRIPT)
    MySourcePath.Text = "C:\media\laure08.mp3"

    ProfilePath.Text = "C:\media\chapter08.prx"

    WebBrowser1.Navigate2 "about:blank"
End Sub

Private Sub StartEncoder_Click()
    MyAudioSource.SetInput (MySourcePath.Text)
    MyAudioSource.Repeat = True
    MyScriptSource.SetInput "UserScript://"

    MySrcGrp.Profile = ProfilePath.Text
    ProfileName.Caption = MySrcGrp.Profile.Name

    For i = 0 To MyProColl.Count - 1
        If MyProColl.Item(i).Name = ProfileName.Caption Then
            Set MyProfile = MyProColl.Item(i)
            MySrcGrp.Profile = MyProfile
            Exit For
        End If
    Next i

    Set MyBroadcast = MyEncoder.Broadcast
    MyBroadcast.PortNumber(WMENC_PROTOCOL_HTTP) = "8080"

    MyEncoder.Start
End Sub
```

```
Private Sub MyEncoder_OnStateChange(ByVal enumState As _
                        WMEncoderLib.WMENC_ENCODER_STATE)
    Select Case enumState
        Case WMENC_ENCODER_RUNNING
            MyState.Caption = "Running"
            WebBrowser1.Navigate2 "http://%computername%/chapter08.htm"
        Case WMENC_ENCODER_STOPPED
            MyState.Caption = "Stopped"
    End Select
End Sub

Private Sub StopEncoder_Click()
    MyEncoder.Stop
End Sub

Private Sub RedButton_Click()
    If MyEncoder.RunState = WMENC_ENCODER_RUNNING Then
        MyEncoder.SendScript 0, "script", "red"
    End If
End Sub

Private Sub GreenButton_Click()
    If MyEncoder.RunState = WMENC_ENCODER_RUNNING Then
        MyEncoder.SendScript 0, "script", "green"
    End If
End Sub

Private Sub BlueButton_Click()
    If MyEncoder.RunState = WMENC_ENCODER_RUNNING Then
        MyEncoder.SendScript 0, "script", "blue"
    End If
End Sub
```

9

Encoding Live Content

Previous encoder chapters showed you how to encode existing files. This chapter will show you how to use Windows Media Encoder to encode live audio and video. The new application is called Live Encoder and it will be able to encode digital media and stream it to Windows Media Player.

Introduction to the Live Encoder Application

Windows Media Encoder is not limited to encoding files from your computer. It can also encode a digital media stream from a camera, microphone, or other capture device. The encoder can then save the encoded stream to a file, or it can broadcast the stream to Windows Media Player or to a server running Windows Media Services for rebroadcasting. Using the encoder with live audio and video gives you the option of streaming live events over the Internet or recording them to a Windows Media file for later use.

This chapter will explain how to configure Windows Media Encoder to receive media streams from media capture devices that are connected to your computer. After the encoder is set up so that it can receive the raw media stream, the encoder can then encode the data by using an appropriate encoding profile and broadcast it to the Player. This chapter will show you how to preview the incoming stream before it is encoded, and see the stream immediately after it is encoded (called *postviewing*). The preview and postview streams will be visible in two separate windows. A third window will display the stream as it is received by the Player.

To create the Live Encoder application, you will use the Visual Basic form you created in Chapter 4 and add new controls and code to perform the new programming tasks required. No later applications in this book will build on the Live Encoder application, but you may want to save it for further use, modification, and study.

The Live Encoder application will perform the following tasks:

■ Let the operator select an encoding profile from a list. The list must include profiles appropriate for the live-capture device. Because a webcam was used to test the code in this chapter, the sample profile includes both audio and video profile information. Other capture devices can be substituted, as long as the correct profile is chosen.

■ After the profile has been chosen, let the operator click a button to start the encoding process. The audio and video from the default audio and video sources will be encoded and the encoding status will be displayed. The operator can stop the encoding at any time by clicking another button.

■ As soon as the encoding process begins, the preview window will display the picture of the media stream before it is encoded. The preview window shows the operator what the video looks like as it comes from the camera or other capture device.

■ As soon as video frames of the encoded stream are created, they are displayed in the postview window. The postview window shows the operator what the video looks like after it has been encoded.

■ After a few moments, the Player will start playing the broadcasted stream in a third window. The window will automatically resize to the height and width specified by the encoding profile. The pixel height and width of the encoded video image will be displayed near the Player window.

Setting Up Your Programming Environment

Before you begin programming, be sure you have installed the following hardware and software and configured it properly.

Installing the Required Hardware

For the example in this chapter, you should have at least one audio and at least one video capture device. The encoder will use the default installed audio and video capture devices.

You can easily change the audio and video sources that the encoder will use. To list all the available audio and video devices on your computer, follow these steps:

1. From the Windows Start menu, select the Run command.

2. Type "cmd" and press the Enter key to launch a new command window.

3. Using the command window, change the working directory to the directory that contains the encoder application. For example, type "cd \Program Files\Windows Media Components\Encoder".

4. Type the following line and then press the Enter key:

```
cscript.exe wmcmd.vbs -devices
```

Installing the Required Software

The following software must be installed on your computer before you can develop the Live Encoder application. If you created the Encoder Broadcast application in Chapter 4, all of these are installed already:

- Windows Server 2003, Standard Edition; Windows Server 2003, Enterprise Edition; or Windows Server 2003, Datacenter Edition. Windows Media Services is a component of all three versions. (The example application in this chapter does not require the server functionality, but using this operating system here enables you to use the same operating system for all example applications in this book.)

- Windows Media Encoder 9 Series. You can install the encoder from the companion CD.

- Windows Media Player 9 Series, if it is not already installed.

- Microsoft Visual Basic 6.0.

> **Note**   You should go to the Windows Update Web site and download any updates available for the required software.

Configuring Visual Basic

To configure Visual Basic for the Live Encoder application, follow these steps:

1. Start Visual Basic and create a new programming project by selecting New Project from the File menu and selecting the Standard EXE option. Click OK.

2. Add a reference to a COM object that contains the Windows Media Encoder functionality. Add the reference by selecting References from the Project menu and scrolling down to Windows Media Encoder. Select the encoder check box and click OK.

3. Add a reference to a COM object that contains the Windows Media Encoder Preview Control. Add the reference by selecting References from the Project menu and scrolling down to Windows Media Encoder Preview Control. Select the preview control check box and click OK.

4. Add the Windows Media Player ActiveX control to the Visual Basic toolbox. Add the Player control by selecting Components from the Project menu and then selecting the Windows Media Player check box. After you click OK in the Components dialog box, the Windows Media Player icon is displayed in the toolbox.

Creating a Visual Basic Form for the Live Encoder Application

In this chapter, you will build on the Encoder Broadcast form that was created in Chapter 4. The Encoder Broadcast form lets Windows Media Encoder broadcast content to the Player. This chapter will use some of the same form but will make several changes. The most important change is that the encoder will broadcast live content from a camera instead of recorded content from a file. In addition, preview and postview windows will be provided for comparing the media stream immediately before and after the encoding process. Finally, Windows Media Player will start automatically when the encoder starts encoding.

Using the Encoder Broadcast Form from Chapter 4

You can start by making a copy of the Encoder Broadcast form that was created in Chapter 4. That form contains the following ten controls:

- **ProfileComboBox**   A ComboBox control to hold all the default encoder profiles.

- **MySourcePath**   A TextBox control to hold the path to the file that is to be encoded. The operator can enter a new source path in this control.

- **StartEncoder**   A CommandButton control to start the encoding process. It has a caption of "Start Encoding".

- **StopEncoder**   A CommandButton control to stop the encoding process. It has a caption of "Stop Encoding".

- **MyState**   A Label control to display the current status of the encoder.

- **Address**   A TextBox control to display the default network port that the broadcast will use. The operator can change this to another port, if needed.

- **PlayPlayer**   A CommandButton control to make Windows Media Player start playing. It has a caption of "Play Player". The button-click procedure checks whether Windows Media Encoder has finished encoding; if it has not finished, the Player will not play.

- **StopPlayer**   A CommandButton control to stop the Player. It has a caption of "Stop Player".

- **BitRate**   A Label control to display the bit rate of the encoded file. The bit-rate data will be supplied by the Player.

- **Player**   A WindowsMediaPlayer ActiveX control to display the default visualization of the audio file that is playing. This will give the operator a visual cue that the file is playing.

Figure 9.1 shows the Encoder Broadcast form created in Chapter 4.

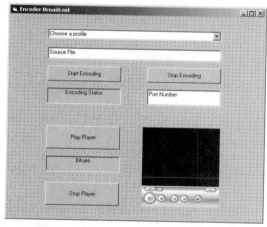

Figure 9.1   Encoder Broadcast form from Chapter 4.

Modifying the Form

To create the Live Encoder application, five controls must be removed from the Encoder Broadcast form. Then six new controls must be added to the form to create preview and postview video windows.

Removing Old Controls

Begin modifying the form by removing the following five controls:

- **MySourcePath**   The MySourcePath TextBox control should be removed. Instead of broadcasting from a source file, the Live Encoder application uses a live audio and video source for the content.

- **Address** The Address TextBox that holds the port number should be removed. The new application sets the port number to the default of 8080 in the code, and the operator cannot change it.

- **PlayPlayer** The PlayPlayer button isn't needed because the Player will now start automatically when the encoder starts encoding.

- **StopPlayer** This button isn't needed because you can stop the Player by stopping the encoding process or by quitting the application.

- **BitRate** The BitRate Label control should be removed. The operator can tell that the Player has started by watching the Player.

Adding New Controls

Next add the following six controls to the form to provide the new functionality needed to send live content to the Player:

- **Label1** A Label control named Label1 to identify the preview window. Give it a caption of "Preview:"

- **Picture1** A PictureBox control named Picture1 to display the video immediately before it is encoded.

- **Label2** A Label control to identify the postview window. Give it a caption of "Postview:"

- **Picture2** A PictureBox control to display the video immediately after it is encoded.

- **Label3** A Label control to identify the Player window. Give it a caption of "Player:"

- **VideoSize** A Label control to display the width and height of the video image, in pixels, after it is encoded. Each encoding profile specifies a default width and height for the encoded video stream.

Figure 9.2 shows the Live Encoder form with the new controls on it.

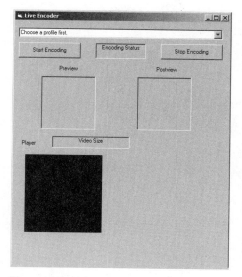

Figure 9.2   Live Encoder form.

Designing the Code for the Live Encoder Application

The code in the Live Encoder application begins with the same code that was used by the Encoder Broadcast application in Chapter 4. The Encoder Broadcast code let the operator select a profile, change the default path to the source file for the encoding, and specify a port number for the broadcast. After Windows Media Encoder began encoding the file, the operator could start the Player and begin receiving the broadcast.

To create the Live Encoder application, the Encoder Broadcast code must be modified to perform the following tasks:

1. Set up the application to use the default audio and video devices in the computer as the audio and video sources of the content to be broadcast.

2. Display a preview image of the video content immediately before it is encoded. To display the preview, the encoder must be running.

3. Display in a separate window a postview image of the video content immediately after it is encoded. To display the postview, the encoder must be running.

4. Automatically start Windows Media Player to receive the content being broadcast.

5. After the Player begins receiving the broadcast, resize the Player window to match the width and height of the video image. This will preserve the aspect ratio of the video image.

6. Display the numeric values of the width and height in pixels.

Adding the Code

To create the Live Encoder application, you must modify the code from the Encoder Broadcast application in Chapter 4. That application included the following eight Visual Basic code blocks:

- General declarations
- Form_Load procedure
- StartEncoder_Click procedure
- StopEncoder_Click procedure
- MyEncoder_OnStateChange procedure
- PlayPlayer_Click procedure
- StopPlayer_Click procedure
- Player_PlayStateChange procedure

The Live Encoder application will keep six of the code blocks but will delete the following two:

- PlayPlayer_Click procedure
- StopPlayer_Click procedure

> **Note**   No new procedures will be added to the Encoder Broadcast code. All the code blocks from the Encoder Broadcast application will be either modified or deleted.

Reusing the Encoder Broadcast Application Code

The following code from the Encoder Broadcast application in Chapter 4 will be reused in the Live Encoder application.

```
Dim WithEvents MyEncoder As WMEncoder
Dim MyProColl As IWMEncProfileCollection
Dim MySrcGrpColl As IWMEncSourceGroupCollection
Dim MySrcGrp As IWMEncSourceGroup
Dim MyAudioSource As IWMEncSource
Dim MyBroadcast As IWMEncBroadcast

Dim DummyText As String

Private Sub Form_Load()

    Set MyEncoder = New WMEncoder

    Dim i As Integer
    Set MyProColl = MyEncoder.ProfileCollection
    For i = 0 To (MyProColl.Count - 1)
      ProfileComboBox.AddItem MyProColl.Item(i).Name, i
    Next i

    Set MySrcGrpColl = MyEncoder.SourceGroupCollection
    Set MySrcGrp = MySrcGrpColl.Add("SG_1")
    Set MyAudioSource = MySrcGrp.AddSource(WMENC_AUDIO)
    MySourcePath.Text = "C:\media\laure04.mp3"

    DummyText = "Choose a profile first."
    ProfileComboBox.Text = DummyText

    Player.uiMode = "none"

    Address.Text = "8080"
End Sub

Private Sub StartEncoder_Click()
    MyAudioSource.SetInput (MySourcePath.Text)
    MyAudioSource.Repeat = True

    Dim MyProfileName As String
    MyProfileName = ProfileComboBox.Text
    If MyProfileName = DummyText Then
        MsgBox ("Please enter a profile before encoding.")
        Exit Sub
    End If

    Dim i As Integer
    Dim MyProfile As IWMEncProfile
    For i = 0 To (MyProColl.Count - 1)
        If MyProColl.Item(i).Name = MyProfileName Then
            Set MyProfile = MyProColl.Item(i)
```

(continued)

```
            MySrcGrp.Profile = MyProfile
            Exit For
        End If
    Next i

    Set MyBroadcast = MyEncoder.Broadcast
    MyBroadcast.PortNumber(WMENC_PROTOCOL_HTTP) = Address.Text

    MyEncoder.Start
End Sub

Private Sub MyEncoder_OnStateChange(ByVal enumState As _
        WMEncoderLib.WMENC_ENCODER_STATE)
    Select Case enumState
        Case WMENC_ENCODER_RUNNING
            MyState.Caption = "Running"
        Case WMENC_ENCODER_STOPPED
            MyState.Caption = "Stopped"
    End Select
End Sub

Private Sub StopEncoder_Click()
    MyEncoder.Stop
End Sub
Private Sub PlayPlayer_Click()
    If MyState.Caption = "Running" Then
        Player.URL = "http://" & Environ("COMPUTERNAME") & ":" _
                    & Address.Text
    Else
        MsgBox "Please start the encoding process."
    End If
End Sub

Private Sub StopPlayer_Click()
    Player.Controls.Stop
End Sub

Private Sub Player_PlayStateChange(ByVal NewState As Long)
    If NewState = 3 Then
        Dim AC As Integer
        Dim MyRate As Long
        AC = Player.currentMedia.getAttributeCountByType _
                        ("Bitrate", "") - 1
        MyRate = Player.currentMedia.getItemInfoByType _
                        ("Bitrate", "", AC)
        BitRate.Caption = "Bitrate = " & CStr(MyRate) & _
                        " bits/second"
    End If
End Sub
```

Modifying the Encoder Broadcast Application Code

Several lines need to be added, removed, or modified to change the Encoder Broadcast code so that the Live Encoder application can make live broadcasts to the Player.

The following code blocks from the Encoder Broadcast application must be modified:

- General declarations
- Form_Load procedure
- StartEncoder_Click procedure
- MyEncoder_OnStateChange procedure
- Player_PlayStateChange procedure

Changing the Declarations Code

You will need to modify declarations to change the generic source to audio and video sources. You will also need to declare the preview and postview objects.

Changing the Audio and Video Source Declarations

Find the following line in the declarations section of the code.

```
Dim MyAudioSource As IWMEncSource
```

Delete the line. The source for the Encoder Broadcast application was a generic audio source. The Live Encoder application will use specific audio and video sources.

Replace the line you just deleted with the following two lines.

```
Dim MyAudioSource As IWMEncAudioSource
Dim MyVideoSource As IWMEncVideoSource
```

These lines set up separate audio and video sources.

Declare the Preview and Postview Data-View Collections

Add the following two lines immediately after the two lines you just added.

```
Dim DVColl_Preview As IWMEncDataViewCollection
Dim DVColl_Postview As IWMEncDataViewCollection
```

These two lines declare the preview and postview data collections. As with other encoder objects, a data-view object must be part of a data-view collection. First the collection is created and then a data view is added to the collection. There will be one collection of preview data objects and another collection of postview data objects. A preview data object defines the stream and display settings needed to generate a preview. The postview data object does the same for postviews.

Declare the Preview and Postview Data-View Objects

Add the following two lines immediately after the two lines you just added.

```
Dim PreView As WMEncDataView
Dim PostView As WMEncDataView
```

The PreView and PostView objects will contain information about the preview and postview stream and display characteristics.

Declare the Preview and Postview Data-Stream Identifiers

Add the following two lines immediately after the two lines you just added.

```
Dim PreviewStream As Long
Dim PostviewStream As Long
```

The data-stream identifiers will help the encoder keep track of the streams for the preview and postview.

Changing the Form_Load Code

The Form_Load procedure must be modified to perform the following tasks:

1. Define the source of the content.

2. Set up the preview and postview objects.

3. Change the scale mode of the Visual Basic form so that the Player control can be resized to match all possible width and height values for the video image.

Adding the Video Source

To add the video source, find the following line in the Form_Load procedure.

```
Set MyAudioSource = MySrcGrp.AddSource(WMENC_AUDIO)
```

Add the following line immediately after it.

```
Set MyVideoSource = MySrcGrp.AddSource(WMENC_VIDEO)
```

This line creates a video source and adds it to the source group.

Removing the File Source

Find the following line and remove it.

```
MySourcePath.Text = "C:\media\laure04.mp3"
```

The source will no longer be a file; so a default file name and path are not needed.

Removing the Default Port Address

Find the following line and remove it.

```
Address.Text = "8080"
```

The port number in the Live Encoder application will always be 8080.

Creating the Data-View Collections

Add the following two lines in place of the line you just deleted.

```
Set DVColl_Preview = MyVideoSource.PreviewCollection
Set DVColl_Postview = MyVideoSource.PostviewCollection
```

These lines create the data-view collections to hold the preview and postview data views. Like many other COM-based technologies, data-view objects are contained in collections and the collections must be created before an individual item can be created.

Creating the Data-View Objects

Add the following two lines immediately after the two lines you just added.

```
Set PreView = New WMEncDataView
Set PostView = New WMEncDataView
```

These two lines create the data-view objects for the preview and postview.

Creating the Stream Identifiers for the Data Views

Next add the following two lines.

```
PreviewStream = DVColl_Preview.Add(PreView)
PostviewStream = DVColl_Postview.Add(PostView)
```

These two lines create identifiers for the preview and postview streams. These identifiers will be used to route the streams to the preview and postview windows.

Setting the Scale Mode of the Form

Add the following line immediately after the two lines you just added.

```
ScaleMode = 3
```

This line changes the *ScaleMode* property to 3, which specifies that pixels will be the default units of measurement on the form. The Live Encoder application needs to resize the Player control to the same width and height that the video was encoded in. The Player can provide the width and height information in *pixels*. Computer monitor screens are measured in pixels, and the absolute size of a pixel depends on which type and size of video monitor your computer uses.

Visual Basic can use several different measurement systems for the layout of controls on a form, including inches, millimeters, pixels, and *twips*. The default measurement system used by Visual Basic is twips. A single twip is 1/20 of a *point*, which is a unit of measure originally used in printing. A point is 1/72 of an inch, so there are 1440 twips in an inch.

Changing the StartEncoder_Click Code

You must change the definition of the source from a file to a device, and you must set up the windows that the preview and postview will use to display the views.

Setting Up the Audio and Video Sources

Find the following two lines in the StartEncoder_Click procedure.

```
MyAudioSource.SetInput (MySourcePath.Text)
MyAudioSource.Repeat = True
```

These lines are no longer needed because the content to be broadcast will no longer be obtained from an audio file.

Replace the two lines you just deleted with the following two lines.

```
MyAudioSource.SetInput ("DEVICE://Default_Audio_Device")
MyVideoSource.SetInput ("DEVICE://Default_Video_Device")
```

These two lines set up the audio and video input sources by using the default devices for the computer you are using. If you have more than one audio or video source that you would like to select from, see the Windows Media Encoder SDK for more information on choosing from multiple sources.

Defining the Port

Find the following line in the StartEncoder_Click procedure.

```
MyBroadcast.PortNumber(WMENC_PROTOCOL_HTTP) = Address.Text
```

Change the value on the right from "Address.Text" to "8080" so the line looks like the following.

```
MyBroadcast.PortNumber(WMENC_PROTOCOL_HTTP) = 8080
```

The port will always be 8080 for the Encoder Live application, so no operator input is required. You may need to change this number if the port is not available for streaming.

Defining the Preview Window

Next find the following line.

```
MyEncoder.Start
```

Add the following two lines immediately after it.

```
PreView.SetViewProperties PreviewStream, Picture1.hWnd
PreView.StartView (PreviewStream)
```

The first line sets the view property of the preview stream by using the preview stream identifier and the handle of the first picture box. A *handle* is a Windows programming term for the indirect address of a window. The *hWnd* property of the picture box provides the handle to the preview window. The second line starts the view by using the stream identifier.

Defining the Postview Window

Add the following two lines immediately after the two lines you just added.

```
PostView.SetViewProperties PostviewStream, Picture2.hWnd
PostView.StartView (PostviewStream)
```

The first line sets the view property of the postview stream by using the postview stream identifier and the handle of the second picture box. The second line starts the view by using the stream identifier.

> **Note**   The video displayed in the preview and postview windows will be stretched to fit whatever size the picture box control has been set to. The view displayed in the Player window, however, will be resized to match the actual width and height, in pixels, of the video that is broadcast to the Player from the encoder. It is possible that none of the views will have the same width and height as the original video signal. For example, if a video camera provides a 640 x 480 stream to the encoder, and the encoder encodes it for Pocket PC (208 x 160 pixels), the preview and postview will be set to 100 x 100 pixels (their size on the form), but the Player control will be resized to the new ratio of 208 x 160 pixels.

Changing the Encoder State-Change Code

You must add a line to the MyEncoder_OnStateChange procedure to start the Player when the encoder begins encoding.

Find the following line.

```
MyState.Caption = "Running"
```

Add the following line immediately after it.

```
Player.URL = "mms://" & Environ("COMPUTERNAME") & ":8080"
```

This line will run when the state of Windows Media Encoder changes to the "Running" state. The Player *URL* property is defined with the URL that requests a stream from the encoder on port 8080. This stream will be whatever the default audio and video devices of your computer are feeding to the encoder, and the stream will be encoded with whatever profile you chose. You may need to replace Environ("COMPUTERNAME") with the network name of your computer as a string.

Changing the Player State-Change Code

You must add code to the Player_PlayStateChange procedure to detect when Windows Media Player is playing, so that the width and height of the Player window can be changed to match the width and height of the video it is receiving.

Deleting the Bit-Rate Code

Find the following lines in the Player_PlayStateChange procedure.

```
Dim AC As Integer
Dim MyRate As Long
AC = Player.currentMedia.getAttributeCountByType _
                    ("Bitrate", "") - 1
MyRate = Player.currentMedia.getItemInfoByType _
                    ("Bitrate", "", AC)
BitRate.Caption = "Bitrate = " & CStr(MyRate) & _
                    " bits/second"
```

These lines are no longer be needed because the application no longer needs to display the bit rate. Delete these lines.

Getting the Width and Height of the Image

Replace the lines you just deleted with the following lines.

```
Dim MyHeight As Long
Dim MyWidth As Long
MyHeight = Player.currentMedia.imageSourceHeight
MyWidth = Player.currentMedia.imageSourceWidth
```

These lines store the width and height of the video stream that is received by the Player. The values are in pixels.

Resizing the Player Control

Add the following two lines immediately after the two lines you just added to the Player_PlayStateChange procedure.

```
Player.Height = MyHeight
Player.Width = MyWidth
```

These two lines resize the Player control to match the width and height of the source video. Because the *ScaleMode* property was set to 3 (for pixels), the width-to-height ratio (known as the aspect ratio) will be correct and the picture will not be distorted. This resizing shows what the video will look like when it is displayed in the full mode of Windows Media Player.

Displaying the Encoded Width and Height

Add the following line immediately after the two lines you just added.

```
VideoSize.Caption = CStr(MyWidth) & " x " & _
        CStr(MyHeight) & " pixels"
```

This line displays the width and height of the encoded video in a label on the form. The following lines show the complete Player_StateChangeChange procedure for this chapter.

```
Private Sub Player_PlayStateChange(ByVal NewState As Long)
    If NewState = 3 Then
        Dim MyHeight As Long
        Dim MyWidth As Long
        MyHeight = Player.currentMedia.imageSourceHeight
        MyWidth = Player.currentMedia.imageSourceWidth
        Player.Height = MyHeight
        Player.Width = MyWidth
        VideoSize.Caption = CStr(MyWidth) & "  x " & _
                CStr(MyHeight) & " pixels"

    End If
End Sub
```

Removing Unneeded Procedures

The following two procedures from the Encoder Broadcast application are not needed by the Live Encoder application:

- **PlayPlayer_Click procedure**   This procedure is not needed because the Player will be started automatically when the encoder starts. Remove the entire PlayPlayer_Click procedure from the code.

- **StopPlayer_Click procedure**   This procedure is not needed because the operator can stop playing by quitting the application. Remove this procedure.

Running the Live Encoder Application

After you have entered all the code, run the project in Visual Basic. From the Run menu, select Start. If there are no errors, the user interface of your application should look like Figure 9.3. You can compare your code to the complete code listing in the next section.

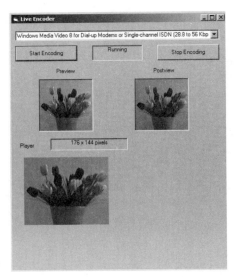

Figure 9.3 Live Encoder application broadcasting to the Player.

Use the following procedure to test your application:

1. Set up your audio and video devices so that they are turned on and working properly. For example, a simple webcam can be used to test this application.

2. Choose a video encoding profile. Do not choose an audio-only profile.

3. Start Windows Media Encoder by clicking the Start Encoding button.

4. You will see a video picture immediately in the preview window on the left.

5. A moment later you will see a video picture in the postview window on the right. The delay between the two views will depend on how complicated the encoding is. For example, the encoding for a Pocket PC stream will happen almost instantly, but the encoding for an NTSC video stream (used for broadband) will take longer.

6. A few seconds later the window for the Player will resize itself to match the new width and height needed for the video.

7. Then the video will appear in the Player window, and you will hear the audio. The sound and picture will be continuously delayed by a few seconds. The width and height (in pixels) will be displayed in the label to the left of the Player.

8. Stop the encoding by clicking the Stop Encoding button. The preview and postview pictures will freeze, and the Player audio and video will stop a few seconds later.

9.   After the encoding has stopped, choose another profile with a different width and height and see the video image change size. You will also be able to detect differences in video encoding quality, depending on the quality of the original source video.

Complete copies of the source code and digital media for this application are on the companion CD.

Source Code for the Live Encoder Application

Here is the complete source code listing for the Live Encoder application.

```
Dim WithEvents MyEncoder As WMEncoder
Dim MyProColl As IWMEncProfileCollection
Dim MySrcGrpColl As IWMEncSourceGroupCollection
Dim MySrcGrp As IWMEncSourceGroup
Dim MyAudioSource As IWMEncAudioSource
Dim MyVideoSource As IWMEncVideoSource
Dim DVColl_Preview As IWMEncDataViewCollection
Dim DVColl_Postview As IWMEncDataViewCollection
Dim PreView As WMEncDataView
Dim PostView As WMEncDataView
Dim PreviewStream As Long
Dim PostviewStream As Long
Dim MyBroadcast As IWMEncBroadcast

Dim DummyText As String

Private Sub Form_Load()
    Set MyEncoder = New WMEncoder

    Dim i As Integer
    Set MyProColl = MyEncoder.ProfileCollection
    For i = 0 To (MyProColl.Count - 1)
      ProfileComboBox.AddItem MyProColl.Item(i).Name, i
    Next i

    Set MySrcGrpColl = MyEncoder.SourceGroupCollection
    Set MySrcGrp = MySrcGrpColl.Add("SG_1")
    Set MyAudioSource = MySrcGrp.AddSource(WMENC_AUDIO)
    Set MyVideoSource = MySrcGrp.AddSource(WMENC_VIDEO)

    DummyText = "Choose a profile first."
    ProfileComboBox.Text = DummyText

    Player.uiMode = "none"
    Set DVColl_Preview = MyVideoSource.PreviewCollection
    Set DVColl_Postview = MyVideoSource.PostviewCollection
```

(continued)

```
        Set PreView = New WMEncDataView
        Set PostView = New WMEncDataView
        PreviewStream = DVColl_Preview.Add(PreView)
        PostviewStream = DVColl_Postview.Add(PostView)

        ScaleMode = 3
    End Sub

    Private Sub StartEncoder_Click()
        MyAudioSource.SetInput ("DEVICE://Default_Audio_Device")
        MyVideoSource.SetInput ("DEVICE://Default_Video_Device")

        Dim MyProfileName As String
        MyProfileName = ProfileComboBox.Text
        If MyProfileName = DummyText Then
            MsgBox ("Please enter a profile before encoding.")
            Exit Sub
        End If

        Dim i As Integer
        Dim MyProfile As IWMEncProfile
        For i = 0 To (MyProColl.Count - 1)
            If MyProColl.Item(i).Name = MyProfileName Then
                Set MyProfile = MyProColl.Item(i)
                MySrcGrp.Profile = MyProfile
                Exit For
            End If
        Next i

        Set MyBroadcast = MyEncoder.Broadcast
        MyBroadcast.PortNumber(WMENC_PROTOCOL_HTTP) = 8080

        MyEncoder.Start
        PreView.SetViewProperties PreviewStream, Picture1.hWnd
        PreView.StartView (PreviewStream)
        PostView.SetViewProperties PostviewStream, Picture2.hWnd
        PostView.StartView (PostviewStream)
    End Sub

    Private Sub MyEncoder_OnStateChange(ByVal enumState As _
            WMEncoderLib.WMENC_ENCODER_STATE)
        Select Case enumState
            Case WMENC_ENCODER_RUNNING
                MyState.Caption = "Running"
                Player.URL = "mms://" & Environ("COMPUTERNAME") _
                        & ":8080"
            Case WMENC_ENCODER_STOPPED
                MyState.Caption = "Stopped"
```

```vb
        End Select
End Sub

Private Sub StopEncoder_Click()
    MyEncoder.Stop
End Sub

Private Sub Player_PlayStateChange(ByVal NewState As Long)
    If NewState = 3 Then
        Dim MyHeight As Long
        Dim MyWidth As Long
        MyHeight = Player.currentMedia.imageSourceHeight
        MyWidth = Player.currentMedia.imageSourceWidth
        Player.Height = MyHeight
        Player.Width = MyWidth
        VideoSize.Caption = CStr(MyWidth) & "  x  " & _
                CStr(MyHeight) & " pixels"

    End If
End Sub
```

Part III

Serving Windows Media

Windows Media Services is the server component of the Windows Media platform. This part of the book will go into depth and detail on how to program a Windows Media server. You will be shown how to develop a series of stand-alone sample applications that you can use and expand on in the future to distribute streaming digital media on a corporate intranet or over the Internet. Detailed step-by-step instructions for every line of code will be provided to enable you to distribute encoded digital media using the three primary methods of streaming digital media over a network. You'll learn how to distribute files to users on demand, make unicast broadcasts of digital streams of live content, and transmit a single multicast stream to all users simultaneously. This chapter will also show you how use XML (Extensible Markup Language) to create playlists of programmed audio and video that can be changed with the click of a button. The sample applications in this part of the book include automation techniques that simplify the user interfaces of the Windows Media components and reduce the number of tasks needed to make the components work together.

10

Creating a Simple Server

This chapter will show you how to create a easy-to-use server application that can deliver digital media files to users on request. The new application is called Simple Server and will allow users to receive audio and video files from the server and play them on Windows Media Player.

Introduction to the Simple Server Application

Windows Media Services enables a Web site owner to deliver large amounts of streaming digital media to many people simultaneously. When an individual uses the Player to request media from a server running Windows Media Services, the server responds by sending out a stream of packets over the network. The Player then assembles the packets into a song or movie and plays them for the user. The server can provide digital media by publishing it in three different ways: on-demand, unicast, and multicast. On-demand publishing is the most common way of serving media. This chapter and the next will show you how to create on-demand publishing points that can distribute files to multiple users on request. Chapter 12 will focus on unicast broadcasts, which send out continuous digital media streams to individual users simultaneously. Chapter 13 covers multicast broadcasts, which send out a single stream that can be received by all users at the same time.

This chapter will show you how to configure a Windows Media server to distribute files over a network when users make on-demand requests through Windows Media Player. To serve files on demand, you must create a publishing point on the server for users to connect to. A publishing point defines a folder on the server that will contain the media files you want to distribute. A server can have many different publishing points, each one associated with a different media folder. When requesting a specific file, all the user needs to know is the name of the server, the name of the publishing point, and the name of the file. Using that information, the Player requests the file from the server, which converts the file to packets and sends them out. As soon as the Player starts receiving the packets, it begins playing the media. If the user wants to rewind or fast forward the media, the Player sends the appropriate request to the server to send earlier or later packets for assembly.

To create the Simple Server application for this chapter, you will create a Visual Basic form and add controls and code to perform the programming tasks required. When you are finished with this chapter, you should copy the Visual Basic project and form to another folder, because you will use parts of that form to create the Serving On-Demand application in Chapter 11.

The Simple Server application will perform the following tasks:

- Let the operator choose the source media path that will be associated with the on-demand publishing point. A default file path will be provided. The server can serve files with the following extensions: .jpg and .mp3, as well as .asf and the standard Windows Media formats, .wma and .wmv. Files that have been encoded into Windows Media Format will provide better quality audio and video.

- Let the operator select a publishing-point name that the server will use for on-demand publishing. A default will be provided. Any valid publishing-point name can be used.

- When the operator has chosen a file path and publishing-point name, let the operator click a button to start the publishing point. The code will check to be sure that the publishing point has not already been created. If another publishing point exists with the same name, the previous publishing point will be deleted and the operator will be notified.

- After the new publishing point has been created, a user can use Windows Media Player to request a media file from the server by using the server name, the publishing-point name, and the name of a file in the folder associated with the publishing point.

Setting Up Your Programming Environment

Before you begin programming, be sure you have installed the following software and configured it properly.

Installing the Required Software

The following software must be installed on your computer before you can develop the Simple Server example application:

- Windows Server 2003, Standard Edition; Windows Server 2003, Enterprise Edition; or Windows Server 2003, Datacenter Edition. Windows Media Services is a component of all three versions.

- Microsoft Visual Basic 6.0.

> **Note**   You should go to the Windows Update Web site and download any updates available for the required software.

Configuring Visual Basic

To configure Visual Basic for the Simple Server application, follow these steps:

1. Start Visual Basic and create a new programming project by selecting New Project from the File menu and selecting the Standard EXE option. Click OK.

2. Add a reference to a COM object that contains the Windows Media Services functionality. Add the reference by selecting References from the Project menu and scrolling down to Windows Media Services. Select the services check box and click OK.

Creating a Visual Basic Form for the Simple Server Application

When Visual Basic loads a new project, a blank form is provided. You will need to modify the form to create the Simple Server application. First you need to add user interface controls to the form and then add programming code for the form and each of the controls.

To create the Simple Server user interface, add the following seven controls to the blank form:

- **PubPath**   Create a TextBox control and name it PubPath. It will contain the path to the new publishing-point folder. The operator can modify this path before the publishing point is created.

- **Label1**   Create a Label control with the default name Label1. Give it a caption of "Pub Point Path:" and place it to the left of the PubPath text box.

- **PubPointName**   Create a TextBox control and name it PubPointName. It will contain the name of the new publishing point. The operator can modify this name before the publishing point is created.

- **Label2**   Create a Label control with the default name Label2. Give it a caption of "Pub Point Name:" and place it to the left of the PubPointName text box.

- **AddPub**   Create a CommandButton control and name it AddPub. Give it a caption of "Add Pub Point". This button will let the operator add a publishing point that has the name and path specified in the two text boxes.

- **NumPoints**   Create a Label control and name it NumPoints. It will display the current number of publishing points. When the operator adds a new publishing point, this number will increase by one.

- **Label3**   Create a Label control with the default name Label3. Give it a caption of "Current number of publishing points:" and place it to the left of the NumPoints label.

When you have added the controls, resize the form and the controls so that the form is easy to read and understand. Figure 10.1 shows the Simple Server form with the controls on it.

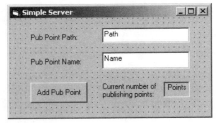

Figure 10.1   Simple Server form with controls.

Designing the Code for the Simple Server Application

The code for the Simple Server must perform the following tasks:

1.   Display the current number of publishing points.

2.   Let the operator select the path to a publishing point that is to be added. A default path is provided.

3.   Let the operator select the name of a publishing point that is to be added. A default name is provided.

4.   Add a new publishing point. If a publishing point with the same name already exists, the new publishing point will not be added and the application will exit.

5.   Display the new number of publishing points. The number will increase by one when the AddPub button is clicked.

Adding the Code

The code for the Simple Server application is divided into these three blocks, which are discussed in the sections that follow:

■   **General declarations**   Variables that can be used in any procedure need to be declared in this block. Variables defined inside a procedure are not available in another procedure.

■   **Form_Load procedure**   This is code that runs when the application starts. After this code has been executed, the application is ready for operator input.

■   **AddPub_Click procedure**   This is code that runs when the operator clicks the button to add a new publishing point.

Adding the Declarations Code

The declarations are located at the top of the form module and are part of the general code object. The variables defined in this declarations area are accessible from any procedure in this form module, because they are declared outside any procedure.

Adding the Server Objects

Put the following declarations at the top of the form module to define the Windows Media Services objects needed for this application. Each line defines a particular server object.

```
Dim Server As WMSServer
Dim MyPubPoint As IWMSOnDemandPublishingPoint
Dim MyPubPoints As IWMSPublishingPoints
```

The following Windows Media Services objects are used in this program:

■   **WMSServer**   This object, named Server in this program, is the primary server object.

■   **IWMSPublishingPoints**   This object, named MyPubPoints, is a collection of publishing points that the server uses to keep track of all publishing points. Before you begin programming, you can look at the Windows Media Services portion of the Microsoft Management Console to see how many publishing points already exist before you run the Simple Server application.

■   **IWMSOnDemandPublishingPoint**   This object, named MyPubPoint, is a single publishing point. There are two basic types of publishing points: on-demand and broadcast. For more information about publishing points, see the Windows Media Services documentation. This application will focus on the on-demand type of publishing point. Essentially, an on-demand publishing point allows the client to receive individual digital media streams by request.

For more information about the object model of Windows Media Services, see the Windows Media Services SDK.

> **Note**   Be sure that you added Windows Media Services as a reference when you set up the project for this application. If you didn't, the objects will not be defined. For more information, see "Configuring Visual Basic" earlier in this chapter.

Adding the Form_Load Code

The Form_Load procedure is code that runs when the form is loaded. The following tasks are performed in this procedure, and each is discussed in the sections that follow:

1.   Create a Windows Media Server object.

2.   Set the default path to the publishing point that is to be created and store it in the PubPath text box so that the operator can modify it if desired.

3.   Set the default name of the publishing point that is to be created and store it in the PubPointName text box so that the operator can modify it if desired.

4.   Create the publishing-points collection object and get the count of the current number of publishing points.

All the Form_Load code must be inserted in the following procedure, which is automatically created in the form's code module when you double-click the form.

```
Private Sub Form_Load()

End Sub
```

Creating the Server Object

To create the server object, add the following line of code as the first line inside the Form_Load procedure.

```
Set Server = New WMSServer
```

In the declarations section, the server object was defined, but the object doesn't exist until you create it with the ***New*** command and assign the new object to the previously defined variable name.

Creating a Default Path to the Publishing Point

Next add the following line to the procedure to assign a default publishing-point path to the PubPath text box.

```
PubPath.Text = "C:\media\"
```

This lets the operator change the location of the publishing point, if desired, but provides a default choice that is the most common location for a publishing point.

Creating a Default Name for the Publishing Point

Add the following line to assign a default publishing-point name to the PubPointName text box.

```
PubPointName.Text = "PubPoint10"
```

This allows the operator to change the name of the publishing point if desired, but provides a default choice. You can use any unique name.

Determining the Current Number of Publishing Points

Add the following lines to create a publishing-points collection object and get the number of publishing points currently contained in the collection.

```
Set MyPubPoints = Server.PublishingPoints
NumPoints.Caption = MyPubPoints.Count
```

The declarations section defined this type of object, but you need to create an instance of a publishing-point collection object here. After the object is created, you can determine the number of publishing points with the *Count* property and display that number in the NumPoints label. The purpose of the second line is to give the operator instant visual feedback that something has happened.

Adding the AddPub_Click Procedure

After the global variables have been declared and the Form_Load procedure has been executed, the application is ready for operator input. The operator can change the default publishing-point name and folder path by typing new values in the text boxes. When ready to add a publishing point, the operator clicks the AddPub button. The following tasks are performed in the AddPub_Click procedure:

1. Determine whether a publishing point with the same name already exists on the server. Each publishing-point name must be unique. If the name has already been used, the application deletes the old publishing point with the same name so that a new one can be created. A message is displayed, notifying

the operator that the old publishing point has been deleted. See the Warning note at the end of this list.

2.   If the name does not already exist, add the publishing point.

3.   Set the option to allow clients to connect. You must set this option or the client won't be able to play digital media from this connection.

4.   Get the new number of publishing points and display it.

> **Warning**   As a convenience to the reader, previous publishing points with the same name will be deleted in step 1. Because each chapter provides a default publishing-point name (for example, this chapter provides a default name of "PubPoint10"), this should not be a problem. If you adapt the application from this chapter for other uses, you may want to modify the code in the AddPub_Click procedure so that instead of automatically deleting the old publishing point, you ask the operator whether to delete it or not.

The code for these tasks must be inserted in the following procedure, which is automatically created in the code module when you double-click the button on the form.

```
Private Sub AddPub_Click()

End Sub
```

Determining Whether the Publishing-Point Name Is Unique

First add the following code lines as the first lines in the AddPub_Click procedure. They determine whether the publishing-point name has already been used.

```
Dim i As Integer
Dim CheckName As String
For i = 0 To (MyPubPoints.Count - 1)
    CheckName = MyPubPoints.Item(i).Name
    If (CheckName = PubPointName.Text) Then
        MyPubPoints.Remove (PubPointName.Text)
        MsgBox ("Deleting previous " & PubPointName.Text)
    End If
Next i
```

These lines loop through the publishing-point collection to determine whether the publishing-point name that was chosen by the operator and stored in PubPointName.Text matches a publishing-point name that is already in the collection. If the name matches, the existing publishing point is deleted.

Adding the Publishing Point

Next enter the following line to add the publishing point after the name has been verified as unique.

```
Set MyPubPoint = Server.PublishingPoints.Add(PubPointName.Text, _
    WMS_PUBLISHING_POINT_CATEGORY.WMS_PUBLISHING_POINT_ON_DEMAND, _
    PubPath.Text)
```

This line adds the publishing point using the name from the ***PubPointsName*** text box, the type of publishing point type (on-demand), and the path from the PubPath text box. Note that this is one line of code using the line-continuation character (_).

Allowing Clients to Connect

Add the following line to the AddPub_Click procedure to let clients connect.

```
MyPubPoint.AllowClientsToConnect = True
```

Even though you have added the publishing point, you must allow clients to connect before you are ready to publish.

Displaying the New Number of Publishing Points

Finally, add the following lines.

```
Set MyPubPoints = Server.PublishingPoints
NumPoints.Caption = MyPubPoints.Count
```

These lines show the operator that a new publishing point has been added. You must create a new publishing-point object to determine the new number of publishing points, now that you have added one.

Running the Simple Server Application

After you have entered all the code, run the project in Visual Basic. From the Run menu, select Start. If there are no errors, the user interface of your application should look like Figure 10.2. You can compare your code to the complete code listing in the next section.

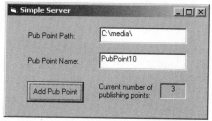

Figure 10.2   Simple Server user interface.

To test the Simple Server application, use the following procedure:

1. Change the default name and path for the publishing point, if desired.

2. Click the Add Pub Point button to add a new publishing point. The number of publishing points will increase by one.

3. Play a file from the new publishing point. Using the URL command from the File menu of Windows Media Player, type in the name of a media file using the MMS protocol. For example, if you have a file named laure10.wma in the publishing point named PubPoint10, you can play it in the Player with the following URL.

    ```
    mms://%computername%/PubPoint10/laure10.wma
    ```

    You may need to replace %computername% with the network name of your computer.

    Another way to verify the new publishing point is to view the Windows Media Services portion of the Microsoft Management Console. It will look similar to Figure 10.3.

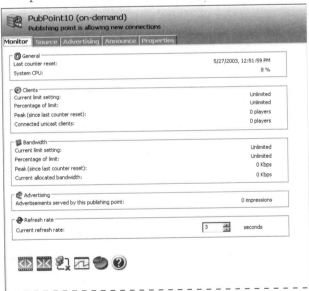

Figure 10.3 Windows Media Services displaying the new publishing point in the Microsoft Management Console.

Complete copies of the source code and digital media for the Simple Server application are on the companion CD.

> **Note**   The number of connected clients for an on-demand delivery is listed under connected unicast clients because the actual packets are sent from the server to the Player using the unicast networking method. However, the server has a method of delivery called unicast broadcast which is very different from on-demand delivery in most respects. Chapter 12 will discuss unicast broadcasting in detail. Also, if the Player has already received a particular file from the server, it will not make another request to the server and you will not see an increase in the number of connected unicast clients.

Source Code for the Simple Server Application

Here is the complete source code listing for the Simple Server application.

```
Dim Server As WMSServer
Dim MyPubPoint As IWMSOnDemandPublishingPoint
Dim MyPubPoints As IWMPublishing Points

Private Sub Form_Load
    Set Server = New WMSServer

    PubPath.Text = "C:\media\"

    PubPointName.Text = "PubPoint10"

    Set MyPubPoints = Server.PublishingPoints
    NumPoints.Caption = MyPubPoints.Count
End Sub

Private Sub AddPub_Click
    Dim i As Integer
    Dim CheckName As String
    For i = 0 To (MyPubPoints.Count - 1)
        CheckName = MyPubPoints.Item(i).Name
        If (CheckName = PubPointName.Text) Then
            MyPubPoints.Remove (PubPointName.Text)
            MsgBox ("Deleting previous " & PubPointName.Text)
        End If
    Next i
```

(continued)

```
Set MyPubPoint = Server.PublishingPoints.Add(PubPointName.Text, _
    WMS_PUBLISHING_POINT_CATEGORY.WMS_PUBLISHING_POINT_ON_DEMAND, _
    PubPath.Text)

MyPubPoint.AllowClientsToConnect = True

Set MyPubPoints = Server.PublishingPoints
NumPoints.Caption = MyPubPoints.Count
End Sub
```

11

Serving Files On-Demand

This chapter will show you how to add Windows Media Player to the simple server you developed in Chapter 10. The new application is called Serving On-Demand and it will let you serve files and play them on-demand.

Introduction to the Serving On-Demand Application

Chapter 10 showed you how to configure a server running Windows Media Services to create on-demand publishing points for distributing digital media files over a network. In that chapter, the only way to know if your publishing point was working properly was to start the full-mode Windows Media Player and make a request to the server using the server name, the name of the publishing point, and the name of the file you wanted to play. Testing your publishing point this way involves steps that can become irritating if you have to do them over and over again each time you create a new publishing point.

This chapter will enable you to embed Windows Media Player inside your application so that the file in your publishing point can be played with one button click. By using programming techniques to automate the repetitive steps, you can make your application easier to use and avoid extra clicks and typing errors.

To create the Serving On-Demand application for this chapter, you will use a copy of the Visual Basic form you created in Chapter 10 and add new controls and code to perform the additional programming tasks required. When you have completed the Serving On-Demand application, copy the Visual Basic project and form to another folder, because you will use parts of that form to create the applications in Chapter 12 and 14.

The Serving On-Demand application will perform the following tasks:

■ Let the operator choose the source media path that will be associated with the on-demand publishing point. A default file path will be provided. The server can serve files with the following extensions: .jpg and .mp3, as well as

.asf and the standard Windows Media formats, .wma and .wmv. Files that have been encoded into Windows Media Format will provide better quality audio and video.

- Let the operator select a publishing-point name that the server will use for on-demand publishing. A default will be provided. Any valid publishing-point name can be used.

- When the operator has chosen a file path and publishing-point name, let the operator click a button to start the publishing point. The code will verify that the publishing point has not already been created. If another publishing point exists with the same name, the previous publishing point will be deleted and the operator will be notified.

- After the new publishing point has been created, the Player will automatically start and request the file using the file name and publishing point the operator selected. After the Player starts playing, it will display the protocol used to send and receive the digital media stream.

Setting Up Your Programming Environment

Before you begin programming, be sure you have installed the following software and configured it properly.

Installing the Required Software

The following software must be installed on your computer before you can develop the Serving On-Demand example application:

- Windows Server 2003, Standard Edition; Windows Server 2003, Enterprise Edition; or Windows Server 2003, Datacenter Edition. Windows Media Services is a component of all three versions.

- Windows Media Player 9 Series, if it is not already installed.

- Microsoft Visual Basic 6.0.

> **Note**   You should go to the Windows Update Web site and download any updates available for the required software.

Configuring Visual Basic

To configure Visual Basic for the Serving On-Demand application, follow these steps:

1. Start Visual Basic and create a new programming project by selecting New Project from the File menu and selecting the Standard EXE option. Click OK.

2. Add a reference to a COM object that contains the Windows Media Services functionality. Add the reference by selecting References from the Project menu and scrolling down to Windows Media Services. Select the services check box and click OK.

3. Add the Windows Media Player ActiveX control to the Visual Basic toolbox. Add the Player control by selecting Components from the Project menu and then selecting the Windows Media Player check box. After you click OK in the Components dialog box, the Windows Media Player icon is displayed in the toolbox.

Creating a Visual Basic Form for the Serving On-Demand Application

In this chapter, you will build on the Simple Server form that was created in Chapter 10. The Simple Server set up the server so it could serve files on demand. This chapter will use some of the same form, but will make several changes. The most important change is that the Player will be added to the form so that when the publishing point is started, the Player will begin playing and also display the transmission protocol used to stream the media from the server to the Player.

Using the Simple Server Form from Chapter 10

Start by making a copy of the form that was created in Chapter 10. That form contains the following seven controls:

- **PubPath**   A TextBox control named PubPath to hold the path to the new publishing-point folder. The operator can modify this path before the publishing point is created.

- **Label1**   A Label control with the default name Label1 and the caption "Pub Point Path:" It is to the left of the PubPath text box.

- **PubPointName**   A TextBox control named PubPointName to contain the name of the new publishing point. The operator can modify this name before the publishing point is created.

- **Label2**   A Label control with the default name Label2 and the caption "Pub Point Name:" It is to the left of the PubPointName text box.

- **AddPub**   A CommandButton control with the name AddPub and the caption "Add Pub Point". It lets the operator add a publishing point that has the name and path specified in the two text boxes.

- **NumPoints**   A Label control named NumPoints to display the current number of publishing points. When the operator adds a new publishing point, this number will increase by one.

- **Label3**   A Label control with the default name Label3 and the caption "Current number of publishing points:" It is to the left of the NumPoints label.

Figure 11.1 shows the Simple Server form created in Chapter 10.

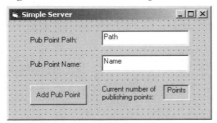

Figure 11.1   Simple Server form from Chapter 10.

Adding New Controls to the Form

First resize the form to make room for the new controls. Click and drag the bottom of the form to make the form approximately twice as tall as it was before. Then add the following five controls:

- **FileName**   A TextBox control named FileName. Initially it will contain the name of the default file to play from the on-demand publishing point. The operator can substitute any media file that exists in the publishing point folder.

- **PlayPlayer**   A CommandButton control named PlayPlayer, to make Windows Media Player start playing. Give the button a caption of "Play Player". The Player will submit to the server an on-demand request to play the file named in the FileName text box.

- **StopPlayer**   A CommandButton control to stop the Player. Give the button a caption of "Stop Player".

- **Protocol**   A Label control named Protocol to display the source protocol of the on-demand file that is received by the Player.

■   **Player**   A WindowsMediaPlayer ActiveX control named Player to display the video portion of the media or the default visualization of an audio file that is playing.

Figure 11.2 shows the Serving On-Demand form with the new controls on it.

Figure 11.2   Serving On-Demand form.

Designing the Code for the Serving On-Demand Application

The code for the Serving On-Demand application begins with the same form and code that was used by the Simple Server application in Chapter 10. The Simple Server code lets the operator select the name and path of a publishing point and provides default values. The operator can add a publishing point, but not before the application determines whether a publishing point with that name already exists. Finally, the number of publishing points is updated and displayed to give visual feedback to the operator that the new publishing point was added.

In this chapter, the Serving On-Demand application must perform the following additional tasks:

1.   Provide a default file name that the Player will use to make an on-demand request from the server. The operator can change this file name at any time.

2.   Start the Player by making an on-demand request.

3.   Stop the Player.

4. .   Display the source protocol of the received file. This will show that the Player is taking the appropriate action.

5.   Display the video of the digital media file, or a default visualization if no video is present.

Adding the Code

The Simple Server application in Chapter 10 included the following three Visual Basic code blocks:

- General declarations

- Form_Load procedure

- AddPub_Click procedure

The Serving On-Demand application will add the following three new procedures:

- **PlayPlayer_Click procedure**   This is code that runs when the operator clicks the Play Player button to start the Player. A flag is checked to determine whether the application has created a publishing point. If not, a message is displayed asking the operator to add a new publishing point before trying to play content through it. If the publishing point has been created, a URL is sent to the Player which starts the on-demand request, using the file name provided.

- **StopPlayer_Click procedure**   This is code that runs when the operator clicks the Stop Player button.

- **Player_PlayStateChange procedure**   This is code that runs when Windows Media Player generates a *PlayStateChange* event.

Reusing the Simple Server Application Code

Here is the code that will be reused from the Simple Server application in Chapter 10.

```
Dim Server As WMSServer
Dim MyPubPoint As IWMSOnDemandPublishingPoint
Dim MyPubPoints As IWMSPublishingPoints

Private Sub Form_Load()
    Set Server = New WMSServer

    PubPath.Text = "C:\media\"

    PubPointName.Text = "PubPoint10"

    Set MyPubPoints = Server.PublishingPoints
    NumPoints.Caption = MyPubPoints.Count
End Sub
```

```
Private Sub AddPub_Click()
    Dim i As Integer
    Dim CheckName As String
    For i = 0 To (MyPubPoints.Count - 1)
        CheckName = MyPubPoints.Item(i).Name
        If (CheckName = PubPointName.Text) Then
            MyPubPoints.Remove (PubPointName.Text)
            MsgBox ("Deleting previous " & PubPointName.Text)
        End If
    Next i

    Set MyPubPoint = Server.PublishingPoints.Add(PubPointName.Text, _
        WMS_PUBLISHING_POINT_CATEGORY.WMS_PUBLISHING_POINT_ON_DEMAND, _
        PubPath.Text)

    MyPubPoint.AllowClientsToConnect = True

    Set MyPubPoints = Server.PublishingPoints
    NumPoints.Caption = MyPubPoints.Count
End Sub
```

Modifying the Simple Server Application Code

Several lines need to be added to the original code to add the Player functionality to the Serving On-Demand application.

Adding New Declarations

Add the following line to declare the publishing point flag.

```
Dim PubPointFlag As Boolean
```

This line defines a flag that will be changed in the AddPub_Click procedure and checked in the PlayPlayer_Click procedure to determine whether the publishing point has been created. Because the button can be clicked at any time, you want to use the flag to be sure that the Player doesn't try to play content from the publishing point before the publishing point exists.

Changing the Form_Load Code

Find the following line in the Form_Load procedure.

```
PubPointName.Text = "PubPoint10"
```

Change it to this.

```
PubPointName.Text = "PubPoint11"
```

To avoid confusion, each sample application in this book uses a different publishing-point name. Publishing points can have any unique name.

Next add the following line at the end of the Form_Load procedure before the *End Sub* line.

```
PubPointFlag = False
```

This line sets the default value of the publishing point flag to *False*. This flag will later be set by the AddPub_Click procedure and checked by the PlayPlayer_Click procedure. Then add the following line after that line.

```
Player.uiMode = "none"
```

This line changes the display of the Windows Media Player control on the form. If you do not add this line, the transport controls will be displayed below the video area. Next add the following line.

```
FileName.Text = "laurel1.wma"
```

This sets the default file for which the Player will make an on-demand request.

> **Note**   Be sure that the file for the default on-demand request is in the directory that the publishing-point path points to. Later chapters show how to use playlists to give the user a choice of items to play from a publishing point.

Changing the AddPub_Click Code

Add the following line at the end of the AddPub_Click procedure before the *End Sub* line.

```
PubPointFlag = True
```

This sets the flag to *True* only if the publishing point was created. This flag will be tested later, in the PlayPlayer_Click procedure.

Adding New Procedures for the Serving On-Demand Application

Three new procedures are needed to complete the Serving On-Demand application: one to start the Player, one to stop the Player, and one to display the protocol.

Adding Code to Start Windows Media Player

The Player start code must perform the following tasks:

1.   Determine whether the publishing point was added.

2. If the new publishing point has been added, start the Player by giving it a URL to the publishing point and including a file name with the request.

3. If the publishing point has not been added yet, do not send the URL to the Player, but, instead, display a message asking the operator to create a publishing point first.

All the code for these tasks must be inserted in the following procedure, which is automatically created in the code module when you double-click the button on the form at design time.

```
Private Sub PlayPlayer_Click()

End Sub
```

Add the following lines to the procedure to determine whether the publishing point was added.

```
If PubPointFlag = True Then
    Dim MyURLPath As String
    MyURLPath = "mms://" & Environ("COMPUTERNAME") & "/" _
                & PubPointName.Text & "/"
    Player.URL = MyURLPath & FileName.Text
Else
    MsgBox "Please add a publishing point."
End If
```

This sets up a simple *If* statement that checks whether PubPointFlag is **True** or **False**. Initially it was set to **False** in the Form_Load procedure, but if the new publishing point was created in the AddPub procedure, the flag was set to **True**.

If the flag is **True**, a URL is created with the following parts:

1. **Protocol**   The Serving On-Demand application uses the MMS (Microsoft Media Server) protocol, which makes a direct connection between the server and the Player. The protocol portion of the URL is "mms://".

2. **Path**   The application creates a path by using the *Environ*("COMPUTER-NAME") function to obtain the name of the computer to connect to. The name of the server could be used instead; for example, if you had a server named laure, you would use that name. The publishing-point name is added to the server name to create the path. For example, if your publishing point is called music, and it's on the server named laureserver, the path portion of the URL would be "laureserver/music/". Be sure to add a forward slash at the end of the publishing-point name to separate it from the file name.

3. **File**   A file name completes the URL. In this case, the file name is laure11.wma but any media file name can be used.

For example, a complete URL for a file named jeanne.wma, on a server named laureserver, with a publishing point called music, would be:

```
mms://laureserver/music/jeanne.wma
```

> **Note** This example creates a general publishing point with an unknown number of files in it. The Player must supply a valid name of a media file contained in the publishing point. You could also set up a playlist of files in the publishing point; then the Player would need to use only the publishing-point name to receive a playlist of the files you wanted to provide to the user. An example of using playlists will be given in Chapter 14.

Adding Code to Stop the Player

The code to stop the Player must be inserted in the following procedure, which is automatically created in the code module when you double-click the Stop Player button on the form at design time.

```
Private Sub StopPlayer_Click()

End Sub
```

Add the following line inside the procedure to stop the Player.

```
Player.Controls.Stop
```

Adding a Player Event Handler to Display the Protocol

For the Serving On-Demand application, it will be useful to display the protocol that is detected by the Player in order to confirm that the Player is receiving the data using the protocol you think it is.

The on-demand publishing in this chapter uses RTSP (Real Time Streaming Protocol) and TCP (Transmission Control Protocol). The Player will display RTSP(TCP) in the Advanced tab of the Statistics dialog box. (If you are using the stand-alone Player, from the View menu, click Statistics.) If the Player has already played this file completely, the protocol is listed as CACHE, meaning that the file is already stored in a temporary location. This assumes that you are using Windows Media Services 9 Series and Windows Media Player 9 Series. For example, if you are using an earlier version of Windows Media Services, RTSP cannot be displayed with the MMS URL.

In this chapter, the *sourceProtocol* property of the Player displays RTSPT for RTSP(TCP), or CACHE if the Player has played the file at least once.

However, after the operator clicks the Play Player button, a brief period of time passes before the Player has enough information not only to play the file but also to supply data about the actual protocol used. If you tried to obtain the protocol data from the Player in the PlayPlayer_Click procedure, you would not get any data because the Player wouldn't be ready to supply it.

The only way to be sure that the Player can supply you with up-to-date information is to create an event handler. This is a code procedure that will be run every time a specific event occurs in the Player. In this case, the event you are interested in is the *PlayState-Change* event.

The Player has several possible play states. The only one that matters in this application is the state that signifies that the Player is playing.

Add the following procedure to your code. Be sure it isn't inside any other procedure.

```
Private Sub Player_PlayStateChange(ByVal NewState As Long)

End Sub
```

This procedure will run every time the *PlayStateChange* event occurs in the Player. Whenever this procedure is called, the current state of the Player is assigned to the *New-State* parameter.

Add the following lines to the procedure.

```
If NewState = 3 Then
    Protocol.Caption = UCase(Player.network.sourceProtocol)
End If
```

This *If* statement checks whether *NewState* is 3, which is the enumeration value that corresponds to the playing state of the Player. For a table of values, see the Player.play-State topic in the Windows Media Player SDK.

If the state is 3, then the *sourceProtocol* property value is displayed in the Protocol label. If the state is anything else, the procedure ends. The *UCase* function is used to change the result into all capital letters.

Note   In this example, on a typical computer, it may take almost a second for the protocol to be displayed and another second for the music to start playing. Using event handlers is necessary when working with software like Windows Media Player that performs tasks that take an unknown amount of time; this is particularly true when the Player is receiving data over a network.

Running the Serving On-Demand Application

After you have entered all the code, run the project in Visual Basic. From the Run menu, select Start. If there are no errors, the user interface of the Serving On-Demand application should look like Figure 11.3. You can compare your code to the complete code listing in the next section.

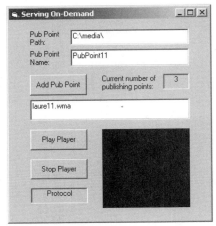

Figure 11.3 Serving On-Demand application.

To test the Serving On-Demand application, use the following procedure:

1. Change the default name and path, if desired.

2. Click the Add Pub Point button to add a new publishing point. The number of publishing points will increase by one.

3. Click the Play Player button. After a moment, you will see the protocol displayed (either RTSPT or CACHE). Shortly after, you should hear the audio playing and see either the video or a visualization.

4. Click the Stop Player button. If you click the Play Player button again, the Player will start playing the file again from the beginning.

Figure 11.4 shows the Serving On-Demand application with a file being served through on-demand publishing.

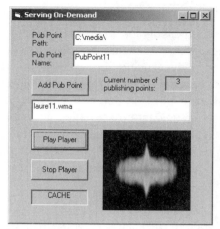

Figure 11.4   Serving On-Demand application playing a file delivered through on-demand publishing.

You can also use the Windows Media Services portion of the Microsoft Management Console to monitor the number of connected clients. Figure 11.5 shows the server displaying the number of connected clients.

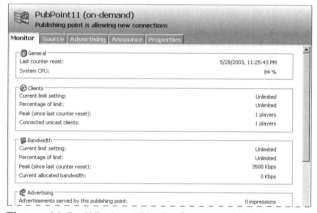

Figure 11.5   Windows Media Services showing the number of connected clients.

> **Note**   The number of connected clients for an on-demand delivery is listed under connected unicast clients because the actual packets are sent from the server to the Player using the unicast networking method. However, the server has a method of delivery called unicast broadcast which is very different from on-demand delivery in most respects. Chapter 12 will discuss unicast broadcasting in detail. Also, if the Player has already received a particular file from the server, it will not make another request to the server and you will not see an increase in the number of connected unicast clients.

Complete copies of the source code and digital media for the Serving On-Demand application are on the companion CD.

Source Code for the Serving On-Demand Application

Here is the complete source code listing for the Serving On-Demand application.

```
Dim Server As WMSServer
Dim MyPubPoint As IWMSOnDemandPublishingPoint
Dim MyPubPoints As IWMSPublishingPoints
Dim PubPointFlag As Boolean

Private Sub Form_Load()
    Set Server = New WMSServer

    PubPath.Text = "C:\media\"

    PubPointName.Text = "PubPoint11"

    Set MyPubPoints = Server.PublishingPoints
    NumPoints.Caption = MyPubPoints.Count

    PubPointFlag = False

    Player.uiMode = "none"

    FileName.Text = "laurel1.wma"
End Sub
```

```vb
Private Sub AddPub_Click()
    Dim i As Integer
    Dim CheckName As String
    For i = 0 To (MyPubPoints.Count - 1)
        CheckName = MyPubPoints.Item(i).Name
        If (CheckName = PubPointName.Text) Then
            MyPubPoints.Remove (PubPointName.Text)
            MsgBox ("Deleting previous " & PubPointName.Text)
        End If
    Next i

    Set MyPubPoint = Server.PublishingPoints.Add(PubPointName.Text, _
        WMS_PUBLISHING_POINT_CATEGORY.WMS_PUBLISHING_POINT_ON_DEMAND, _
        PubPath.Text)

    MyPubPoint.AllowClientsToConnect = True

    Set MyPubPoints = Server.PublishingPoints
    NumPoints.Caption = MyPubPoints.Count

    PubPointFlag = True
End Sub

Private Sub PlayPlayer_Click()
    If PubPointFlag = True Then
        Dim MyURLPath As String
        MyURLPath = "mms://" & Environ("COMPUTERNAME") & "/" _
                    & PubPointName.Text & "/"
        Player.URL = MyURLPath & FileName.Text
    Else
        MsgBox "Please add a publishing point."
    End If
End Sub

Private Sub StopPlayer_Click()
    Player.Controls.Stop
End Sub

Private Sub Player_PlayStateChange(ByVal NewState As Long)
    If NewState = 3 Then
        Protocol.Caption = UCase(Player.network.sourceProtocol)
    End If
End Sub
```

12

Serving Unicast Broadcasts

This chapter will show you how to use Windows Media Services to broadcast digital media to Windows Media Player. The new application is called Serving Unicasts and it will let you send out continuous media streams to the Player by using the unicast method of network distribution.

Introduction to the Serving Unicasts Application

Chapters 10 and 11 showed you how to use a server running Windows Media Services to stream digital media files to users on demand. Publishing files on demand allows the server to deliver files to users at their convenience. In addition to on-demand publishing, Windows Media Services can also *broadcast* a constant stream of digital media. The user still initiates the request for the media, but instead of asking for a file by name, the user makes a request to a named *publishing point*. Unlike on-demand publishing, a broadcast does not allow users to fast forward or rewind the broadcast media. Broadcasts are most useful for transmitting live events or in situations where the intent of the transmission is to give all users the same experience at the same time. Broadcasting is very efficient for the server because the server does not have to process requests to fast forward or rewind the media.

The server has several choices for the source of the media it broadcasts; the source can be an encoder, a file, or a playlist. When it streams live audio and video from Windows Media Encoder, the server can either request data from the encoder (called encoder pull) or receive requests from the encoder to transmit (called encoder push). The server can also read data directly from a file, which is the method of sourcing used in the example of this chapter. See Chapter 9 for more information about streaming live content, and see Chapters 6 and 7 for more details about pushing and pulling content between servers and encoders. See Chapter 14 for more information about using playlists with the server.

Windows Media Services provides two methods of broadcasting: *unicasting* and *multicasting*. The method discussed in this chapter is called *unicasting*. A unicast broadcast sends out an identical copy of a media stream to each user. This is the most common type of broadcast. The server can also send out a single stream to all users with a method called *multicasting*. Instead of making a request to the server, the Player will "listen" to all incoming network traffic and when it detects a stream containing a specific set of multicast addresses, the Player will play the media. Multicasting is more efficient than unicasting, but is not as popular because it requires specific hardware and software. For more information about multicasting, see Chapter 13.

Publishing points are used to access a unicast broadcast. The publishing point contains information about the source of the media to be broadcast. To use a publishing point, the Player must request a unicast broadcast using the server name and the name of the publishing point. When the server receives the request, it gets the media from an encoder, a file, or a playlist.

This chapter will show you how to configure the server to create a publishing point for a unicast broadcast. The operator will choose a publishing-point name and a path to a digital media file. After the publishing point is started, the operator can click a button to begin playing the broadcast. The Player will display the protocol used to receive the stream to show that the unicast network method was used.

To create the Serving Unicasts application for this chapter, you will use a copy of the Visual Basic form you created in Chapter 11 and add new controls and code to perform the additional programming tasks required. When you have completed the Serving Unicasts application, copy the Visual Basic project and form to another folder, because you will use parts of that form to create the application in Chapter 13.

The Serving Unicasts application will perform the following tasks:

- Let the operator choose the source media path and file that will be associated with the unicast broadcast publishing point. A default file path and name will be provided. The server can serve files with the following extensions: .jpg and .mp3, as well as .asf and the standard Windows Media formats, .wma and .wmv. Files that have been encoded into Windows Media Format will provide better quality audio and video.

- Let the operator select a publishing-point name that the server will use for unicast broadcast publishing. A default will be provided. Any valid publishing-point name can be used.

- When the operator has chosen a file path and name and a publishing-point name, let the operator can click a button to start the publishing point. The code will verify that the publishing point has not already been created. If another publishing point exists with the same name, the previous publishing point will be deleted and the operator will be notified.

■   After the new publishing point has been created, let the operator start the Player by clicking a button. The Player will send a request to the server using the server name and the publishing-point name. After the Player starts playing, it will display the protocol used to send and receive the digital media stream.

> **Note**   By default, the first Player to request a unicast broadcast stream will start the broadcast. Players that tune in after the broadcast has started will recieve the broadcast already in progress.

Setting Up Your Programming Environment

Before you begin programming, be sure you have installed the following software and configured it properly.

Installing the Required Software

The following software must be installed on your computer before you can develop the Serving Unicasts example application. If you created the Serving On-Demand application in Chapter 11, all of these are installed already:

■   Windows Server 2003, Standard Edition; Windows Server 2003, Enterprise Edition; or Windows Server 2003, Datacenter Edition. Windows Media Services is a component of all three versions.

■   Windows Media Player 9 Series, if it is not already installed.

■   Microsoft Visual Basic 6.0.

> **Note**   You should go to the Windows Update Web site and download any updates available for the required software.

Configuring Visual Basic

To configure Visual Basic for the Serving On-Demand application, follow these steps:

1.   Start Visual Basic and create a new programming project by selecting New Project from the File menu and selecting the Standard EXE option. Click OK.

2. Add a reference to a COM object that contains the Windows Media Services functionality. Add the reference by selecting References from the Project menu and scrolling down to Windows Media Services. Select the services check box and click OK.

3. Add the Windows Media Player ActiveX control to the Visual Basic toolbox. Add the Player control by selecting Components from the Project menu and then selecting the Windows Media Player check box. After you click OK in the Components dialog box, the Windows Media Player icon is displayed in the toolbox.

Creating a Visual Basic Form for the Serving Unicasts Application

In this chapter, you will build on the Serving On-Demand form that you created in Chapter 11. That form demonstrated using the Player to make an on-demand publishing request and receive the requested stream. This chapter uses most the same form, but modifies it so that the server can broadcast a unicast stream and the Player can receive it.

Using the Serving On-Demand Form from Chapter 11

Start by making a copy of the Serving On-Demand form that you created in Chapter 11. That form contains the following twelve controls:

- **PubPath**   A TextBox control named PubPath to hold the path to the new publishing-point folder. The operator can modify this path before the publishing point is created.

- **Label1**   A Label control with the default name Label1 and the caption "Pub Point Path:" It is to the left of the PubPath text box.

- **PubPointName**   A TextBox control named PubPointName to contain the name of the new publishing point. The operator can modify this name before the publishing point is created.

- **Label2**   A Label control with the default name Label2 and the caption "Pub Point Name:" It is to the left of the PubPointName text box.

- **AddPub**   A CommandButton control with the name AddPub and the caption "Add Pub Point". It lets the operator add a publishing point that has the name and path specified in the two text boxes.

- **NumPoints**   A Label control named NumPoints to display the current number of publishing points. When the operator adds a new publishing point, this number will increase by one.

- **Label3**   A Label control with the default name Label3 and the caption "Current number of publishing points:" It is to the left of the NumPoints label.

- **FileName**   A TextBox control named FileName. Initially it contains the name of the default file to play from the on-demand publishing point. The operator can substitute any media file that exists in the publishing-point folder.

- **PlayPlayer**   A CommandButton control with the name PlayPlayer and a caption of "Play Player". It makes Windows Media Player start playing.

- **StopPlayer**   A CommandButton control to stop the Player. It has a caption of "Stop Player".

- **Protocol**   A Label control named Protocol to display the source protocol of the on-demand file that is received by the Player.

- **Player**   A WindowsMediaPlayer ActiveX control to display the video portion of the media or the default visualization of an audio file that is playing.

Figure 12.1 shows the Serving On-Demand form created in Chapter 11 to demonstrate on-demand publishing.

Figure 12.1   Serving On-Demand form from Chapter 11.

Modifying the Form

Most of the user interface is the same as the Serving On-Demand form used in Chapter 11. Make the following two minor changes in the form:

- **FileName**   Delete the text box named FileName. For the Serving Unicasts application, the Player will simply use the publishing point name without a file name. This will cause the server to send whatever stream, playlist, or file is associated with the publishing point. In this chapter, a file will be broadcast.

■   **Label1**   Change the caption for Label1, which identifies the PubPath text box. The new caption should read "Path and File Name:"

Figure 12.2 shows the Serving Unicasts form.

Figure 12.2   Serving Unicasts form.

Designing the Code for the Serving Unicasts Application

The code in the Serving Unicasts application begins with the same code that was used in Chapter 11. The Serving On-Demand code lets the operator select the name and path of a publishing point and provides default values. The operator can add a publishing point, and the new number of publishing points is displayed. The application also provides a default file name for on-demand requests, play and stop buttons for the Player, a label to display the source protocol, and a window for video and visualizations.

In this chapter, the Serving Unicasts code must perform the following new tasks:

1.   Include in the publishing point a file to be broadcast.

2.   Change the kind of publishing point from on-demand to unicast broadcast.

3.   Make the Player request a publishing point without a file name.

Adding the Code

The Serving On-Demand application in Chapter 11 included the following six Visual Basic code blocks:

■   General declarations

■   Form_Load procedure

- AddPub_Click procedure
- PlayPlayer_Click procedure
- StopPlayer_Click procedure
- Player_PlayStateChange procedure

No new procedures will be added, but the following blocks will be modified to create the Serving Unicasts application:

- General declarations
- Form_Load procedure
- AddPub_Click procedure
- PlayPlayer_Click procedure

Reusing the Serving On-Demand Application Code

Here is the code that will be reused from the Serving On-Demand application in Chapter 11.

```
Dim Server As WMSServer
Dim MyPubPoint As IWMSOnDemandPublishingPoint
Dim MyPubPoints As IWMSPublishingPoints
Dim PubPointFlag As Boolean

Private Sub Form_Load()
    Set Server = New WMSServer

    PubPath.Text = "C:\media\"

    PubPointName.Text = "PubPoint11"

    Set MyPubPoints = Server.PublishingPoints
    NumPoints.Caption = MyPubPoints.Count

    PubPointFlag = False

    Player.uiMode = "none"

    FileName.Text = "laurel1.wma"
End Sub

Private Sub AddPub_Click()
    Dim i As Integer
    Dim CheckName As String
    For i = 0 To (MyPubPoints.Count - 1)
        CheckName = MyPubPoints.Item(i).Name
```

(continued)

```
            If (CheckName = PubPointName.Text) Then
                MyPubPoints.Remove (PubPointName.Text)
                MsgBox ("Deleting previous " & PubPointName.Text)
            End If
        Next i

    Set MyPubPoint = Server.PublishingPoints.Add(PubPointName.Text, _
        WMS_PUBLISHING_POINT_CATEGORY.WMS_PUBLISHING_POINT_ON_DEMAND, _
        PubPath.Text)

    MyPubPoint.AllowClientsToConnect = True

    Set MyPubPoints = Server.PublishingPoints
    NumPoints.Caption = MyPubPoints.Count

    PubPointFlag = True
End Sub

Private Sub PlayPlayer_Click()
    If PubPointFlag = True Then
        Dim MyURLPath As String
        MyURLPath = "mms://" & Environ("COMPUTERNAME") & "/" _
                    & PubPointName.Text & "/"
        Player.URL = MyURLPath & FileName.Text
    Else
        MsgBox "Please add a publishing point."
    End If
End Sub

Private Sub StopPlayer_Click()
    Player.Controls.Stop
End Sub

Private Sub Player_PlayStateChange(ByVal NewState As Long)
    If NewState = 3 Then
        Protocol.Caption = UCase(Player.network.sourceProtocol)
    End If
End Sub
```

Modifying the Serving On-Demand Application Code

Several lines need to be added to the original code to change the application from on-demand publishing to unicast broadcasting.

Changing the Declarations Code

Find the following line in the declarations section of the code.

```
Dim MyPubPoint As IWMSOnDemandPublishingPoint
```

Change it to this.

```
Dim MyPubPoint As IWMSBroadcastPublishingPoint
```

This changes the type of publishing point from on-demand to broadcast.

Changing the Form_Load Code

Find the following line in the Form_Load procedure.

```
PubPath.Text = "C:\media\"
```

Change it to this.

```
PubPath.Text = "C:\media\laure12.wma"
```

This changes the behavior of the publishing point. In the Serving On-Demand application, the Player could request any media file in the directory governed by the publishing point. But in the Serving Unicasts application, the Player does not have to provide the name of the file, only the name of the publishing point.

> **Note**   Be sure that the file you set as a default exists in the directory you are choosing for the publishing-point path.

Next find the following line.

```
PubPointName.Text = "PubPoint11"
```

Change it to this.

```
PubPointName.Text = "PubPoint12"
```

To avoid confusion, each sample application in this book uses a different publishing-point name. Publishing points can have any unique name.

Find the following line and delete it.

```
FileName.Text = "laure11.wma"
```

The file name is no longer chosen by the Player but will be defined as part of the publishing point.

Changing the AddPub_Click Code

Find the following line.

```
Set MyPubPoint = Server.PublishingPoints.Add(PubPointName.Text, _
    WMS_PUBLISHING_POINT_CATEGORY.WMS_PUBLISHING_POINT_ON_DEMAND, _
    PubPath.Text)
```

Change it to this.

```
Set MyPubPoint = Server.PublishingPoints.Add(PubPointName.Text, _
    WMS_PUBLISHING_POINT_CATEGORY.WMS_PUBLISHING_POINT_BROADCAST, _
    PubPath.Text)
```

This changes the publishing point from an on-demand to a unicast-broadcast publishing point.

Changing the PlayPlayer_Click Code

Find the following lines.

```
Dim MyURLPath As String
MyURLPath = "mms://" & Environ("COMPUTERNAME") & "/" _
            & PubPointName.Text & "/"
Player.URL = MyURLPath & FileName.Text
```

Replace them with this line.

```
Player.URL = "mms://" & Environ("COMPUTERNAME") & "/" _
            & PubPointName.Text
```

This will create a request to the server from the Player to play whatever is in the playlist in the publishing point. You may need to replace Environ("COMPUTERNAME") with the network name of your computer.

Running the Serving Unicasts Application

After you have entered all the code, run the project in Visual Basic. From the Run menu, select Start. If there are no errors, the user interface of the Serving Unicasts application should look like Figure 12.3. You can compare your code to the complete code listing in the next section.

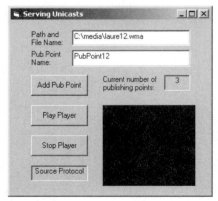

Figure 12.3 Serving Unicasts application.

To test the Serving Unicasts application, use the following procedure:

1.   Change the default publishing-point file name and path and the publishing-point name, if desired.

2.   Click the Add Pub Point button to add a new publishing point. The number of publishing points will increase by one.

3.   Click the Play Player button. After a moment, the protocol is displayed. Instead of RTSPT or CACHE, as was displayed in the Serving On-Demand application in the last chapter, the protocol will read RTSPU. This indicates that the RTSP (Real Time Streaming Protocol) is being used with UDP (User Datagram Protocol). Soon, you will hear the audio playing and see either the video or a visualization.

4.   Click the Stop Player button. If you click the Play Player button again, the Player will start playing the file again from the beginning if no other Players are receiving the broadcast.

If you compare the behavior of the on-demand and unicast applications in these samples, one difference is that the audio and video of unicast takes a little longer to start playing than it does with on-demand publishing. Also, if you use the Full Mode of the Player to connect to the publishing point using the URL you created in this application, you will notice that the seek bar is not operational. The most important difference is that if a user tunes in to a broadcast after the broadcast has started, they will miss the first part of the broadcast. Figure 12.4 shows the Serving Unicasts application with a file being served through unicast broadcasting.

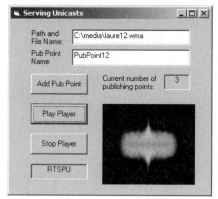

Figure 12.4   Serving Unicasts application playing a file delivered through unicast broadcasting.

You can also use the Windows Media Services portion of the Microsoft Management Console to monitor the number of connected clients. Figure 12.5 shows the server displaying the number of connected clients.

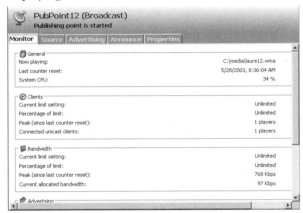

Figure 12.5   Windows Media Services showing the number of connected clients.

Complete copies of the source code and digital media for the Serving Unicasts application are on the companion CD.

Source Code for the Serving Unicasts Application

Here is the complete source code for the Serving Unicasts application.

```
Dim Server As WMSServer
Dim MyPubPoint As IWMSBroadcastPublishingPoint
Dim MyPubPoints As IWMSPublishingPoints
Dim PubPointFlag As Boolean

Private Sub Form_Load()
    Set Server = New WMSServer

    PubPath.Text = "C:\media\laure12.wma"

    PubPointName.Text = "PubPoint12"

    Set MyPubPoints = Server.PublishingPoints
    NumPoints.Caption = MyPubPoints.Count

    PubPointFlag = False

    Player.uiMode = "none"
End Sub
```

```
Private Sub AddPub_Click()
    Dim i As Integer
    Dim CheckName As String
    For i = 0 To (MyPubPoints.Count - 1)
        CheckName = MyPubPoints.Item(i).Name
        If (CheckName = PubPointName.Text) Then
            MyPubPoints.Remove (PubPointName.Text)
            MsgBox ("Deleting previous " & PubPointName.Text)
        End If
    Next i

    Set MyPubPoint = Server.PublishingPoints.Add(PubPointName.Text, _
        WMS_PUBLISHING_POINT_CATEGORY.WMS_PUBLISHING_POINT_BROADCAST, _
        PubPath.Text)

    MyPubPoint.AllowClientsToConnect = True

    Set MyPubPoints = Server.PublishingPoints
    NumPoints.Caption = MyPubPoints.Count

    PubPointFlag = True
End Sub

Private Sub PlayPlayer_Click()
    If PubPointFlag = True Then
        Player.URL = "mms://" & Environ("COMPUTERNAME") & "/" _
                    & PubPointName.Text
    Else
        MsgBox "Please add a publishing point."
    End If
End Sub
Private Sub StopPlayer_Click()
    Player.Controls.Stop
End Sub

Private Sub Player_PlayStateChange(ByVal NewState As Long)
    If NewState = 3 Then
        Protocol.Caption = UCase(Player.network.SourceProtocol)
    End If
End Sub
```

13

Serving Multicast Broadcasts

This chapter will explain how to use Windows Media Services to broadcast digital media using the multicast method of network transmission. The new application is called Serving Multicasts, and it will let you send out a single digital media stream to many Players simultaneously.

Introduction to the Serving Multicasts Application

Chapter 12 showed you how to broadcast a continuous stream of digital media from a server to Windows Media Player by using the *unicast* method of network transmission. Unicasts send out a separate data stream simultaneously to each user that requests one. But there is another method of networking called *multicast* that transmits a single stream to multiple Players all at the same time. To do this, the server publishes an announcement that defines the multicast, and it is up to the user to "tune in" to the multicast at the time it begins streaming over the network. If users tune in late, they will miss the beginning of the multicast.

The advantage of multicasting is that it is more efficient than unicasting. If thousands of people try to receive a unicast broadcast from a server at the same time, the server may not be able to keep up with the demand. But multicasting needs to send out only one stream, and that eases the load on the server and can help to reduce network traffic considerably. The disadvantage of multicasting is that users must tune in to the multicast when it starts, the same way that they tune in to a live radio show. Another disadvantage is that the network must have a specific type of hardware router that can process multicast packets correctly. For these reasons, multicasting is more popular on a corporate network where all the routers are compatible and people can be available to receive a multicast at a fixed date and time. In addition, multicasting over the Internet is more difficult because intermediate routers aren't always upgraded, so there may not be appropriate routes open for multicast packets. For example, you may be able to multicast to 90 percent of the computers that are hooked up to the Internet in Los Angeles, but that same multicast might not be able to be received by anyone in rural Washington state.

This chapter will show you how to configure Windows Media Services to stream a multicast broadcast and announce it. The operator will choose a publishing point, a path to the digital media that will be multicast, a multicast address, the name of the server, and the name and path of the announcement file for the multicast. After the publishing point is started, the operator can click a button to begin receiving the multicast. To verify that the multicast network method was used, the Player will display the protocol used to receive the stream.

To create the Serving Multicasts application for this chapter, you will use a copy of the Visual Basic form you created in Chapter 12 and add new controls and code to perform the additional programming tasks required. No later applications in this book will build on the Serving Multicasts application, but you may want to save it for further use, modification, and study.

The Serving Multicasts application will perform the following tasks:

- Let the operator choose the source media path and file that will be associated with the multicast broadcast publishing point. A default file path and name will be provided. A server running Windows Media Services can serve files with the following extensions: .jpg and .mp3, as well as .asf and the standard Windows Media formats, .wma and .wmv. Files that have been encoded into Windows Media Format will provide better quality audio and video.

- Let the operator select a publishing-point name that the server will use for multicast broadcast publishing. A default will be provided. Any valid publishing-point name can be used.

- Let the operator choose the name of the host computer for the multicast. The default name of the computer will be provided, but the operator can change it, if needed.

- Let the operator choose the file path and name for the announcement file. A default will be provided, but any valid file path and name can be used.

- When the operator has chosen the announcement file path and name, the media file path and name, and the names of the computer and the publishing point, the operator can click a button to start the publishing point. The code will verify that the publishing point has not been created already. If another publishing point exists with the same name, the previous publishing point will be deleted and the operator will be notified. The announcement file will then be created.

■   After the new publishing point has been created, the operator can start the Player by clicking a button. The Player will send a request to the Web server for the announcement file name and use the announcement file to start listening for multicast packets.

Setting Up Your Programming Environment

Before you begin programming, be sure you have installed the following software and configured it properly.

Installing the Required Software

The following software must be installed on your computer before you can develop the Serving Multicasts example application.

> **Important**   If you used Windows Server 2003, Standard Edition, to create applications in previous chapters, you must install a different version of that operating system to create the application in this chapter. Read the first bulleted item carefully.

■   Windows Server 2003, Enterprise Edition; or Windows Server 2003, Datacenter Edition. Windows Media Services is a component of all three versions, but the multicast plug-in required for the application described in this chapter is not included in Windows Server 2003, Standard Edition.

■   Windows Media Player 9 Series, if it is not already installed.

■   Microsoft Visual Basic 6.0.

> **Note**   You should go to the Windows Update Web site and download any updates available for the required software.

Configuring Visual Basic

To configure Visual Basic for the Serving Multicasts application, follow these steps:

1. Start Visual Basic and create a new programming project by selecting New Project from the File menu and choosing the Standard EXE option. Click OK.

2. Add a reference to a COM object that contains the Windows Media Services functionality. Add the reference by selecting References from the Project menu and scrolling down to Windows Media Services. Select the services check box and click OK.

3. Add the Windows Media Player ActiveX control to the Visual Basic toolbox. Add the Player control by selecting Components from the Project menu and then selecting the Windows Media Player check box. After you click OK in the Components dialog box, the Windows Media Player icon is displayed in the toolbox.

Creating a Visual Basic Form for the Serving Multicasts Application

In this chapter, we will build on the Serving Unicasts form used in Chapter 12. That form was used to prepare a publishing point for a unicast broadcast that Windows Media Player could request and receive. This chapter uses most of the same form, but modifies it to make Windows Media Services broadcast a multicast stream and let the Player tune in to it.

Using the Serving Unicasts Form from Chapter 12

Begin by making a copy of the Serving Unicasts form that you created in Chapter 12. That form contains the following 11 controls:

- **PubPath**   A TextBox control named PubPath to hold the path to a digital media file in a publishing point folder. The operator can modify this path and file name before the publishing point is created.

- **Label1**   A Label control with the default name Label1 and the caption "Path and File Name:"

- **PubPointName**   A TextBox control named PubPointName to contain the name of the new publishing point. The operator can modify this name before the publishing point is created.

- **Label2** A Label control with the default name Label2 and the caption "Pub Point Name:" It is to the left of the PubPointName text box.

- **AddPub** A CommandButton control with the name AddPub and the caption "Add Pub Point". It lets the operator add a publishing point that has the path and name specified in the two text boxes.

- **NumPoints** A Label control named NumPoints to display the current number of publishing points. When the operator adds a new publishing point, this number will increase by one.

- **Label3** A Label control with the default name Label3 and the caption "Current number of publishing points:" It is to the left of the NumPoints label.

- **PlayPlayer** A CommandButton control with the name PlayPlayer and a caption of "Play Player". It makes Windows Media Player start playing.

- **StopPlayer** A CommandButton control to stop the Player. It has a caption of "Stop Player".

- **Protocol** A Label control named Protocol to display the source protocol of the file that is received by the Player.

- **Player** A WindowsMediaPlayer ActiveX control named Player to display the video portion of the media or the default visualization of an audio file that is playing.

Figure 13.1 shows the Serving Unicasts form created in Chapter 12 to demonstrate unicast broadcasting.

Figure 13.1   Serving Unicasts form from Chapter 12.

Adding New Controls to the Form

All of the user interface controls from the Serving Unicasts form in Chapter 12 will be reused in the Serving Multicasts application. Three more controls need to be added to let the operator supply the name of the server and the path and name of the announcement file for the multicast.

Resize the form to make it a little larger, and move the controls around to make room for the new text boxes. See Figure 13.2. Then add the following controls to the form:

- **Host**   A TextBox control named Host. Type the name of your server in the *Text* property of the Host text box. In the Serving Unicasts application of Chapter 12, the environment variable, COMPUTERNAME, could be used for the name of the server. But multicasting requires the actual name of the server. In this example, the environment variable will be used, but you may need to supply the name of your own server.

- **AnnouncePath**   A TextBox control named AnnouncePath. This will hold the default path to the announcement file used to announce the multicast.

- **AnnounceFile**   A TextBox control named AnnounceFile. This will hold the default name of the announcement file.

You can also add labels to identify these three text boxes. See Figure 13.2, which shows the Serving Multicasts form with the new controls on it.

Figure 13.2   Serving Multicasts form.

Designing the Code for the Serving Multicasts Application

The code in the Serving Multicasts application begins with a copy of the same code that was used by the Serving Unicasts application in Chapter 12. The Serving Unicasts code lets the operator modify or use the default file path and name of a publishing point. The operator can add a publishing point and see that the number of publishing points on the server has increased by one. The operator can then send a request from the Player to play a digital media file from the publishing point and see the video or visualization of the file. The source protocol is displayed to show the protocol used by Windows Media Player to receive the broadcast.

To create the Serving Multicasts application, new code must be added to perform the following tasks:

1. Provide the name of the server in a text box for the operator to accept or modify. A default server name will be provided by the *hostname* string.

2. Provide the path to the announcement file in a text box for the operator to accept or modify. A default path will be provided.

3. Provide the name of the announcement file in a text box for the operator to accept or modify. A default file name will be provided.

4. Change the broadcast publishing-point type from unicast to multicast.

Adding the Code

The Serving Unicasts application in Chapter 12 included the following six Visual Basic code blocks:

- General declarations
- Form_Load procedure
- AddPub_Click procedure
- PlayPlayer_Click procedure
- StopPlayer_Click procedure
- Player_PlayStateChange procedure

No new procedures will be added, but the following blocks will be modified to create the Serving Multicasts application:

- General declarations
- Form_Load procedure

- ■ PlayPlayer_Click procedure

- ■ AddPub_Click procedure

Reusing the Serving Unicasts Application Code

Here is the Serving Unicasts application code from Chapter 12 that will be reused and modified.

```
Dim Server As WMSServer
Dim MyPubPoint As IWMSBroadcastPublishingPoint
Dim MyPubPoints As IWMSPublishingPoints
Dim PubPointFlag As Boolean

Private Sub Form_Load()
    Set Server = New WMSServer

    PubPath.Text = "C:\media\laure12.wma"

    PubPointName.Text = "PubPoint12"

    Set MyPubPoints = Server.PublishingPoints
    NumPoints.Caption = MyPubPoints.Count

    PubPointFlag = False

    Player.uiMode = "none"
End Sub

Private Sub AddPub_Click()
    Dim i As Integer
    Dim CheckName As String
    For i = 0 To (MyPubPoints.Count - 1)
        CheckName = MyPubPoints.Item(i).Name
        If (CheckName = PubPointName.Text) Then
            MyPubPoints.Remove (PubPointName.Text)
            MsgBox ("Deleting previous " & PubPointName.Text)
        End If
    Next i

    Set MyPubPoint = Server.PublishingPoints.Add(PubPointName.Text, _
        WMS_PUBLISHING_POINT_CATEGORY.WMS_PUBLISHING_POINT_BROADCAST, _
        PubPath.Text)

    MyPubPoint.AllowClientsToConnect = True

    Set MyPubPoints = Server.PublishingPoints
    NumPoints.Caption = MyPubPoints.Count
```

```
        PubPointFlag = True
End Sub


Private Sub PlayPlayer_Click()
    If PubPointFlag = True Then
        Player.URL = "mms://" & Environ("COMPUTERNAME") & "/" _
                     & PubPointName.Text
    Else
        MsgBox "Please add a publishing point."
    End If
End Sub


Private Sub StopPlayer_Click()
    Player.Controls.Stop
End Sub


Private Sub aPlayer_PlayStateChange(ByVal NewState As Long)
    If NewState = 3 Then
      SourceProtocol.Caption = UCase(Player.network.SourceProtocol)
    End If
End Sub
```

Modifying the Serving Unicasts Application Code

Several lines need to be added to, removed from, or modified in the original code to change the application from unicast to multicast broadcasting.

Changing the Declarations Code

New definitions need to be added to the declarations code for the server multicast plug-in. This plug-in is available only with the Windows Server 2003, Enterprise Edition and Windows Server 2003, Datacenter Edition operating systems.

Adding Multicast Definitions

Add the following two lines at the end of the declarations section to define the objects needed for a multicast broadcast.

```
Dim Plugin As IWMSPlugin
Dim AdminMulticastSink As IWMSAdminMulticastSink
```

The first line defines the plug-in object. Windows Media Services uses plug-in modules to extend the functionality beyond the normal tasks required.

The second line creates an object that administers the plug-in for multicasting.

Changing the Form_Load Code

The Form_Load procedure must be changed to update the names of the media file and publishing point, and to create a default path and name for the announcement file.

Updating the Media File Name

Each chapter uses a different media file.

Find the following line in the Form_Load procedure.

```
PubPath.Text = "laurel2.wma"
```

Change it to this.

```
PubPath.Text = "laurel3.wma"
```

Now the file name for the broadcast will be laurel3.wma.

Updating the Publishing-Point Name

Each sample server application in this book uses a different name for its publishing point to be sure that no settings from previous applications can cause errors.

Find the following line in the Form_Load procedure.

```
PubPointName.Text = "PubPoint12"
```

Change it to this.

```
PubPointName.Text = "PubPoint13"
```

Now the publishing point will be called PubPoint04.

Adding the Host Name

Later in this application the Player will need the name of the server. Add the following line.

```
Host.Text = Environ("COMPUTERNAME")
```

This line will get the name of the computer and store it in the Host text box. You may need to replace Environ("COMPUTERNAME") with the network name of your computer.

Adding the Announcement File Path and Name

Multicasts require announcements. You can create announcements for on-demand publishing and unicast broadcasts, but you must create one for a multicast. The announcement contains information that notifies the Player what address to "listen" to.

Add the following two lines to the Form_Load procedure to create a default path and file for the announcement.

```
AnnouncePath.Text = "C:\Inetpub\wwwroot\"
AnnounceFile.Text = "announce.nsc"
```

This will create a default file name, announce.nsc, and put it in the default Web publishing path, C:\Inetpub\wwwroot\. You can modify the path to point to any location that can be accessed on the Web server. You can call the announcement file any valid file name, but you must use the extension .nsc, which is always used for announcement files.

Be sure that Windows Media Services has write permission for the folder you want to store the announcement file in. If the server does not have write permission, an error will result when the server attempts to write the file.

Changing the AddPub_Click Code

Several new lines must be added to the AddPub_Click procedure to configure the multicast server properly. The broadcast is still a broadcast, but must be changed from a unicast broadcast to a multicast broadcast.

A number of tasks must be performed:

1. Notify Windows Media Services not to allow individual clients to start and stop the multicast broadcast.

2. Configure and enable the multicast plug-in.

3. Configure the multicast address, port, and TTL (time-to-live). The multicast address is the address that the server will broadcast the multicast to.

4. Configure the local address that the server will use to make the multicast from. This address may be different from the hostname of the computer on the network.

5. Publish the announcement file.

6. Start the server.

The lines that you need to add to the AddPub_Click procedure should be inserted after the following line.

```
PubPointFlag = True
```

Preventing the First Client from Starting the Server

To put the server instead of the client in control of starting and stopping the broadcast, add the following line to the AddPub_Click procedure.

```
MyPubPoint.AllowClientToStartAndStop = False
```

The default value for the *AllowClientToStartAndStop* property is **True**. If you don't change this to **False**, the server will wait until the first client connects before starting the broadcast. This is acceptable behavior for on-demand publishing or a unicast broadcast, but it will not work for a multicast. Allowing a client to start and stop the multicast would be okay for one listener, but not for multiple listeners. If the first person could start the multicast by connecting to it, that person would also stop the multicast by disconnecting, ending the broadcast for any other listeners.

Configuring the Multicast Plug-in

To configure the multicast plug-in, add the following four lines to the procedure, immediately after the line you just added.

```
MyPubPoint.AnnouncementStreamFormats.Add (PubPath.Text)
Set Plugin = MyPubPoint.BroadcastDataSinks _
             ("WMS Multicast Data Writer")
Set AdminMulticastSink = Plugin.CustomInterface
Plugin.Enabled = True
```

The first line adds required format information to the announcement about the digital media to be multicast.

The second line creates a multicast plug-in.

The third line creates a custom *AdminMulticastSink* interface for the multicast plug-in.

The forth line enables the plug-in.

Configuring the Address, Port, and TTL

In typical TCP or UDP networking, the client and server each have a different address, and they communicate to each other through each other's addresses. But a multicast is sent out from a server, and the clients "listen" to a special address that isn't the address of any client or server computer but is chosen from a reserved block of addresses. If the client receives a broadcast that contains the multicast address it is listening for, the client will start decoding it; otherwise the client ignores the packets.

A multicast broadcast should always contain a destination address, a destination port, and a TTL (time-to-live). Add the following lines to the AddPub_Click procedure to configure these three settings.

```
AdminMulticastSink.DestinationMulticastIPAddress = _
    "239.192.13.92"
AdminMulticastSink.DestinationMulticastPort = 30587
AdminMulticastSink.MulticastTTL = 64
```

The first line creates the destination address. A multicast address is always in the range 224.0.0.0 through 239.255.255.255.

The second line creates the destination port. Port numbers can be any number from 0 to 65535.

The third line sets the TTL (time-to-live) value for the multicast packets. Each time the packets go through a router, the TTL count is decremented. If the count reaches zero, the packets are deleted. The purpose of this is to be sure that multicast packets don't stay on the network forever.

Configuring a Local Address

In addition to configuring the multicast address, port, and TTL, you may want to include the network internet protocol (IP) address of the computer that the multicast broadcast is coming from. If you specify the IP address that the multicast is coming from, the Player will accept a multicast only from your computer and will reject other packets that may be using the same multicast address. In other words, you can use the address of the computer that is sending the multicast to filter out other packets that are using the multicast address but do not originate from you. To include the IP address of the computer that will send the multicast, add the following line to your code immediately after the lines you just added.

```
AdminMulticastSink.LocalIPAddress = "192.168.47.54"
```

This number is chosen from a range of network addresses that are considered private and will not duplicate the address of a legitimate Internet Web site. If you want to modify this application to send out multicasts to other computers, you can eliminate this line. If you do want to filter by using the originating IP address, then use this line, but you may want to specify the IP address of the network interface card you are multicasting from to avoid duplication.

Creating the Announcement

A multicast must have an announcement file that Windows Media Player can use to determine how to receive the multicast. Add the following lines to the AddPub_Click procedure to create the announcement.

```
MyPubPoint.Announce
Dim AnnounceFilePath As String
AnnounceFilePath = AnnouncePath.Text & AnnounceFile.Text
MyPubPoint.AnnounceToNSCFile AnnounceFilePath, True
```

The first line creates the announcement with all the details that have just been defined (address, port, TTL, local address).

The next two lines gets the path and file name that were chosen by the operator for the announcement (or the defaults if no choice was made).

The fourth line writes the announcement information to the chosen path and file.

Starting the Server

Now that the Server has been configured and the announcement is ready, all that remains is to start the Windows Media Services. Add the following line.

```
MyPubPoint.Start
```

This line starts the publishing point. The multicast begins and users can start listening any time they tune in.

Changing the PlayPlayer_Click Code

The code in the PlayPlayer_Click procedure needs to be changed so that Windows Media Player can receive a multicast broadcast. Multicasting requires changing the protocol from MMS to HTTP. Also, because the operator can change the computer name, the new computer name must be part of the string that the Player uses to receive the multicast.

Changing the Player URL Command

In the Serving Unicasts application, the Player used the MMS protocol to make a request to the server for a specific publishing point. In the Serving Multicasts application, the Player must use the HTTP protocol and must request an announcement file.

Find the following line in the PlayPlayer_Click procedure.

```
Player.URL = "mms://" & Environ("COMPUTERNAME") & "/" _
             & PubPointName.Text
```

Change it to this.

```
Player.URL = "http://" & Host.Text & "/" & AnnounceFile.Text
```

Multicast announcements are provided by the Web server through the use of the announcement file. The name of the server is provided by `Host.Text` and the name of the announcement file as stored in `AnnounceFile.Text`.

For example, if your server was named laure and the announcement file was named periwinkle.nsc, the syntax for the line you would supply to the *URL* property would be `http://laure/periwinkle.nsc`.

The announcement file will notify the Player what network address and port to listen to for the multicast.

Running the Serving Multicasts Application

After you have entered all the code, run the project in Visual Basic. From the Run menu, select Start. If there are no errors, the user interface of your application should look like Figure 13.3. You can compare your code to the complete code listing in the next section.

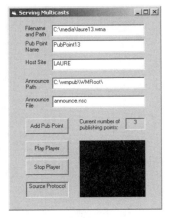

Figure 13.3   Serving Multicasts application.

To test the Serving Multicasts application, use the following procedure:

1. Accept or change the default values for these items:
    - ❏   Publishing-point path and file name
    - ❏   Publishing-point name
    - ❏   Host site
    - ❏   Announcement path
    - ❏   Announcement file name

2. Click the Add Pub Point button to add a new publishing point. You will see the number of publishing points increase by one.

3. Click the Play Player button. After a moment, you will see the protocol displayed. Instead of RTSPT, CACHE, or RTSPU, as was displayed in the applications from Chapters 11 and 12, the protocol should read ASFM. This indicates that the multicast protocol is being used. Soon, you will hear the audio playing and see either the video or a visualization. Unless you click the Play button immediately after adding the publishing point, the audio and video will not start at the beginning. Because this is a multicast, the Player receives the content at whatever point the server has reached in the file, not necessarily at the beginning of the file.

4. Click the Stop Player button. If you click the Play Player button again, the Player resumes playing the file again, but not at the beginning. Because this is a multicast broadcast, the audio and video resume playing farther along in the file. The Player does not play the part of the file that the server is broadcasting while the Player is stopped. This is similar to the idea of a radio: if you turn off a radio and turn it back on again, you will pick up the broadcast in progress.

If you compare the behavior of the multicast to on-demand and unicast applications, the main difference to the user is that the audio and video of a multicast continues (in the server, at least) whether the Player is playing or not. And, as with a unicast, you cannot seek to a location within the content.

Figure 13.4 shows the Serving Multicasts application with a file being served through multicast broadcasting.

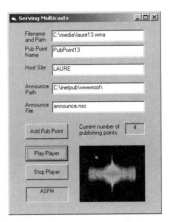

Figure 13.4   Serving Multicasts application playing a file delivered
through multicast broadcasting.

Complete copies of the source code and digital media for the Serving Multicasts
application are on the companion CD.

Source Code for the Serving Multicasts Application

Here is the complete source code listing for the Serving On-Demand application.

```
Dim Server As WMSServer
Dim MyPubPoint As IWMSBroadcastPublishingPoint
Dim MyPubPoints As IWMSPublishingPoints
Dim PubPointFlag As Boolean

Dim Plugin As IWMSPlugin
Dim AdminMulticastSink As IWMSAdminMulticastSink

Private Sub Form_Load()
    Set Server = New WMSServer
    PubPath.Text = "C:\media\laure13.wma"

    PubPointName.Text = "PubPoint13"
    Host.Text = Environ("COMPUTERNAME")

    Set MyPubPoints = Server.PublishingPoints
    NumPoints.Caption = MyPubPoints.Count

    PubPointFlag = False
```

```
        Player.uiMode = "none"
        AnnouncePath.Text = "C:\Inetpub\wwwroot\"
        AnnounceFile.Text = "announce.nsc"
End Sub

Private Sub AddPub_Click()
    Dim i As Integer
    Dim CheckName As String
    For i = 0 To (MyPubPoints.Count - 1)
        CheckName = MyPubPoints.Item(i).Name
        If (CheckName = PubPointName.Text) Then
            MyPubPoints.Remove (PubPointName.Text)
            MsgBox ("Deleting previous " & PubPointName.Text)
        End If
    Next i

    Set MyPubPoint = Server.PublishingPoints.Add(PubPointName.Text, _
        WMS_PUBLISHING_POINT_CATEGORY.WMS_PUBLISHING_POINT_BROADCAST, _
        PubPath.Text)

    Set MyPubPoints = Server.PublishingPoints
    NumPoints.Caption = MyPubPoints.Count

    PubPointFlag = True

    MyPubPoint.AllowClientToStartAndStop = False

    MyPubPoint.AnnouncementStreamFormats.Add (PubPath.Text)

    Set Plugin = MyPubPoint.BroadcastDataSinks _
                    ("WMS Multicast Data Writer")
    Set AdminMulticastSink = Plugin.CustomInterface
    Plugin.Enabled = True

    AdminMulticastSink.DestinationMulticastIPAddress = _
            "239.192.13.92"
    AdminMulticastSink.DestinationMulticastPort = 30587
    AdminMulticastSink.MulticastTTL = 64
    AdminMulticastSink.LocalIPAddress = "127.0.0.1"

    Dim AnnounceFilePath As String
    MyPubPoint.Announce
    AnnounceFilePath = AnnouncePath.Text & AnnounceFile.Text
    MyPubPoint.AnnounceToNSCFile AnnounceFilePath, True

    MyPubPoint.Start
End Sub
```

(continued)

```
Private Sub PlayPlayer_Click()
    If PubPointFlag = True Then
        Player.URL = "http://" & Host.Text & "/" & AnnounceFile.Text
    Else
        MsgBox "Please add a publishing point."
    End If
End Sub

Private Sub StopPlayer_Click()
    Player.Controls.Stop
End Sub

Private Sub Player_PlayStateChange(ByVal NewState As Long)
    If NewState = 3 Then
        Protocol.Caption = UCase(Player.network.sourceProtocol)
    End If
End Sub
```

14

Creating Server Playlists

This chapter will show you how to use Windows Media Services to create playlists. The new application is called Server Playlists and it will let you create Windows Media playlists by using XML.

Introduction to the Server Playlists Application

In addition to serving digital media streams and files, Windows Media Services can also supply playlists to Windows Media Player. A playlist is a list of media items arranged in a predefined sequence. There are two main types of Windows Media playlists. This chapter will cover server-side playlists, which are playlists that are processed by the server and have the file name extension .wsx. Chapter 18 will cover client-side playlists, which are processed by Windows Media Player and have the file name extension .asx. Playlists can also contain additional information about the media items and instructions on how the Player should process them. For example, a playlist could contain a list of 20 jazz songs and include links to Web sites related to each song. It could also be programmed to interrupt the music sequence for advertisements.

To provide playlists for the server to publish, you can either type up a playlist in a text editor or use Extensible Markup Language (XML) programming to create dynamic playlists in memory and save them to disk for later use. This chapter will show you how to create a dynamic playlist in memory using the Document Object Model (DOM) and XML technologies. You will learn how to add media items to the playlist and specify how many seconds each media item will play. When the playlist is created, the server will create an on-demand publishing point to provide the playlist to users who request it. For more information about playlists, also referred to as Windows Media metafiles, see the Windows Media Player SDK.

This chapter also shows you how to use Windows Management Instrumentation (WMI) as a way to provide feedback from the server to your application. After the publishing point starts, the server notifies WMI, which in turn notifies your application, allowing you to display the status of the server and start the Player automatically. Because the server may have other tasks and may not be able to start the publishing point immediately, it is best to use a WMI event handler to be sure that you don't start the Player before the publishing point is ready.

To create the Server Playlists application for this chapter, you will use a copy of the Visual Basic form you created in Chapter 11 and add new controls and code to perform the additional programming tasks required. No later applications in this book will build on the Server Playlists application, but you may want to save it for further use, modification, and study.

The Server Playlists application will perform the following tasks:

- Let the operator choose the source media path that will be associated with a publishing point. A default path will be provided. Any valid file path can be used.

- Let the operator choose a publishing-point name that the server will use for publishing the playlist. A default will be provided. Any valid publishing-point name can be used.

- Let the operator choose the name of a playlist. A default will be provided. Any valid playlist file name and extension can be used.

- Let the operator specify the names of two digital media files to be added to the playlist and the duration (in seconds) that each file should play. Defaults will be provided. Any valid media file names can be used and the durations can be any positive number.

- When a publishing-point path and name, a playlist name, and media items and durations have been chosen, let the operator click a button to start the publishing point. The code will verify that the publishing point has not been created already. If another publishing point exists with the same name, the previous publishing point will be deleted and the operator will be notified.

- After the new publishing point has been started, create the playlist with the specified media items and durations. The playlist will be saved to disk. Next the Player will automatically send a request to the server for the new playlist. The Player will play the media items in the playlist for the specified durations.

Setting Up Your Programming Environment

Before you begin programming, be sure you have installed the following software and configured it properly.

Installing the Required Software

The following software must be installed on your computer before you can develop the Server Playlists example application.

- Windows Server 2003, Standard Edition; Windows Server 2003, Enterprise Edition; or Windows Server 2003, Datacenter Edition. Windows Media Services is a component of all three versions.

- Windows Media Player 9 Series, if it is not already installed.

- Microsoft Visual Basic 6.0.

> **Note**   You should go to the Windows Update Web site and download any updates available for the required software.

Configuring Visual Basic

To configure Visual Basic for the Server Playlists application, follow these steps:

1. Start Visual Basic and create a new programming project by selecting New Project from the File menu and selecting the Standard EXE option. Click OK.

2. Add a reference to a COM object that contains the Windows Media Services functionality. Add the reference by selecting References from the Project menu and scrolling down to Windows Media Services. Select the services check box and click OK.

3. Add a reference to a COM object that contains the Microsoft XML functionality. Add the reference by selecting References from the Project menu and scrolling down to Microsoft XML. Select the XML 3.0 check box and click OK. (Use XML version 3.0 or later.) You will use XML to create a playlist for the server to send to the Player.

4. Add a reference to a COM object that contains the Microsoft WMI Scripting Library. First select References from the Project menu and then click Browse. Next load the Wbemdisp.tlb file, which is usually in the Windows/System32/

Wbem folder. Then be sure that Microsoft WMI Scripting Library is selected in the list of references. This will happen automatically when you load the .tlb file. (Use Microsoft WMI Scripting Library version 1.2 or later.) You will use the WMI Scripting Library to create a server event handler.

5.   Add the Windows Media Player ActiveX control to the Visual Basic toolbox by selecting Components from the Project menu and then selecting the Windows Media Player check box. After you click OK in the Components dialog box, the Windows Media Player icon is displayed in the toolbox.

Creating a Visual Basic Form for the Server Playlists Application

In this chapter, we will build on the Serving On-Demand form used in Chapter 11. That chapter showed how to use the Windows Media Services to prepare a publishing point for an on-demand request from Windows Media Player. This chapter uses some of the same form, but modifies it to create a multiple-item playlist using XML.

Using the Serving On-Demand Form from Chapter 11

Begin by making a copy of the form that was created in Chapter 11. That form contains the following twelve controls:

- **PubPath**   A TextBox control named PubPath to hold the path to the new publishing-point folder. The operator can modify this path before the publishing point is created.

- **Label1**   A Label control with the default name Label1 and the caption"Pub Point Path:" It is to the left of the PubPath text box.

- **PubPointName**   A TextBox control named PubPointName to hold the name of the new publishing point. The operator can modify this name before the publishing point is created.

- **Label2**   A Label control with the default name Label2 and the caption "Pub Point Name:" It is to the left of the PubPointName text box.

- **AddPub**   A CommandButton control with the name AddPub and the caption "Add Pub Point". It lets the operator add a publishing point that has the name and path specified in the two text boxes.

- **NumPoints**   A Label control named NumPoints to display the current number of publishing points. When the operator adds a new publishing point, this number will increase by one.

- **Label3**   A Label control with the default name Label3 and the caption "Current number of publishing points:" It is to the left of the NumPoints label.

- **FileName**   A TextBox control named FileName. Initially it contains the name of the default file to play from the on-demand publishing point. The operator can substitute any media file that exists in the publishing-point directory.

- **PlayPlayer**   A CommandButton control with the name PlayPlayer and a caption of "Play Player". It makes Windows Media Player start playing.

- **StopPlayer**   A CommandButton control to stop the Player. It has a caption of "Stop Player".

- **Protocol**   A Label control named Protocol to display the source protocol of the on-demand file that is received by the Player.

- **Player**   A WindowsMediaPlayer ActiveX control to display the video portion of the media or the default visualization of an audio file that is playing.

Figure 14.1 shows the Serving On-Demand form created in Chapter 11.

Figure 14.1   Serving On-Demand form from Chapter 11.

Modifying the Form

To create the Server Playlists application, eight old controls must be removed from the Serving On-Demand form. Then nine new controls must be added to the form to provide input for the playlist and to display status information about the server and the Player.

Removing Old Controls

Begin modifying the form by removing the following eight controls:

- **Label1** The "Pub Point Path:" label should be removed to make room for more important new controls.

- **Label2** The "Pub Point Name:" label should be removed for the same reason.

- **Label3** The "Current number of publishing points" label should be removed. Instead of using a counter to give feedback that a publishing point has been added, the new application will use an event handler.

- **NumPoints** This label should be removed because the number of publishing points will no longer be displayed.

- **FileName** This text box should be removed. Instead of specifying a single file, the new application will use two files and their durations to create a dynamic playlist.

- **PlayPlayer** This button should be removed because the Player will start automatically when the publishing point is created.

- **StopPlayer** This button should be removed because you can stop the Player by quitting the Player.

- **Protocol** This label should be removed because the Player protocol will not be displayed in this application.

Adding New Controls

Next add the following nine controls to the form to provide playlist input and to display status from the server and the Player:

- **PlayListName** A TextBox control named PlayListName to hold the default file name of the playlist to be created. The operator can change this to any valid playlist file name.

- **PubStatus** A Label control to display the status of the publishing point.

- **PlayStatus** A Label control to display the name of the playlist that is currently playing on the Player.

- **Label1** A Label control to identify the column that contains the file names for the playlist to be created. Give it a caption of "Filenames".

- **Label2** A Label control to identify the column that contains the durations for the items in the playlist to be created. Give it a caption of "Durations".

- **Filename1**   A TextBox control to hold the default file name of the first item to be added to the playlist.

- **Filename2**   A TextBox control to hold the default file name of the second item to be added to the playlist.

- **Dur1**   A TextBox control to hold the default duration of the first item to be added to the playlist.

- **Dur2**   A TextBox control to hold the default duration of the second item to be added to the playlist.

Figure 14.2 shows the Server Playlists form with the new controls.

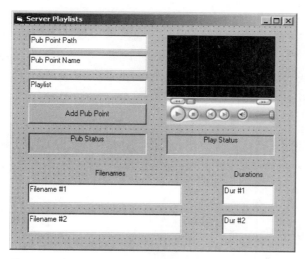

Figure 14.2   Server Playlists form.

Designing the Code for the Server Playlists Application

The code for the Server Playlists application begins with the same code that was used by the Serving On-Demand application in Chapter 11. The Serving On-Demand code let the operator add a publishing point with a specified name and a default digital media file. After the publishing point was created, the operator could start the Player and receive the file.

In this chapter, modifications must be made to the Serving On-Demand application code to make the Server Playlists application code perform the following tasks:

1.   Provide default file names and durations for two media files that will be used to create a playlist.

2. Create the playlist by using XML (Extensible Markup Language) and the Document Object Model (DOM).

3. Create a server event handler by using Windows Management Instrumentation (WMI) to notify the Server Playlists application that the server has added a publishing point.

4. Start the Player after the publishing point has been created.

5. Use a Player event handler to display the name of the file that is currently playing.

Adding the Code

To create the Server Playlists application, you must modify the code from the Serving On-Demand application in Chapter 11. That application included the following six Visual Basic code blocks:

- General declarations
- Form_Load procedure
- AddPub_Click procedure
- PlayPlayer_Click procedure
- StopPlayer_Click procedure
- Player_PlayStateChange procedure

To create the Server Playlists application, the following code blocks will be modified:

- General declarations
- Form_Load procedure
- AddPub_Click procedure
- Player_PlayStateChange procedure

The following procedure will be added:

- **EventSink_OnObjectReady procedure** This procedure will use the *EventSink* object with the *ObjectReady* procedure to process events registered with WMI.

And the following procedures will be removed because the Player will be started automatically when the publishing point is created:

- PlayPlayer_Click procedure
- StopPlayer_Click procedure

Reusing the Serving On-Demand Application Code

Here is the code that will be reused from the Serving On-Demand application in Chapter 11.

```
Dim Server As WMSServer
Dim MyPubPoint As IWMSOnDemandPublishingPoint
Dim MyPubPoints As IWMSPublishingPoints
Dim PubPointFlag As Boolean

Private Sub Form_Load()
    Set Server = New WMSServer
    PubPath.Text = "C:\media\"

    PubPointName.Text = "PubPoint11"

    Set MyPubPoints = Server.PublishingPoints
    NumPoints.Caption = MyPubPoints.Count

    PubPointFlag = False

    Player.uiMode = "none"

    FileName.Text = "laurie11.wma"
End Sub

Private Sub AddPub_Click()
    Dim i As Integer
    Dim CheckName As String
    For i = 0 To (MyPubPoints.Count - 1)
        CheckName = MyPubPoints.Item(i).Name
        If (CheckName = PubPointName.Text) Then
            MyPubPoints.Remove (PubPointName.Text)
            MsgBox ("Deleting previous " & PubPointName.Text)
        End If
    Next i

    Set MyPubPoint = Server.PublishingPoints.Add(PubPointName.Text, _
        WMS_PUBLISHING_POINT_CATEGORY.WMS_PUBLISHING_POINT_ON_DEMAND, _
        PubPath.Text)

    MyPubPoint.AllowClientsToConnect = True
    Set MyPubPoints = Server.PublishingPoints
    NumPoints.Caption = MyPubPoints.Count

    PubPointFlag = True
End Sub
```

(continued)

```
Private Sub PlayPlayer_Click()
    If PubPointFlag = True Then
        Dim MyURLPath As String
        MyURLPath = "mms://" & Environ("COMPUTERNAME") & "/" _
                    & PubPointName.Text & "/"
        Player.URL = MyURLPath & FileName.Text
    Else
        MsgBox "Please add a publishing point."
    End If
End Sub

Private Sub StopPlayer_Click()
    Player.Controls.Stop
End Sub
Private Sub Player_PlayStateChange(ByVal NewState As Long)
    If NewState = 3 Then
        Protocol.Caption = UCase(Player.network.sourceProtocol)
    End If
End Sub
```

Modifying the Serving On-Demand Application Code

Several lines need to be added to, removed from, or modified in the Serving On-Demand code so that the Server Playlists application can create dynamic playlists for the Player.
The following code blocks must be modified:

- General declarations

- Form_Load procedure

- AddPub_Click procedure

- Player_PlayStateChange procedure

Changing the Declarations Code

Code must be added to declare the objects needed for XML playlists and for the WMI event handler.

Adding the XML Playlist Declarations

Find the following line and delete it.

```
Dim PubPointFlag As Boolean
```

The PubPointFlag will not be used in this application.
Replace the line you just deleted with the following line.

```
Dim MyPlaylist As IXMLDOMDocument
```

This line declares the playlist object as an XML Document Object Model document. XML is a markup language that defines structured documents. Windows Media 9 Series technologies use XML to create playlists for multiple media items to be sent to Windows Media Player in a structured order. For more information about the playlists created by the server, see the Windows Media Services SDK. Additional information about playlists (also known as Windows Media metafiles) is available in the Windows Media Player SDK.

The Document Object Model (DOM) is a framework for defining specific structures for documents. Many Web pages, for example, use the DOM to define their structure. By using XML to specify the structure of the DOM, you can create and manipulate the data in a playlist in real time as conditions change. For example, you can create a playlist of items you want to broadcast and then change that playlist as conditions change. For more information about XML and the DOM, see the World Wide Web Consortium (W3C) Web site at *http://www.w3.org/*.

Next add the following four lines immediately after the declaration you added for MyPlaylist.

```
Dim MyProcNode As IXMLDOMNode
Dim Root As IXMLDOMNode
Dim Node As IXMLDOMNode
Dim Seq As IXMLDOMNode
```

These lines declare nodes for the playlist. A DOM document consists of nodes and elements. The nodes define the hierarchy of the document, and the elements define the types of data that are stored in the document.

Every Windows Media playlist DOM document must contain a procedure node, which is used by Windows Media to process the document as a playlist. In the Server Playlists application, this node is named MyProcNode.

Every DOM document has a root node that all other nodes branch from. You can think of a DOM document as a tree with a single root and one or more branches. Each branch is a node. The root of the playlist DOM document is named Root.

The node named Node will be used to create new nodes for each item in the playlist.

Finally, the playlist created for this application will put the media items in a sequence. A node named Seq is used to define the beginning and end of the sequence.

Next add the following three lines of code.

```
Dim RootElement As IXMLDOMElement
Dim SequenceElement As IXMLDOMElement
Dim MediaItem As IXMLDOMElement
```

These lines define elements that will be used in the DOM document to specify different types of data that are stored in the document.

The first line declares the root element, which is needed to define the root of the document. This element is named RootElement.

The second line declares a sequence element, which is needed to define the sequence portions of the document. This element is named SequenceElement.

The third line declares a media element, which is used to define the specific media items in the document. These media items will use the MediaItem element.

Adding the Server Plug-in Declarations

Add the following two lines immediately after the lines you just added.

```
Dim Plugin As IWMSPlugin
Dim WMIBridgeAdmin As IWMSWMIBridgeAdmin
```

These lines declare a plug-in object and its administrative interface that will be used to notify the sever which events you want to send to Windows Management Instrumentation (WMI). WMI is a standards-based technology that provides a way to pass events in an enterprise environment. The server uses a plug-in to pass the events to WMI, which can then pass them along to other applications. For more information, see the Windows Management Instrumentation SDK.

Adding the WMI Declarations

Add the following three lines immediately after the lines you just added.

```
Dim Services As SWbemServices
Dim WithEvents EventSink As SWbemSink
Dim Prop As SWbemPropertySet
```

These lines declare the objects needed to communicate to WMI. WMI is the Microsoft implementation of the Web-based Enterprise Management (WBEM) standard. In the Server Playlists application, WBEM services will be used to connect to WMI and to process events with an event sink named EventSink. An event sink is a namespace that can be used to register and process events. When the event occurs, the sink will cause specific code to run. The WBEM property set will be used to determine specific properties for the event that is processed.

Next add the following three lines.

```
Dim MyQuery As String
Dim Flag As Integer
Dim MyName As String
```

The first line declares a string that will be used to hold a query to WMI for event information.

The second line declares a flag that will be used to determine whether a new publishing point was added.

The third line declares a string that will hold the name of the publishing point that was added.

Changing the Form_Load Code

Several lines must be added, deleted, or modified in the Form_Load procedure to notify the server which events to send to WMI, to notify WMI which events to send back to the Server Playlists application, to make changes is the publishing point, and to set defaults for the playlist values.

Adding the Bridge to WMI

Find the following line in the Form_Load procedure.

```
Set Server = New WMSServer
```

Add the following three lines immediately after it.

```
Set Plugin = Server.EventHandlers.Item("WMS WMI Event Handler")
Set WMIBridgeAdmin = Plugin.CustomInterface
WMIBridgeAdmin.ExposedEventClasses = _
        WMS_WMI_CLASS_PUBLISHING_POINT
```

These lines tell the server to create a WMI Event Handler plug-in to handle publishing-point events. Whenever anything happens in the server that relates to publishing points, the server will send an event notification to WMI.

The first line creates the plug-in and defines it to be a WMI Event Handler plug-in.

The second line creates a custom interface for the plug-in that will be used to modify the plug-in through code.

The third line modifies the plug-in by setting it to register publishing-point events.

Later, when you have finished creating the Server Playlists application, you will be able to see the effect of these three lines of code by looking at the Windows Media Services user interface. After you have run the Server Playlists application at least once, you can click the Properties tab of the Windows Media Services, select Event Notification, and right-click WMS WMI Event Handler to see that the server is now reporting publishing-point events. Figure 14.3 shows the WMS WMI Event Handler properties tab.

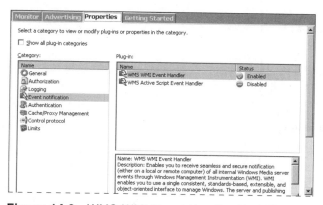

Figure 14.3   WMS WMI Event Handler Properties tab in Windows Media Services.

Adding the WMI Services Code

Add the following four lines immediately after the lines you just added.

```
Set EventSink = New SWbemSink
Set Services = GetObject("winmgmts://./root/cimv2")
MyQuery = "select * from WMS_PublishingPoint_Event"
Services.ExecNotificationQueryAsync EventSink, MyQuery
```

These lines create the objects that will query WMI for information about specific events. Using WMI makes it easy to process server events in a complex enterprise environment with many computers. WMI also makes it easy to process events asynchronously, that is, where the timing of events may not be easily predicted.

The first line creates an event sink named EventSink. This sink will be used as a gateway between WMI and the Server Playlists application.

The second line creates the WMI services object by using the *GetObject* method. The WINMGMTS protocol is used. The syntax of the protocol in this example is used to define the local computer. For more information about the syntax of the WINMGMTS protocol, see the Windows Management Instrumentation SDK.

The third line sets up a query string. As in structured query language (SQL), the WMI query will request all data (signified by the asterisk) relating to the *WMS_PublishingPoint_Event*.

The fourth line sends the query to WMI services.

After WMI receives the query, it will register the request. When the server sends an event to WMI that matches the type of event that was registered by the query, WMI sends a notification to the event sink called EventSink. This notification will be processed in the EventSink_OnObjectReady procedure of the Server Playlists application.

Changing the Publishing-Point Path

Find the following line in the Form_Load procedure.

```
PubPath.Text = "C:\media\"
```

Change it to the following line.

```
PubPath.Text = "C:\wmpub\wmroot\"
```

The publishing-point path for this chapter will change to the server root for security reasons. The server automatically has permission to write files to this folder. If you attempt to write files to another folder, you may not have permission.

Changing the Publishing-Point Name

Find the following line in the Form_Load procedure.

```
PubPointName.Text = "PubPoint11"
```

Change it to the following line.

```
PubPointName.Text = "PubPoint14"
```

The publishing-point name will be different for every chapter.

Removing the PubPointFlag Variable

Find the following line in the Form_Load procedure and remove it.

```
PubPointFlag = False
```

This flag is not needed.

Removing the Previous File Name

Find the following line in the Form_Load procedure and remove it.

```
FileName.Text = "lauriell.wma"
```

This line is not needed because two new file names will be provided instead.

Adding the Playlist Defaults

Add the following line immediately after the line you just added.

```
PlayListName.Text = "myplaylist.wsx"
```

This line defines the default name of the playlist file and stores it in the PlayList-Name text box. The file name extension is .wsx, which is the file name extension used by Windows Media for playlists that will be used by the server to determine what to distribute next. Playlists that are meant to be used by the Player use the .asx extension.

Next add the following four lines.

```
FileName1.Text = "C:\wmpub\wmroot\laure14.wma"
FileName2.Text = "C:\wmpub\wmroot\jeanne14.wma"
Dur1.Text = "20s"
Dur2.Text = "10s"
```

These four lines define defaults for the two file names and associated durations that will make up the playlist. You should use paths that point to files on your computer. The duration values are in seconds. For more information about playlist time values, see the Windows Media Services SDK.

Next add the following four lines.

```
Set MyPlaylist = Server.CreatePlaylist
Set MyProcNode = MyPlaylist.createNode(7, "wsx", "")
MyPlaylist.appendChild MyProcNode
MyProcNode.Text = "version = '1.0'"
```

These lines create the playlist and add a processing node named MyProcNode that defines the playlist as a Windows Media playlist.

The first line creates the playlist object as an object named MyPlaylist.

The second line creates a node for the document and defines it as a node for processing instructions. The first parameter defines the node as a procnode, the second parameter defines the name of the node to be wsx, and the third parameter is left blank. It is not used by Windows Media but is reserved for future use with namespaces.

The third line appends the newly created node to the playlist.

The fourth line adds text to the procnode to define the playlist format version.

The result of these four lines is to create a playlist that starts with the following line.

```
<?wsx version = '1.0'?>
```

Next add the following two lines.

```
Set RootElement = MyPlaylist.createElement("smil")
Set Root = MyPlaylist.appendChild(RootElement)
```

These two lines create the *SMIL* element in the playlist. SMIL stands for Synchronized Multimedia Integration Language and is the technology used in Windows Media 9 Series to provide synchronization of the items in a playlist. For more information about SMIL, see the Windows Media Services SDK and the World Wide Web Consortium (W3C) Web site at *http://www.w3.org/*. Windows Media playlists use Version 2.0 of SMIL.

The first line creates the *SMIL* element, and the second line adds the element to the root of the document. All additional elements will be added inside the *SMIL* element.

The playlist document now looks like this.

```
<?wsx version = '1.0'?>
<smil>

</smil>
```

All further additions to the document will be inserted between the two SMIL tags.

Changing the AddPub_Click Code

Find the following line in the AddPub_Click procedure.

```
NumPoints.Caption = MyPubPoints.Count
```

Remove it. The number of publishing points will not be displayed in this application.

Several lines must be added to create the playlist when the publishing point is created. You want to wait until the publishing point is created before letting the operator change the default values of the playlist items and durations.

Find the following line in the AddPub_Click procedure.

```
Set MyPubPoints = Server.PublishingPoints
```

Add the following two lines after it.

```
Set SequenceElement = MyPlaylist.createElement("seq")
Set Seq = Root.appendChild(SequenceElement)
```

These two lines create the sequence element. This element will define a linear sequence in which the media items will play. The first line creates the element and the second adds it to the root element. Because the root element is the *SMIL* element, the *SEQ* element will be embedded inside the *SMIL* element.

The playlist created by the application code will now look like this.

```
<?wsx version = '1.0'?>
<smil>
    <seq>

    </seq>
</smil>
```

Next add the following eight lines of code.

```
Set MediaItem = MyPlaylist.createElement("media")
MediaItem.SetAttribute "src", FileName1.Text
MediaItem.SetAttribute "dur", Dur1.Text
Set Node = Seq.appendChild(MediaItem)

Set MediaItem = MyPlaylist.createElement("media")
MediaItem.SetAttribute "src", FileName2.Text
MediaItem.SetAttribute "dur", Dur2.Text
Set Node = Seq.appendChild(MediaItem)
```

These lines define the media items in the playlist.

The first line creates a media element.

The second line sets an attribute of the element. The attribute name is *src* and the value of the element will be the name of the first file in the list as stored in the FileName1 text box.

The third line sets another attribute of the element. The attribute name is *dur* and the value of the element will be the duration of the content in the first digital media file. This will determine how long the media item will play in the sequence.

The fourth line creates a node for the media item and makes it a child of the *SEQ* element.

The last four lines do the same process for the next media item.

The playlist now is complete and looks like the following, assuming that the default values were used for file names and durations.

```
<?wsx version = '1.0'?>
<smil>
    <seq>
        <media src="C:\wmpub\wmroot\laurel14.wma" dur="20s"/>
        <media src="C:\wmpub\wmroot\jeanne14.wma" dur="10s"/>
    </seq>
</smil>
```

The two media items are embedded inside the *SEQ* elements, making them a sequence. The first item (laure14.wma) will play for 20 seconds, and then the second item (jeanne14.wma) will play for ten seconds.

Add the following line immediately after the lines you just added.

```
MyPlaylist.save (PubPath.Text + PlayListName.Text)
```

This saves the playlist your code has created in the folder and file indicated by the names in the PubPath and PlayListName text boxes.

Find the following line.

```
PubPointFlag = True
```

Remove it. The flag is no longer used by this application.

Changing the Player_PlayStateChange Code

Find the following line in the Player_PlayStateChange procedure.

```
Protocol.Caption = UCase(Player.network.sourceProtocol)
```

Replace it with the following line.

```
PlayStatus.Caption = Player.currentMedia.Name
```

This displays the name of the playlist that the currently playing digital media file is in.

Adding the EventSink_OnObjectReady Event Code

A new procedure must be added to process the event notifications that will be sent from WMI.

Add the following two lines after all other code in your module. Leave a few lines of space between these two lines for additional lines that will be inserted.

```
Private Sub EventSink_OnObjectReady(ByVal obj As ISWbemObject, _
        ByVal ctx As ISWbemNamedValueSet)



End Sub
```

This sets up the procedure that will handle the WMI event notification. Whenever WMI sends a notification to the Server Playlists application, it will be processed by this procedure. The procedure has two parameters.

The first parameter is the object that defines the event, and the second parameter defines additional details about the event. For more information about these parameters, see the Windows Management Instrumentation SDK. In this application, only the first parameter is processed.

Next insert the following three lines between the two lines you just added.

```
Set Prop = obj.Properties_
MyName = Prop("PublishingPointName").Value
Flag = Prop("SubEvent").Value
```

The first line creates a properties object that will be used to determine specific properties of the notification object. There is an underscore at the end of the name, Properties, but it does not signify the continuation of the line. The name of the property is *Properties_* and not *Properties*.

The second line gets the name of the publishing point that the event notification refers to.

The third line gets a number that further defines the type of event. There are several types of publishing-point events, and the *SubEvent* type will determine the exact nature of the event. For example, the event could be a notification of a publishing point being created, deleted, started, stopped, and so on.

Next add the following lines immediately after the lines you just added.

```
If Flag = 0 Then
    Dim MyURLPath As String
    PubStatus.Caption = MyName & " added."
    MyURLPath = "mms://" & Environ("COMPUTERNAME") & "/" _
                & PubPointName.Text & "/"
    Player.URL = MyURLPath & PlayListName.Text
Else
    PubStatus.Caption = "Status unknown."
End If
```

This sets up an ***If…Then…Else*** statement that determines what type of event was passed to the event handler. The type of event is defined by the value of the Flag variable. If the value is 0 (zero), then a publishing point was added.

If a publishing point was added, then two things will happen. First, the name of the publishing point will be displayed in the PubStatus label control. Second, the Player will be started by sending it the URL of the playlist that was created earlier. You may need to replace Environ("COMPUTERNAME') with the network name of your computer.

If another type of event is received, the Player will not start, and the status of the unknown event will be displayed.

Removing Unneeded Procedures

Because the Player will be started automatically when the publishing point is created, you can remove the following two procedures:

- PlayPlayer_Click procedure
- StopPlayer_Click procedure

Running the Server Playlists Application

After you have entered all the code, run the project in Visual Basic. From the Run menu, select Start. If there are no errors, the user interface of the Server Playlists application should look like Figure 14.4. You can compare your code to the complete code listing in the next section.

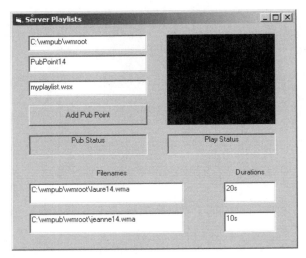

Figure 14.4   Server Playlists application.

To test the Server Playlists application, use the following procedure:

1. Change the default name and path of the publishing point, if desired.

2. Change the name of the playlist file, if desired.

3. Change the file names, paths, and durations of the two media items, if desired.

4. Click the Add Pub Point button.

5. You will see the status of the server change to show the name of the publishing point that was added.

6. You will see and hear the Player begin playing the first item on the playlist. It should play for the duration specified.

7. When the first item finishes playing, the second item will begin playing and play for the duration specified.

8. The name of each media item is displayed while it is playing.

9. Using a text editor, such as Notepad, you can read the playlist on the disk to see how it is structured.

Figure 14.5 shows the Server Playlists application with one of the two media items being played.

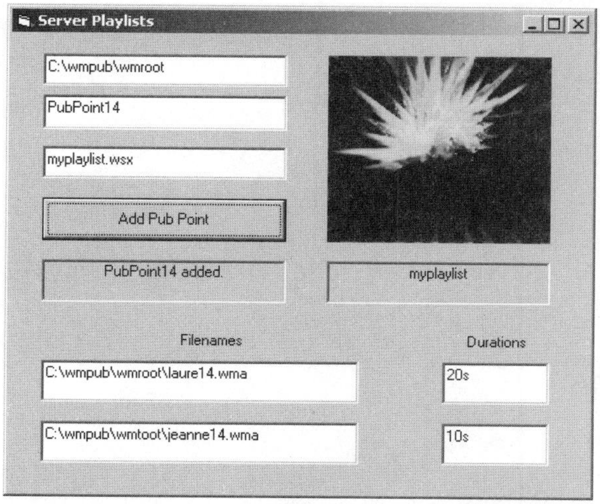

Figure 14.5   Server Playlists application playing a playlist.

Complete copies of the source code and digital media for this application are on the companion CD.

Source Code for the Server Playlists Application

Here is the complete source code listing for the Server Playlists application.

```
Dim Server As WMSServer
Dim MyPubPoint As IWMSOnDemandPublishingPoint
Dim MyPubPoints As IWMSPublishingPoints

Dim MyPlaylist As IXMLDOMDocument

Dim MyProcNode As IXMLDOMNode
Dim Root As IXMLDOMNode
Dim Node As IXMLDOMNode
Dim Seq As IXMLDOMNode

Dim RootElement As IXMLDOMElement
Dim SequenceElement As IXMLDOMElement
Dim MediaItem As IXMLDOMElement

Dim Plugin As IWMSPlugin
Dim WMIBridgeAdmin As IWMSWMIBridgeAdmin
```

(continued)

```
Dim Services As SWbemServices
Dim WithEvents EventSink As SWbemSink
Dim Prop As SWbemPropertySet
Dim MyQuery As String
Dim Flag As Integer
Dim MyName As String

Private Sub Form_Load()
    Set Server = New WMSServer

    Set Plugin = Server.EventHandlers.Item("WMS WMI Event Handler")
    Set WMIBridgeAdmin = Plugin.CustomInterface
    WMIBridgeAdmin.ExposedEventClasses = _
            WMS_WMI_CLASS_PUBLISHING_POINT

    Set EventSink = New SWbemSink
    Set Services = GetObject("winmgmts://./root/cimv2")
    MyQuery = "select * from WMS_PublishingPoint_Event"
    Services.ExecNotificationQueryAsync EventSink, MyQuery

    PubPath.Text = "C:\wmpub\wmroot\"
    PubPointName.Text = "PubPoint14"

    Set MyPubPoints = Server.PublishingPoints

    Player.uiMode = "none"
    PlayListName.Text = "myplaylist.wsx"
    FileName1.Text = "C:\wmpub\wmroot\laure14.wma"
    FileName2.Text = "C:\wmpub\wmroot\jeanne14.wma"
    Dur1.Text = "20s"
    Dur2.Text = "10s"

    Set MyPlaylist = Server.CreatePlaylist
    Set MyProcNode = MyPlaylist.createNode(7, "wsx", "")
    MyPlaylist.appendChild MyProcNode
    MyProcNode.Text = "version = '1.0'"

    Set RootElement = MyPlaylist.createElement("smil")
    Set Root = MyPlaylist.appendChild(RootElement)
End Sub

Private Sub AddPub_Click()
    Dim i As Integer
    Dim CheckName As String
    For i = 0 To (MyPubPoints.Count - 1)
        CheckName = MyPubPoints.Item(i).Name
        If (CheckName = PubPointName.Text) Then
            MyPubPoints.Remove (PubPointName.Text)
            MsgBox ("Deleting previous " & PubPointName.Text)
```

```
            End If
        Next i

        Set MyPubPoint = Server.PublishingPoints.Add(PubPointName.Text, _
            WMS_PUBLISHING_POINT_CATEGORY.WMS_PUBLISHING_POINT_ON_DEMAND, _
            PubPath.Text)

        MyPubPoint.AllowClientsToConnect = True

        Set MyPubPoints = Server.PublishingPoints

        Set SequenceElement = MyPlaylist.createElement("seq")
        Set Seq = Root.appendChild(SequenceElement)

        Set MediaItem = MyPlaylist.createElement("media")
        MediaItem.SetAttribute "src", FileName1.Text
        MediaItem.SetAttribute "dur", Dur1.Text
        Set Node = Seq.appendChild(MediaItem)

        Set MediaItem = MyPlaylist.createElement("media")
        MediaItem.SetAttribute "src", FileName2.Text
        MediaItem.SetAttribute "dur", Dur2.Text
        Set Node = Seq.appendChild(MediaItem)

        MyPlaylist.save (PubPath.Text & PlayListName.Text)
End Sub
Private Sub Player_PlayStateChange(ByVal NewState As Long)
    If NewState = 3 Then
        PlayStatus.Caption = Player.currentMedia.Name
    End If
End Sub

Private Sub EventSink_OnObjectReady(ByVal obj As ISWbemObject, _
                ByVal ctx As ISWbemNamedValueSet)
    Set Prop = obj.Properties_
    MyName = Prop("PublishingPointName").Value
    Flag = Prop("SubEvent").Value

    If Flag = 0 Then
        Dim MyURLPath As String
        PubStatus.Caption = MyName + " added."
        MyURLPath = "mms://" & Environ("COMPUTERNAME") & "/" _
                    & PubPointName.Text & "/"
        Player.URL = MyURLPath & PlayListName.Text
    Else
        PubStatus.Caption = "Status unknown."
    End If
End Sub
```

Part IV

Playing
Windows Media

This part of the book will show you how to develop a series of sample applications that you can use and expand on in the future to enhance, modify, and extend the capabilities of Windows Media Player. Detailed step-by-step instructions for every line of code will be provided to enable you to: build a stand-alone media player by using Visual Basic; provide a customized user interface for the Player by embedding it in a Web page with Microsoft JScript and HTML; and create a graphical user interface for the Player by using the skin programming language of the Player. You will then expand on these techniques to use Windows Media metafiles to add interactive banners to the Player interface and embed Web pages inside the Player, enabling the user to surf the Web while listening to music. Finally, you'll learn how to use the border technology of Windows Media Player to add additional buttons, links, and extra video panes to the existing Player user interface. The sample applications in this part of the book include automation techniques that simplify the user interfaces of the Windows Media components and reduce the number of tasks needed to make the components work together.

15

Creating a Simple Player

This chapter will demonstrate how to customize the user interface of Windows Media Player. The new application is called Simple Player, and it will show you how to create a custom user interface and attach it to the Windows Media Player ActiveX control.

Introduction to the Simple Player Application

Windows Media Player makes it possible to put music and video on your computer, Pocket PC, or portable digital media device. It can play files, unicast and multicast streams, and playlists of digital media items. In previous chapters, Windows Media Player was used as part of a server or encoder application. This chapter will show you how to create a custom user interface for the Player that lets you play digital media how, when, and where you want.

You can make your own player interface by using the methods, properties, and events of Windows Media Player with the ActiveX control version of the Player. Developing a customized player application isn't a complicated process. You will start with the Player control and add your own user interface of text boxes and buttons, making it possible to develop your own versions of the Player for your specific needs and circumstances.

To create the Simple Player application for this chapter, create a new project and form in Visual Basic and add controls and code to perform the programming tasks required. No later applications in this book will build on the Simple Player application, but you may want to save it for further use, modification, and study.

The Simple Player application will perform the following tasks:

■ Let the user choose the path and file name of the digital media that is to be played. A default file path and name will be provided. Any valid path and file name can be used.

- When a path and file name have been chosen, let the user click the Play button to play the file. Stop and Pause buttons will also be provided.

- After the media begins playing, display the name of the media item, the duration (in seconds), and the current position in the file. A visualization will be displayed in a window if an audio file was selected. If a video file was chosen, the video image will be displayed instead of the visualization.

Setting Up Your Programming Environment

Before you begin programming, be sure you have installed the following software and configured it properly.

Installing the Required Software

The following software must be installed on your computer before you can develop the Simple Player example application:

- Windows Server 2003, Standard Edition; Windows Server 2003, Enterprise Edition; or Windows Server 2003, Datacenter Edition. Windows Media Services is a component of all three versions. (The example application in this chapter does not require the server functionality, but using this operating system here enables you to use the same operating system for all example applications in this book.)

- Windows Media Player 9 Series, if it is not already installed.

- Microsoft Visual Basic 6.0.

> **Note**   You should go to the Windows Update Web site and download any updates available for the required software.

Configuring Visual Basic

To configure Visual Basic for the Simple Player application, follow these steps:

1. Start Visual Basic and create a new programming project by selecting New Project from the File menu and selecting the Standard EXE option. Click OK.

2. Add the Windows Media Player ActiveX control to the Visual Basic toolbox. Add the Player control by selecting Components from the Project menu and

then selecting the Windows Media Player check box. After you click OK in the Components dialog box, the Windows Media Player icon is displayed in the toolbox.

Creating a Visual Basic Form for the Simple Player Application

When Visual Basic loads a new project, a blank form is provided. You will need to modify the form to create the Simple Player application. First you need to add user interface controls to the form, and then add programming code for the form and each of the controls.

To create the Simple Player user interface, add the following nine controls to the blank form:

- **FilePlay**   A TextBox control named FilePlay to hold the path to the file that is to be played. The user can enter a new file path to any digital media file.

- **PlayPlayer**   A CommandButton control named PlayPlayer to start playing a digital media file. Give it a caption of "Play".

- **PausePlayer**   A CommandButton control named PausePlayer to pause the playing of a media file. Give it a caption of "Pause". If a user clicks the Play button after clicking the Pause button, the file will resume playing at the point where it was paused.

- **StopPlayer**   A CommandButton control named StopPlayer to stop playing a digital media file. Give it a caption of "Stop". If you click the Play button after clicking the Stop button, the file will start playing at the beginning of the file.

- **Player**   A WindowsMediaPlayer ActiveX control named Player to display the video portion of the file as it is playing. If there is audio but no video, a default visualization will be displayed.

- **ClipName**   A Label control to display the name of the digital media clip being played. The name will be obtained by the Player.

- **Position**   A Label control to display the position in the content as it is playing. This is the number of seconds played.

- **MyDuration**   A Label control to display the duration of the digital media file.

- **Timer1**   A Timer control to time the requests for updates to the position in the content being played.

You can also add labels with captions such as "Position" and "Duration" to show the purpose of the Position and MyDuration labels. See Figure 15.1.

When you have added the controls, resize the form and the controls so that the form is easy to read and understand. The timer control can be placed anywhere because it will not be displayed when the form is loaded. Figure 15.1 shows the Simple Player form with the controls on it.

Figure 15.1   Simple Player form with controls.

Designing the Code for the Simple Player Application

The code for the Simple Player application must perform the following tasks:

1. Let the user select a digital media file to play.

2. Play the file.

3. Pause the file.

4. Stop playing the file.

5. Display the name of the content being played. This is not necessarily the same as the name of the file.

6. Display the video portion of the content. If no video is present, the default visualization is displayed.

7. Display the duration (length) of the content.

8. Display the number of seconds played.

Adding the Code

The code for the Simple Player application is divided into these six blocks, which are discussed in the sections that follow:

- **Form_Load procedure**   This is code that runs when the application starts. After this code has been executed, the application is ready for user input.

- **PlayPlayer_Click procedure**   This is code that runs when the user clicks the Play button to start playing the digital media file.

- **PausePlayer_Click procedure**   This is code that runs when the user clicks the Pause button to pause the Player.

- **StopPlayer_Click procedure**   This is code that runs when the user clicks the Stop button to stop the Player.

- **Timer1_Timer procedure**   This is code that runs periodically, every time the timer finishes counting a specified number of seconds.

- **Player_PlayStateChange procedure**   This is code that runs every time the state of the Player changes.

Adding the Form_Load Code

The Form_Load procedure is code that runs when the form is loaded. The following tasks are performed in this procedure, and each is discussed in the sections that follow:

1. Set the user-interface mode of the Player control.

2. Set the default file name of the digital media file to be played.

3. Set the time interval of the timer control.

All the Form_Load code must be inserted in the following procedure, which is automatically created in the form's code module when you double-click the form.

```
Private Sub Form_Load()

End Sub
```

Changing the Player UI Mode

Add the following line inside the Form_Load procedure to change the user-interface mode of Windows Media Player.

```
Player.uiMode = "none"
```

When you place the Player control on a form, a window is created. This window displays the Player video window. Below the video window, the status window and the transport controls (Play, Pause, Stop, Seek, and so on) normally appear. To simplify the custom user interfaces that you are creating, you can hide the status window and the transport controls by changing the UI mode of the player to "none".

Setting the Default File to be Played

Add the following line to the Form_Load procedure to create the default file path and name.

```
FilePlay.Text = "C:\media\laurel5.wma"
```

This puts a default file path and file name into the *Text* property of the FilePlay text box. The user can change this file path or name at any time before clicking Play.

Setting the Timer Interval

Add the following line to set the timer interval.

```
Timer1.Interval = 1000
```

This determines how often the timer code will run. The number 1000 sets the timer to call the Timer1_Timer procedure every 1000 milliseconds; that is, once every second.

Adding the PlayPlayer_Click Code

After the Form_Load procedure has been executed, the application is ready for user input. The user can change the file to be played by typing new values in a text box. When ready to play the file, the user can click the Play button. The following tasks are performed in the PlayPlayer_Click procedure:

1. Pass the path and name of the digital media file to the *URL* property. This will cause the Player to start playing.

2. In the ClipName label, display the name of the content that is playing.

All the code for these tasks must be inserted in the following procedure, which is automatically created in the code module when you double-click the PlayPlayer button on the form.

```
Private Sub PlayPlayer_Click()

End Sub
```

Getting the URL

Add the following three lines inside the procedure to get the URL that will be used to inform the Player what to play.

```
If Player.Controls.currentPosition = 0 Then
    Player.URL = FilePlay.Text
End If
```

This checks whether the position of the digital media is 0. If the position is 0, the Player has not started, and you can send the path and file name from the FilePlay text box to the *URL* property of the Player. If the path leads to a file that the Player can play, the content will start playing from the beginning of the media file.

You must check to see if the Player is already running, or the Pause procedure will not work correctly. Because the *URL* property starts the Player playing at the beginning of a file, you want to avoid using *URL* unless the Player position is at 0, indicating that the Player has not begun, or that the Player has been stopped by the StopPlayer_Click procedure.

Starting Windows Media Player

Add the following line after the lines you just added.

```
Player.Controls.Play
```

This makes the Player start playing at the current playback position within the digital media file. If the Player has not played any file yet, or was stopped by the StopPlayer_Click procedure, the media will start playing from the beginning of the file. If the Player was paused by the PausePlayer_Click procedure, the media will play from the position at which it was paused.

Displaying the Name of the Content

Add the following line to display the name of the digital media being played.

```
ClipName.Caption = Player.currentMedia.Name
```

This line gets the name of the digital media currently playing and displays the result in the ClipName label. This line of code will be repeated in the *PlayStateChange* event handler of the Player, discussed later in this chapter. However, because of the way that Windows Media Player loads information, it is most likely that the file name will be displayed here and that the *Title* of the content will be displayed later when the event handler runs.

Adding the PausePlayer_Click Code

The Pause button lets the user stop the Player temporarily, at any position in the content.

The PausePlayer_Click code must be inserted in the following procedure, which is automatically created in the code module when you click the Pause button on the form.

```
Private Sub PausePlayer_Click()

End Sub
```

Add the following line of code inside the PausePlayer_Click procedure.

```
Player.Controls.Pause
```

This pauses the Player. Clicking the Play button afterwards will resume playing from the same position in the content where it was paused.

Adding the StopPlayer_Click Code

The Stop button stops the Player and resets it to the beginning of the content. The StopPlayer_Click code must be inserted in the following procedure, which is automatically created in the code module when you double-click the Stop button on the form.

```
Private Sub StopPlayer_Click()

End Sub
```

Add the following line inside the StopPlayer_Click procedure.

```
Player.Controls.Stop
```

This stops the Player. Clicking the Play button afterwards will resume playing at the beginning of the content.

Adding the Timer Code

To display the current position within the content while the content is playing requires a way to query the Player at regular intervals for the current position. The Timer control can do this easily.

The timer code must be inserted in the following procedure, which is automatically created in the code module when you double-click the timer on the form.

```
Private Sub Timer1_Timer()

End Sub
```

Add the following line inside the procedure.

```
Position.Caption = _
    Format(Player.Controls.currentPosition, "0") & " seconds"
```

This gets the current position from the Player once every second and displays it in the Position label. The *Format* function cuts off the fractional values of the answer because the updates appear only every second. Note that this is one line of code wrapped over to two lines.

If you want to see the position value every tenth of a second, you could change the interval to 100 and change the second parameter of the *Format* function to "0.0".

Adding a Player Event Handler to Display Duration

For the Simple Player application, it will be useful to display the duration of the digital media file so that the user knows how many seconds it will take for the file to play. However, the *Duration* property is not immediately available to the Player when it receives a command to start playing the file.

Because it takes Windows Media Player a few seconds to start playing, some methods and properties are not immediately available. The *Duration* property of the currently playing digital media is not available until after the Player has been playing a few moments. If you attempt to read the duration in the PlayPlayer_Click procedure, the Player will not be ready to give you the answer immediately.

What is needed is a way to determine when the Player has completed its start-up processes. Fortunately, the Player provides an event that can trigger a procedure to determine when the Player is done loading and has entered the play state. This is the *Play-StateChange* event.

The Player has several play states. The only one that matters in this application is the state that signifies that the Player is actually playing.

Add the following complete procedure to your code. Be sure it isn't part of any other procedure.

```
Private Sub Player_PlayStateChange(ByVal NewState As Long)
    If NewState = 3 Then
        ClipName.Caption = Player.currentMedia.Name

        Dim NumDur As Double
        NumDur = Player.currentMedia.duration
        MyDuration.Caption = Format(NumDur, "0.0") & " seconds"
    End If
End Sub
```

This procedure will run every time the *PlayStateChange* event occurs in the Player.

Whenever this code is called, the current state of the Player is assigned to *NewState*. The first line inside the procedure checks whether *NewState* is equal to 3, which is the enumeration value that indicates the playing state. For a table of play-state values, see the Player.playState topic in the Windows Media Player SDK.

If the state is 3, the duration of the current digital media is obtained from the Player and displayed in the Duration label. The *Format* function is used to round the number displayed to tenths of a second.

Also, the name of the media content currently playing is displayed in the ClipName label. The actual name stored in the metadata will be displayed, not the file name. When this same line of code was used in the PlayPlayer_Click module, the name of the file was displayed instead. If the two names are the same, the display will not change. But most of the time the file name is shorter than the title of the clip. The reason that the two are different is that the Player immediately assigns the name of the file to the *Name* property, but later changes the *Name* property to the value in the *Title* attribute, after the Player gets up to speed.

Running the Simple Player Application

After you have entered all the code, run the project in Visual Basic. From the Run menu, select Start. If there are no errors, the user interface of your application should look like Figure 15.2. You can compare your code to the complete code listing in the next section.

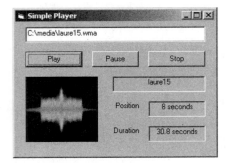

Figure 15.2   Simple Player application.

To test the Simple Player application, use the following procedure:

1.   Change the file to play, if desired, by changing the file path and name in the text box at the top of the form.

2.   Click Play. You will see the video or visualization and hear the audio. The duration will be displayed and the current position should change every second to indicate how many seconds of the file have been played.

3.   You can use the Pause and Stop buttons to pause or stop the Player.

4.   The ClipName label will first display the name of the file being played and then change to display the actual title of the content. This is a good illustration of why you should always use an event handler to obtain information from the Player.

Complete copies of the source code and digital media for the Simple Player application are on the companion CD.

Source Code for the Simple Player Application

Here is the complete source code listing for the Simple Player application.

```
Private Sub Form_Load()
    Player.uiMode = "none"
    FilePlay.Text = "C:\media\laure15.wma"
    Timer1.Interval = 1000
End Sub
Private Sub PlayPlayer_Click()
    If Player.Controls.currentPosition = 0 Then
        Player.URL = FilePlay.Text
    End If
    Player.Controls.Play
    ClipName.Caption = Player.currentMedia.Name
End Sub

Private Sub PausePlayer_Click()
    Player.Controls.Pause
End Sub

Private Sub StopPlayer_Click()
    Player.Controls.Stop
End Sub

Private Sub Timer1_Timer()
    Position.Caption = _
        Format(Player.Controls.currentPosition, "0") & " seconds"
End Sub

Private Sub Player_PlayStateChange(ByVal NewState As Long)
    If NewState = 3 Then
        ClipName.Caption = Player.currentMedia.Name

        Dim NumDur As Double
        NumDur = Player.currentMedia.duration
        MyDuration.Caption = Format(NumDur, "0.0") & " seconds"
    End If
End Sub
```

16

Embedding Windows Media Player in a Web Page

This chapter will demonstrate how to embed Windows Media Player in a Web page. The new application is called Web Player and it will show you how to create a custom user interface for the Player by embedding an ActiveX control in a Web page instead of in a Visual Basic form.

Introduction to the Web Player Example

In Chapter 15, you were shown how to create a custom user interface for Windows Media Player by embedding a smaller version of the Player, known as an ActiveX control, into a form in Visual Basic. This chapter will continue with the concept of embedding the Player, but it will discuss how to embed the Player in a Web page. You can create a custom user interface for the Player with the techniques in this chapter, but instead of running your Player on the desktop, it will now be part of a Web page on a Web site.

The advantage of embedding the Player in a Web page is that you can put the Player controls directly into your Web page design, instead of having the Player in a separate window. When you embed the Player, you can scale down and redesign the Player interface so that you can insert it into a small portion of your Web page. Doing this will avoid the inconvenience of having to open a separate window to use the Player. With this method, the user can stay on your Web page and easily click a song and play it though the embedded Player on your site. While they are listening to the music, people can read information that you have provided about each song, and they can view details about how to buy a copy, all without ever leaving your page.

Another advantage of using Internet Explorer is that it makes available such technologies as HTML, DHTML, Microsoft JScript, Microsoft Visual Basic Scripting

Edition (VBScript), XML, VML, and many others. If a user doesn't have Internet Explorer or doesn't have the Player installed on their computer, your Web page can detect this and ask the user to download them.

To create the Web Player for this chapter, you will create a Web page using the text editor of your choice. No later examples in this book will build on the Web Player, but you may want to save it for further use, modification, and study.

The Web Player application will perform the following tasks.

- Let the user choose the file path and name of the digital media that is to be played. A default file path and name will be provided. Any valid file path and name can be used.

- When a file path and name have been chosen, let the user click a Start button to play the file. Stop and Pause buttons can also be used.

- After the media begins playing, display the name of the media item, the duration (in seconds), and the current position of the media. A visualization will be displayed in a window if an audio file has been selected. If a video file was chosen, the video image will be displayed instead of the visualization.

Setting Up Your Programming Environment

Before you begin programming, be sure you have installed the following software.

Installing the Required Software

The following software must be installed on your computer before you can develop the Web Player example Web page:

- Windows Media Player 9 Series, if it is not already installed.

- Microsoft Internet Explorer version 6.0 or later. Previous versions and other browsers may also work, but have not been tested.

- Microsoft JScript. Other similar scripting languages may also work, but have not been tested.

- While it is not required, a Web page editor such as Microsoft FrontPage is recommended.

You do not need to have Visual Basic installed on your computer to create the example in this chapter.

> **Note** You should go to the Windows Update Web site and download any updates available for the required software.

Creating the Web Page

When you start a new Web page with the Web page editor of your choice, be sure that your page begins with the following minimum code.

```
<HTML>
<HEAD>
</HEAD>
<BODY>
</BODY>
</HTML>
```

All your code will be inserted between the following two lines.

```
<BODY>
</BODY>
```

These are known as the body tags, and everything between them is the body of the Web page.

Adding Form Elements

To let the user interact with the Web page, you must provide form elements (buttons, text boxes, windows, and so on). This Web page will provide a custom user interface for the simple task of playing a digital media file on a Windows Media Player embedded in the page.

Adding New Controls

To create the custom user interface, the following eight controls will be added to the Web page:

- **FilePlay** A text input control named FilePlay that contains the name of the file to be played. A default file name will be provided. The user can enter any valid file or path to a Windows Media file on the local computer or on a network.

- **BtnPlay** A button input control named BtnPlay to start the Player.

- **BtnPause** A button input control named BtnPause to pause the Player.

- **BtnStop** A button input control named BtnStop to stop the Player.

- **Player**   A Windows Media Player ActiveX control to play the audio and video. If there is no video in the file, a default visualization will be displayed with the audio.

- **ClipName**   A text input control named ClipName to display the name of the digital media clip that is currently playing.

- **Position**   A text input control named Position to display the position of the clip.

- **Duration**   A text input control named Duration to display the duration of the clip.

Adding Code to Create the Controls

This section explains the code you must add to the Web page to make each control appear on the page.

Adding the FilePlay Control

Add the following lines after the opening <BODY> tag to create the FilePlay text input control.

```
<INPUT TYPE="text" NAME="FilePlay" SIZE="21"
       VALUE="c:\media\laure16.wma" ONCHANGE="NewURL()">
<BR><BR>
```

The first two lines use the standard HTML text input control. The value of the control is the name of the file you want to play. If no path is provided, it is assumed that the file is in the same directory as the Web page. The file path and name c:\media\laure16.wma is given as a default, but you can substitute the name of any valid media file.

This code also uses the *OnChange* attribute that calls the NewURL function whenever the contents of the text box changes. This will be useful if the user wants to provide a new file path or name. The code for the NewURL function will be provided later in this chapter. Note that two BREAK tags are inserted for spacing.

Adding the BtnPlay Button

Immediately after the lines you just added, add the following lines to create the BtnPlay control.

```
<INPUT TYPE="BUTTON" NAME="BtnPlay"
       VALUE="Play" ONCLICK="StartMeUp()">
```

This code uses the standard button input control. The *OnClick* attribute will cause the StartMeUp function to run when the user clicks the BtnPlay button. The code for the StartMeUp function will be provided later.

Adding the BtnPause Button

Next add the following lines to create the BtnPause control.

```
<INPUT TYPE="BUTTON" NAME="BtnPause"
       VALUE="Pause" ONCLICK="PauseMeNow()">
```

This code uses the standard button input control. The *OnClick* attribute will cause the PauseMeNow function to run when the user clicks the BtnPause button. The code for the PauseMeNow function will be provided later.

Adding the BtnStop Button

Add the following lines to create the BtnStop control.

```
<INPUT TYPE="BUTTON" NAME="BtnStop"
       VALUE="Stop" ONCLICK="ShutMeDown()">
<BR><BR>
```

The first two lines of code use the standard button input control. The *OnClick* attribute will cause the ShutMeDown function to run when the user clicks the BtnStop button. The code for the ShutMeDown function will be provided later. Add two BREAK tags for extra vertical spacing.

Adding the Player ActiveX Control

Add the following lines to create the Windows Media Player ActiveX control.

```
<OBJECT ID="Player" HEIGHT="150" WIDTH="150"
        CLASSID="CLSID:6BF52A52-394A-11d3-B153-00C04F79FAA6">
  <PARAM NAME="uiMode" VALUE="none">
  <PARAM NAME="autoStart" VALUE="false">
</OBJECT>
<BR><BR>
```

This code uses the *Object* element to create the Player control on the Web page. The *Id* attribute provides the name that will be used to refer to the Player; in this case it is Player, but the name could be any name that has not already been used on the Web page. The *Height* and *Width* attributes can be any values but were sized to fit with the rest of the elements on the form.

The *ClassID* attribute is used to be sure that you are using the correct ActiveX object. Only version 7.0 and later of the Windows Media Player control use that definition. It is recommended that you copy and paste the number from the Windows Media Player SDK rather than type it yourself, to avoid typographical errors.

The *Param* elements allow you to pass specific values to specific properties of the Player before any other code runs.

The *uiMode* is set to "none" so that the Player will not display any user interface controls when it first appears on the page.

The autoStart parameter is set to "false" so that the Player will not start playing when you supply a value to the *URL* property.

For more information about the Player control, see the Windows Media Player SDK.

Adding the ClipName Control

Add the following lines to create the ClipName control.

```
<INPUT TYPE="text" NAME="ClipName" SIZE="21"
       VALUE="ClipName" READONLY>
<BR><BR>
```

This code uses the standard text input control to display the string "ClipName" as a placeholder. The actual name will be set later by the *PlayStateChange* event code. The *ReadOnly* attribute prevents the user from changing the value. Add two BREAK tags for extra vertical spacing.

Adding the Position Control

Add the following lines to create the Position control.

```
<INPUT TYPE="text" NAME="Position" SIZE="21"
       VALUE="Position" READONLY>
<BR><BR>
```

This code uses the standard text input control to display the string "Position" as a placeholder. The actual value of the file position will be set by the GetPosition function, which will be explained later. The *ReadOnly* attribute prevents the user from changing the value. Add two BREAK tags for extra vertical spacing.

Adding the Duration Control

Add the following lines to create the Duration control.

```
<INPUT TYPE="text" NAME="Duration" SIZE="21"
       VALUE="Duration" READONLY>
```

This code uses the standard text input control to display the string "Duration" as a placeholder. The actual value of the file duration will be set later by the *PlayStateChange* event code. Again, the *ReadOnly* attribute prevents the user from changing the value.

Viewing the Web Page

Figure 16.1 shows the Web Player Web page with the controls added.

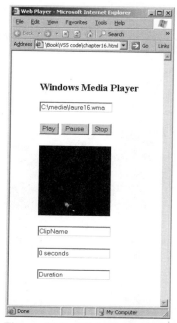

Figure 16.1   Web Player Web page with controls.

Designing the Code for the Web Player Web Page

The code for this Web page must perform the following tasks:

1. Let the user select a digital media file to play.

2. Play the file.

3. Pause the file.

4. Stop playing the file.

5. Display the name of the content that is being played. This is not necessarily the same as the name of the file.

6. Display the video portion of the content. If no video is present, display the default visualization.

7. Display the duration (length) of the content.

8. Display the position in the content, in seconds, relative to the starting time.

Adding the Code

The Web Player requires two script code blocks, both written in Microsoft JScript:

- **General code**   Statements and functions are placed here that will load when the Web page loads.

- **Event code**   This is code that runs only when Windows Media Player has a *PlayStateChange* event.

Adding the General Script Code

The general script code contains statements that will be run when the Web page loads, and functions that will be loaded but not run until they are called by another part of the program.

The general script code will be inserted after the code that created the forms in the body of the code. Add the following lines just before the </BODY> tag to create the code block for the general script.

```
<SCRIPT>
<!--

-->
</SCRIPT>
```

The rest of the general script code will be added between the following two lines.

```
<!--

-->
```

These comment lines prevent the browser from trying to render the code between them as if it were HTML.

Adding the Initial Script Code

Add the following two lines to the general script code.

```
setTimeout('GetPosition()', 1000);
NewURL();
```

These lines will run before any other JScript code.

The first line sets a JScript timer with the *setTimeout* method. The timer will run for 1000 milliseconds (one second) and then call the GetPosition function, which will be explained later. The purpose of this is to set up a timing procedure that allows the code to query the Player for some data once every second.

The second line calls the NewURL function, which will give the Player the value from the FilePlay control before the user can click the BtnPlay button. The NewUrl function will also be called any time the user modifies the value in the FilePlay control.

Adding the Code for Each Function

Besides the two initial lines, the general script block contains the following five functions.

Adding the NewURL Code

Add the following lines to create the NewURL function.

```
function NewURL ()
{
    Player.URL = FilePlay.value;
}
```

The body of the function takes whatever value is entered in the FilePlay control and passes it to the *URL* property of the Player. Because the *autoStart* property was set to false, the Player will not begin playing immediately.

This function is called by a line in the initial code block and will also be called every time the user changes the contents of the FilePlay control.

Adding the StartMeUp Code

Add the following lines to create the StartMeUp function.

```
function StartMeUp()
{
    Player.controls.play();
}
```

The body of the function calls the *Play* method of the Player, using whatever value was given to the *URL* property.

This function will be called when the user clicks the BtnPlay button.

Adding the PauseMeNow Code

Add the following lines to create the PauseMeNow function.

```
function PauseMeNow()
{
    Player.controls.pause();
}
```

The body of the function calls the *Pause* method of the Player. If the user clicks the Play button next, the Player will start playing from the position at which it was paused.

This function will be called when the user clicks the BtnPause button.

Adding the ShutMeDown Code

Add the following lines to create the ShutMeDown function.

```
function ShutMeDown()
{
    Player.controls.stop();
}
```

The body of the function calls the *Stop* method of the Player. If the user clicks the Play button next, the Player will start playing from the beginning of the file.

This function will be called when the user clicks the BtnStop button.

Adding the GetPosition Code

Add the following lines to create the GetPosition function.

```
function GetPosition()
{
    MyPosition = Math.round(Player.controls.currentPosition);
    Position.value = MyPosition + " seconds";
    setTimeout('GetPosition()',1000);
}
```

The body of the function performs two tasks: getting the position, and resetting the timer.

The first two lines get the current position in the content from the Player by using the *currentPosition* property. The value is rounded to the nearest integer by using the *Math.round* JScript function and displayed in the Position text box.

The third line resets the timer for another 1000 milliseconds, after which the Get-Position function will be called again. Essentially this function calls itself every second, using the technique of *recursion*, which is very useful in this kind of situation.

The GetPosition function is called by the initial code portion of the script block, and then calls itself every 1000 milliseconds thereafter.

Adding the PlayStateChange Event Script Code

The Web Player example uses a second script block that runs only when the play state of the Player changes.

The event script code will be inserted after the closing </SCRIPT> tag of the general script code. Add the following lines to create the event script code.

```
<SCRIPT LANGUAGE="JScript"  FOR="Player"
    EVENT="playStateChange(NewState)">
<!--

-->
</SCRIPT>
```

The rest of the event script code will be added between these two lines.

```
<!--

-->
```

Add the following lines to the event script code.

```
if (NewState == 3)
{
    ClipName.value = Player.currentMedia.Name;
    Duration.value =
        Math.round(Player.currentMedia.duration) + " seconds";
}
```

Every time the Player has a new kind of play-state event (start, stop, and so on), this code block will be called, and the type of event will be assigned to the NewState variable. If the NewState value is 3, this means that the Player has started playing. For more information on the play states of Windows Media Player, see Chapter 15 and the Windows Media Player SDK.

If the Player is playing, the next two statements are executed.

The first statement gets the content title of the current clip and displays it in the ClipName text box.

The second statement gets the duration of the media file, rounds it off to the nearest second, and displays it in the Duration text box.

Running the Web Player

After you have entered all the code, load your page in Internet Explorer. If there are no errors, your Web page should look like Figure 16.2. You can compare your code to the complete code listing in the next section.

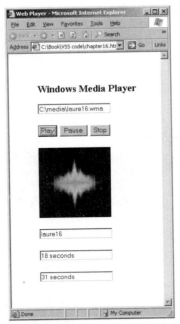

Figure 16.2 Custom Web Player in a Web page.

To test the Web Player, use the following procedure:

1. Change the file to play, if desired, by changing the file path and name in the text box at the top of the form.

2. Click Play. You will see the video or visualization and hear the audio. The duration will be displayed and the current position should change every second to indicate how many seconds of the file have been played.

3. You can use the Pause and Stop buttons to pause or stop the Player.

4. The ClipName control will display the content title of the file being played.

Complete copies of the source code and digital media for the Web Player Web page are on the companion CD.

Source Code for the Web Player Web Page

Here is the complete source code listing for the Web Player.

```
<HTML>
<HEAD>
<TITLE>Web Player</TITLE>
</HEAD>
<BODY>
```

```
<H4>Windows Media Player</H4>
<INPUT TYPE="text" NAME="FilePlay" SIZE="21"
        VALUE="C:\media\laure16.wma" ONCHANGE="NewURL()">
<BR><BR>

<INPUT TYPE="BUTTON" NAME="BtnPlay"
        VALUE="Play" ONCLICK="StartMeUp()">
<INPUT TYPE="BUTTON" NAME="BtnPause"
        VALUE="Pause" ONCLICK="PauseMeNow()">
<INPUT TYPE="BUTTON" NAME="BtnStop"
        VALUE="Stop" ONCLICK="ShutMeDown()">
<BR><BR>

<OBJECT ID="Player" HEIGHT="150" WIDTH="150"
        CLASSID="CLSID:6BF52A52-394A-11d3-B153-00C04F79FAA6">
  <PARAM NAME="uiMode" VALUE="none">
  <PARAM NAME="autoStart" VALUE="false">
</OBJECT>
<BR><BR>

<INPUT TYPE="text" NAME="ClipName" SIZE="21"
        VALUE="ClipName" READONLY>
<BR><BR>
<INPUT TYPE="text" NAME="Position" SIZE="21"
        VALUE="Position" READONLY>
<BR><BR>
<INPUT TYPE="text" NAME="Duration" SIZE="21"
        VALUE="Duration" READONLY>

<SCRIPT>
<!--
setTimeout('GetPosition()', 1000);
NewURL();

function NewURL()
{
  Player.URL = FilePlay.value;
}

function StartMeUp()
{
  Player.controls.play();
}

function PauseMeNow()
{
  Player.controls.pause();
}
```

(continued)

```
function ShutMeDown()
{
  Player.controls.stop();
}

function GetPosition()
{
  MyPosition = Math.round(Player.controls.currentPosition);
  Position.value = MyPosition + " seconds";
  setTimeout('GetPosition()', 1000);
}
-->
</SCRIPT>

<SCRIPT LANGUAGE="JScript" FOR="Player"
        EVENT="playStateChange(NewState)">
<!--
if (NewState == 3)
{
  ClipName.value = Player.currentMedia.Name;
  Duration.value =
        Math.round(Player.currentMedia.duration) + " seconds";
}
-->
</SCRIPT>

</BODY>
</HTML>
```

17

Creating Skins for Windows Media Player

This chapter will teach you how to customize the user interface of Windows Media Player by using the skin technology within the Player. The new applications are called Simple Skin and Advanced Skin, and they will show you how to use skin programming techniques that will allow you to design artistic and secure custom user interfaces for the Player.

Introduction to Skins

In Chapters 15 and 16, you were taught how to create custom user interfaces for Windows Media Player by embedding an ActiveX control in a Visual Basic application and in a Web page. This chapter will show you a third way to create custom user interfaces by using the skin programming language provided by the Player. Because this language uses XML and JScript to build the user interface components, it has greater graphics capabilities, making it possible to develop more unique user interface designs than you can with many other programming languages.

These unique interface designs are developed with the Player programming technique called *skins*. A skin is a type of custom user interface that has more creative and unusual artwork than generic user interfaces that have standard Windows features. A skin can provide all the necessary components to operate the Player, but it can be made out of any artwork you want. It can be either abstract or realistic. It can have simple shapes or elaborate detail. It can even look like a hot air balloon, a deck of cards, or a bag full of donuts. To create a skin, you must first assemble as many art files as your design requires, and then write one or more text files containing XML and JScript code. When you have created all the files, you will then compress them into a single file that can be loaded into the Player.

In addition to the graphic design advantages of using a skin, skins are more secure than other custom user interface technologies, because skin code runs in a protected "sandbox" similar to other secure scripting languages. As a result, the Windows Media Player can help prevent a hacker's malicious code from attacking a user's operating system or hard disk.

To create the Simple Skin and Advanced Skin examples for this chapter, you will create a skin file using the text editor of your choice. No later applications in this book will build on these examples, but you may want to save them for further use, modification, and study.

The Simple Skin will perform the following task:

- Let the user start and stop the default digital media. The default media will be whatever was played last by Windows Media Player.

The Advanced Skin application will perform the following tasks:

- Let the user choose the file path and name of the digital media that is to be played. A default file path and name will be provided. Any valid file path and name can be used.

- When a file path and name have been chosen, let the operator click a Start button to play the file. Stop and Pause buttons can also be used to stop or pause the media.

- After the media begins playing, display the name of the media item, the duration and current position (in seconds), and the status of the media. Display a visualization if an audio file was selected, or the video image if a video file was chosen.

Setting Up Your Programming Environment

Before you begin programming, be sure you have installed the following software.

Installing the Required Software

The following software must be installed on your computer before you can develop the example skins in this chapter:

- Windows Media Player 9 Series, if it is not already installed.

- While it is not required, a text editor such Microsoft Notepad is recommended. You must save text files in the ASCII file format. Do not use a word processor such as Microsoft Word that saves formatting along with text.

> **Note**   You should go to the Windows Update Web site and download any updates available for the required software.

Installing JScript

You do not need to install Microsoft JScript or be concerned about which version of JScript is installed. Windows Media Player will check for the version of JScript that is installed and will install a later version of JScript if it is needed for Player skins.

To find out what version of JScript is installed, you can use the following Web page code to display the JScript version.

```
<HTML>
<HEAD>
</HEAD>
<BODY>
<SCRIPT>
    var myInfo = "Microsoft " + ScriptEngine() + " version ";
    myInfo += ScriptEngineMajorVersion() + ".";
    myInfo += ScriptEngineMinorVersion() + ".";
    myInfo += ScriptEngineBuildVersion();
    alert(myInfo);
</SCRIPT>
</BODY>
</HTML>
```

Creating Skin Files

Skins use one or more file types, including skin definition files, JScript code files, and art files.

Skin Definition File

There can be only one skin definition file for a skin. The contents of the file must be written in ASCII text, and the file name must have the .wms extension. The programming code in the file consists of XML elements and embedded JScript statements. For more information about programming skins, see the Windows Media Player 9 Series SDK or the *Microsoft Windows Media Player for Windows XP Handbook,* by Seth McEvoy.

Art Files

Depending on the type of skin you create, you may want to include one or more art files. The skin is this chapter does not use any art. For more information about creating art for skins, see the Windows Media Player 9 Series SDK or the *Microsoft Windows Media Player for Windows XP Handbook*, by Seth McEvoy.

JScript Files

If you want to include more than a line or two of JScript, you should put it in an auxiliary file with the file name extension .js. The .js file is a plain text file that contains JScript code in ASCII text format.

Formatting Code for Skins

A typical skin is created by using a combination of both XML and JScript. And every skin must include an XML skin definition file.

Formatting Skin Definition Files with XML

The code for a skin definition file consists of XML elements and attributes. Elements are objects that correspond to user interface items, such as buttons, sliders, and so on. Each element can have one or more attributes that define and modify the element. Typical attributes include color, size, and so on.

The code in the skin definition file consists of four different types of elements:

1. A THEME element, with THEME tags at the beginning and end of every skin.

2. At least one VIEW element. Each view defines a window that contains one or more user interface elements.

3. User interface elements to let the user interact with the skin. Some user interface elements provide a way for the user to send messages to the Player, and other elements display information from the Player to the user.

4. Elements that have event attributes (such as *onClick*) that contain embedded script code that will take some action when triggered by a user or by the Player.

Adding the THEME Element

The THEME element tags begin and end the skin definition code. Your skin must always have a THEME element and can have no more than one THEME element. All other code for the skin is placed between these two tags. The THEME code block looks like this.

```
<THEME>


</THEME>
```

This code is similar to the <HTML> and </HTML> code tags that every Web page uses. Using standard XML notation, angle brackets (< and >) are used to enclose the element names, and the forward slash is used to indicate a closing tag. For more information on XML in skins, see the Windows Media Player 9 Series SDK or the *Microsoft Windows Media Player for Windows XP Handbook*, by Seth McEvoy.

Adding the VIEW Element

Every skin must have at least one VIEW element. A skin can contain more than one view only if certain parts are not shown to the user all the time. A second view might be used for a drawer that slides out or a separate window that pops up.

Here is what the VIEW tags look like when they are embedded inside the THEME element for a simple example.

```
<THEME>
    <VIEW>


    </VIEW>
</THEME>
```

> **Note**   It is common XML coding practice to indent nested elements.

Adding User Interface Elements

You must add user interface elements to your skin code so that the user can control the Player through your skin. The user interface elements must be placed between the opening and closing tags for the view you want them displayed in.

For example, to add two TEXT elements to a view, write the code between the opening and closing VIEW tags. The simple example should now look like the following.

```
<THEME>
    <VIEW>

        <TEXT
            top = "10"
            left = "10"
            value = "Play"
        />

        <TEXT
            top = "30"
            left = "10"
            value = "Stop"
        />

    </VIEW>
</THEME>
```

Unlike the THEME and VIEW elements, the TEXT element uses a slightly different bracketing syntax. The THEME and VIEW elements use angle brackets (< and >) to enclose an opening tag and a closing tag because the THEME and VIEW elements will have other elements enclosed within them. TEXT, however, is a complete element with only attributes and no subelements. Elements that do not enclose other elements do not use separate opening and closing tags. Instead, the entire element is contained inside a single tag, using only an opening bracket (<) on the left side and a forward slash and closing bracket (/>) on the right.

Elements almost always have one or more attributes. An attribute modifies the element; for example, by defining a color or size. The TEXT elements in this example have the attributes of *top* and *value*. The *top* attribute defines the distance, in pixels, from the top of the skin down to the location where the element will be placed. The *left* attribute defines the distance, in pixels, from the left edge of the skin over to the location where the element will be placed. The *value* attribute defines the text that will be displayed by the TEXT element.

If you save this simple example to a text file and change the file name extension to .wms, you will have a skin file. Double-click the file name in Windows Explorer to start it. You will see a window that looks like Figure 17.1, but nothing will happen within the window. You must add some scripting code to make it play.

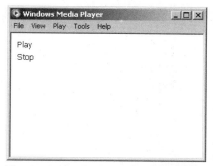

Figure 17.1   Simple Skin for Windows Media Player.

Adding Scripting Code

When you double-clicked the skin file of the Simple Skin example, the Player started and displayed your skin, but nothing happened. This is because all the code you entered so far is static. It creates user interface elements, but there is nothing to let the Player know what the user wants to do.

You must add JScript code to the two TEXT elements to connect them to the Player and give the Player a command when the user clicks a TEXT element.

Adding the Play Code

You need to enter code to make the Player begin playing when the user clicks the TEXT element that has the value "Play".

Find the following line in that TEXT element.

```
value = "Play"
```

Immediately after that line, and before the closing bracket (/>), add the following line.

```
onClick = "JScript:player.controls.play();"
```

This code uses the *onClick* attribute and defines a line of code that runs when the TEXT element is clicked. The line begins with the word JScript to indicate that JScript is the language used. The rest of the line is a command to the Player to call the *play* method of the *controls* object, which is part of the *player* object.

For more details about the Windows Media Player object model, see the Windows Media Player 9 Series SDK. Note that for skins, the name of the *player* object is always lowercase; also, because the language is JScript, every object, method, and property name is case-sensitive.

Adding the Stop Code

You need to enter additional code to make the Player stop playing when the user clicks the TEXT element that has the value "Stop".

Find the following line in that TEXT element.

```
value = "Stop"
```

Immediately after that line, and before the closing bracket (/>), add the following line.

```
onClick = "JScript:player.controls.stop();"
```

This code is almost the same as the code for the first TEXT element except that it uses the *stop* method of the Player.

Viewing the Code

The complete Simple Skin code should look like the following.

```
<THEME>
    <VIEW>

    <TEXT
        top = "10"
        left = "10"
        value = "Play"
        onClick = "JScript:player.controls.play();"
    />

    <TEXT
        top = "30"
        left = "10"
        value = "Stop"
        onClick = "JScript:player.controls.stop();"
    />

    </VIEW>
</THEME>
```

This is the minimum code needed to create a skin that will start and stop the Player.

Testing the Simple Skin

To test the Simple Skin, use the following procedure:

1. In Windows Explorer, double-click the name of the saved file that has the .wms extension. The window shown in Figure 17.1 should appear on your screen.

2. Click the word "Play" to start the Player.

3. Click the word "Stop" to stop the Player.

This Simple Skin example assumes that Windows Media Player has played at least one media item on your computer at least one time in the past. This skin finds the last thing you played and plays it again.

Formatting JScript Files

If you want to go beyond simple skins, you will run out of room when trying to write an embedded command that runs when a user interface element receives an event that, for example, calls the *onClick* attribute. You can add more than one code statement in a skin event attribute by separating each statement with a semicolon. However, too many lines of embedded code quickly become unreadable and difficult to deal with.

The solution is to put more complex code in a separate file. If you have a JScript file that has the same name as the skin definition file, it will be loaded automatically. You can also load JScript files by using the *scriptFile* attribute of the VIEW element, and you can have a different script file for each view.

A JScript file consists of two sections: initial code and functions.

Using JScript Initial Code

When the JScript file is loaded, each line is processed in order from top to bottom. Each line is processed only once. Put code at the top of each file that you want to run just once. This is similar to the declarations and form-load code in Visual Basic. Here you can define global variables, initialize parameters, and do any other tasks that help to set up and initialize your skin.

Using JScript Functions

When JScript encounters code that defines a function, it reads the code but does not run it. The code inside the function will be run only when the function is called by name from another part of the program. A function looks like this:

```
function functionname() {

}
```

For example, in the Simple Skin code, the line

```
player.controls.play();
```

could be placed in a function like this:

```
function playme() {
    player.controls.play();
}
```

You would then call the code in the function from the skin definition file by using this line

```
onClick = "JScript:playme();"
```

instead of this line:

```
onClick = "JScript:player.controls.play();"
```

Creating an Advanced Skin

The rest of this chapter will show you how to create an advanced skin that will do the same tasks as the Simple Player and Web Player of Chapters 15 and 16. All you need to do is create two text files and add skin programming code to them.

The Advanced Skin application will perform the following tasks:

1. Get a playlist name.

2. Get a file path and name for a digital media file.

3. Add the media file to the playlist.

4. Add the playlist to the media collection in Windows Media Player.

5. Start the Player.

6. Pause and stop the Player.

7. Be sure that the file is not added to the playlist again if the user clicks Play twice.

Adding User Interface Elements

To let the user interact with the skin, you must provide user interface elements (buttons, text boxes, windows, and so on). The Advanced Skin will provide a custom user interface for the simple task of playing a media file.

To create the custom user interface, the following elements need to be added to the VIEW of the skin. Each element has an *id* attribute which will be used to refer to the element.

Adding EDITBOX Elements

An EDITBOX lets the user provide text input, much like a TextBox control in Visual Basic.

The following two EDITBOX elements need to be added to the skin:

- **playlist_name** An EDITBOX element named playlist_name to let the user enter the name of a playlist that will be added to the Media Library in Windows Media Player.

■ **filepath_name**   An EDITBOX element named filepath_name to let the user enter the path and file name for a digital media file that will be added to the playlist.

Adding TEXT Elements

Ten TEXT elements are used in the Advanced Skin. Each of the TEXT elements is used in one of three ways:

■ Display text as an unchanging label. This is similar to the Label control in Visual Basic.

■ Display text that can run code when clicked. This is similar to a Command-Button control in Visual Basic.

■ Display changeable information from the application. This is similar to the Visual Basic Label control when used to display information that can be updated while the application is running.

The following TEXT elements will be added to the Advanced Skin application:

■ **play_button**   A TEXT element named play_button to display the word "PLAY" and let the user click it to start the Player.

■ **pause_button**   A TEXT element to display the word "PAUSE" and let the user click it to pause the Player.

■ **stop_button**   A TEXT element to display the word "STOP" and let the user click it to stop the Player.

■ **position_display**   A TEXT element to display the current position (number of seconds played) in the digital media file being played.

■ **duration_display**   A TEXT element to display the duration (total length) of the digital media file being played.

■ **status_display**   A TEXT element to display the status of the media file being played.

■ **label01**   A TEXT element to label the EDITBOX that holds the playlist name.

■ **label02**   A TEXT element to label the EDITBOX that holds the file path and name of the media file that will be added to the playlist.

■ **label03**   A TEXT element to label the position_display element.

■ **label04**   A TEXT element to label the duration_display element.

Adding the XML Code for Each Element

To create the EDITBOX and TEXTBOX elements listed in the previous section, you must write some XML code.

Adding the Default Code

The following code must always be part of a skin.

```
<THEME>
    <VIEW>

    </VIEW>
</THEME>
```

Insert all other code inside the VIEW element tags.

Adding VIEW Attributes

You need to change the opening tag of the VIEW element by adding two attributes to modify the VIEW element. They set the size of the view to 320 pixels wide and 320 pixels high. A pixel is a unit of measurement on a computer screen and is equivalent to one dot. Change the opening VIEW tag to look like the following.

```
<VIEW
    width = "320"
    height = "320"
>
```

Adding the Playlist Input and Label

Add the following code to create an EDITBOX element where the user can provide a name for the new playlist to be added.

```
<EDITBOX
    id = "playlist_name"
    top = "10"
    left = "140"
    width = "160"
    value = "A Playlist for Laure"
/>
```

This creates an EDITBOX control with the *id* attribute "playlist_name". Because skins don't allow comments in the body of the code, *id* attributes can be used as a way to remember what a particular element does.

In this case, the *id* value will be referenced later when the name of the new playlist is sent to the Player. A default value of "A Playlist for Laure" is supplied, but any text string can be used for a playlist name.

The upper-left corner of the EDITBOX is ten pixels down from the top of the skin and 140 pixels to the right of the left edge of the skin. The EDITBOX is 160 pixels wide.

A TEXT label for the EDITBOX control helps the user understand the purpose of the EDITBOX. Add the following code to display the label.

```
<TEXT
    id = "label01"
    top = "10"
    left = "10"
    value = "Playlist name:"
    enabled = "false"
/>
```

This TEXT element displays text at the position indicated by the attributes. Every element on a skin needs *top* and *left* attributes to position it on the skin. Sometimes the width and height are defined, but if they are not defined, the width and height of the TEXT element will be dictated by the default values.

Adding the Input and Label for the File Name and Path

Add the following code to create an EDITBOX element where the user can provide a path and name for the digital media file to be added to the playlist.

```
<EDITBOX
    id = "filepath_name"
    top = "40"
    left = "140"
    value = "C:\media\laure17.wma"
/>
```

This creates an EDITBOX control with the *id* attribute "filepath_name". The *id* value will be referenced later when the name of the file is sent to the Player. A default value of "C:\media\laure17.wma" is supplied, but any valid path and media file name can be used.

Add the following code to create a TEXT label that identifies the filepath_name EDITBOX.

```
<TEXT
    id = "label02"
    top = "40"
    left = "10"
    value = "Filename and path:"
    enabled = "false"
/>
```

Adding the PLAY Button

Add the following code to create a TEXT element that has an *onClick* attribute and can function as a PLAY button.

```
<TEXT
    id = "play_button"
    top = "70"
    left = "10"
    width = "90"
    value = "PLAY"
    fontStyle = "bold"
    fontSize = "20"
    backgroundColor = "green"
    hoverFontStyle = "bold"
    justification = "center"
    hoverForegroundColor = "white"
    onClick = "JScript:getNewItem();"
/>
```

Most of the attributes of this button are used to display the word PLAY:

- The position is set with the *top* and *left* attributes.

- The width of the element is set with the *width* attribute.

- The height is determined by the *fontSize* attribute.

- The font is set to "bold" with the *fontStyle* attribute.

- The foreground color is automatically set to the default value, black.

- The background color is set to "green" with the *backgroundColor* attribute.

- The text is centered with the *justification* attribute.

The *hoverForegroundColor* attribute is set to "white". Setting this attribute to any color value except black will change the color of the text from the default black to the color specified whenever the user hovers the mouse cursor over the TEXT element. This is useful because it provides a visual cue that the user can take some action at that location on the skin. Color names such as "white" are used in this example, but color values can also use numbers, such as "#FFFFFF" for white. For more information on color values for skins, see the Windows Media Player 9 Series SDK.

The *onClick* attribute will call the JScript function named getNewItem, which is defined later in this chapter. This function will get the new playlist name, add a file to it, add the playlist to the Player, and start playing the file. Earlier examples of using the Player showed how to play a file, but by using a playlist, you can start learning how to work with playlists, which are a powerful way to add media in groups.

Adding the PAUSE Button

Add the following code to create a TEXT element that has an *onClick* attribute and can function as a PAUSE button.

```
<TEXT
    id = "pause_button"
    top = "70"
    left = "107"
    width = "95"
    value = "PAUSE"
    fontStyle = "bold"
    fontSize = "20"
    backgroundColor = "orangeRed"
    hoverFontStyle = "bold"
    justification = "center"
    hoverForegroundColor = "white"
    onClick = "JScript:player.controls.pause();"
/>
```

Most of the attribute settings are similar to the settings for the PLAY button. The attributes that determine color and position are different so that the button will appear to the right of the PLAY button and be a different color.

The main difference is that the *onClick* attribute calls only one line of code to pause the Player. It uses the *pause* method of the *controls* object, which is part of the *player* object. The PLAY button needs several lines of JScript code to perform its tasks, but only one short line is needed to pause the Player.

Adding the STOP Button

Add the following code to create a TEXT element that has an *onClick* attribute and can function as a STOP button.

```
<TEXT
    id = "stop_button"
    top = "70"
    left = "210"
    width = "90"
    value = "STOP"
    fontStyle = "bold"
    fontSize = "20"
    backgroundColor = "magenta"
    hoverFontStyle = "bold"
    justification = "center"
    hoverForegroundColor = "white"
    onClick = "JScript:player.controls.stop();"
/>
```

Most of the attribute settings are similar to the settings for the PAUSE button. The attributes that determine color and position are different so that the button will appear to the right of the PAUSE button and be a different color.

The main difference is that the *onClick* attribute uses the *stop* method of the *controls* object, which is part of the *player* object.

Adding the Position Display and Label

Add the following code to create a TEXT element to display the current position in the digital media file.

```
<TEXT
    id = "position_display"
    top = "110"
    left = "80"
    value="wmpprop:player.controls.currentPositionString"
    enabled = "false"
/>
```

The value of this TEXT element is provided by the Player. The **wmpprop** keyword will "listen" to the Player and update the value of the TEXT element every time the Player changes the particular property. In this case, it is the *currentPositionString* property of the *controls* object, which is part of the *player* object.

If you compare this to the code used in the sample applications of Chapters 15 and 16, you'll see that it is much easier to get the position of the media from within a skin. You do not have to use event handlers because the skin is more tightly bound to Windows Media Player and does not use the ActiveX control to provide communication between the Player and the external programming code.

Add the following label using a TEXT element.

```
<TEXT
    id = "label03"
    top = "110"
    left = "10"
    value = "Position:"
    enabled = "false"
/>
```

This is a simple label for the position display to the right of it.

Adding the Duration Display and Label

Add a TEXT element to display the duration of the media.

```
<TEXT
    id = "duration_display"
    top = "110"
    left = "265"
```

```
        value="wmpprop:player.currentMedia.durationString"
        enabled = "false"
/>
```

The value of this TEXT element is provided by the Player. The ***wmpprop*** keyword will "listen" to the Player and update the value of the TEXT element every time the Player changes the particular property. Every time the *DurationString* property of the *currentMedia* object changes, the value of this TEXT element will be changed and the duration will be displayed.

Add the following label using a TEXT element.

```
<TEXT
      id = "label04"
      top = "110"
      left = "200"
      value = "Duration:"
      enabled = "false"
/>
```

This is a simple label for the duration display to the right of it.

Adding a Visualization Window

If you are using just audio files, it is useful to display the default visualization of Windows Media Player when it is playing so that you can tell that everything is functioning properly, especially in noisy environments.

You can add a visualization window with the following code.

```
<EFFECTS
      id = "visualization_window"
      top = "140"
      left = "10"
      width = "130"
      height = "130"
 />
```

This code uses the EFFECTS element to set up a window, and the attributes to specify the position and size of the window.

In the applications of Chapters 15 and 16, the visualization was displayed in the window provided by the Windows Media Player ActiveX control.

Adding a Video Window

It is very important that you add a video window to your skin. Even if you aren't planning to always use video, you must provide a window for it. If your skin does not provide a video window, and digital media files containing video are played, Windows Media Player will not use your skin, but will use the Full Mode of the Player instead.

Add a video window by adding the following code.

```
<VIDEO
    id = "video_display"
    top = "140"
    left = "170"
    width = "130"
    height = "130"
/>
```

This uses the VIDEO element to set up a window, and the attributes to position and size it. The video will be displayed in this window. If there is no video, the window will be transparent. Even if there is a video, the visualization will still play in the EFFECTS element window to the right.

In the applications of Chapters 15 and 16, the video was displayed in the window provided by the Windows Media Player ActiveX control.

Adding a Scrolling Status Window

It can be useful to see the status of the Player as it starts, stops, and pauses. A TEXT element can be used to display the status (state) of the Player.

The following code creates a status window that will appear at the bottom of the Player skin.

```
<TEXT
    id = "status_display"
    top = "290"
    left = "10"
    width = "290"
    scrolling = "true"
    backgroundColor = "gold"
    value = "wmpprop:player.status"
/>
```

This element is similar to the other display elements. The main difference is that it sets the scrolling attribute to "true". This scrolls the text continuously, allowing you to display information that may be longer than the width of the display.

This code also uses the **wmpprop** keyword to "listen" to the *status* property of the *player* object. The value of the status property will be reported constantly to the TEXT element and displayed there.

Complete XML Code for the Advanced Skin

Here is the complete XML code listing for the Advanced Skin. You will also need an auxiliary JScript file, but that will be explained in the sections following this code.

```
<THEME>
    <VIEW
        width = "320"
        height = "320"
    >

        <EDITBOX
            id = "playlist_name"
            top = "10"
            left = "140"
            width = "160"
            value = "A Playlist for Laure"
        />

        <TEXT
            id = "label01"
            top = "10"
            left = "10"
            value = "Playlist name:"
            enabled = "false"
        />

        <EDITBOX
            id = "filepath_name"
            top = "40"
            left = "140"
            width = "160"
            value = "C:\media\laure17.wma"
        />
        <TEXT
            id = "label02"
            top = "40"
            left = "10"
            value = "Filename and path:"
            enabled = "false"
        />

        <TEXT
            id = "play_button"
            top = "70"
            left = "10"
            width = "90"
            value = "PLAY"
            fontStyle = "bold"
            fontSize = "20"
            backgroundColor = "green"
```

(continued)

```
        hoverFontStyle = "bold"
        justification = "center"
        hoverForegroundColor = "white"
        onClick = "JScript:getNewItem();"
    />

    <TEXT
        id = "pause_button"
        top = "70"
        left = "107"
        width = "95"
        value = "PAUSE"
        fontStyle = "bold"
        fontSize = "20"
        backgroundColor = "orangeRed"
        hoverFontStyle = "bold"
        justification = "center"
        hoverForegroundColor = "white"
        onClick = "JScript:player.controls.pause();"
    />

    <TEXT
        id = "stop_button"
        top = "70"
        left = "210"
        width = "90"
        value = "STOP"
        fontStyle = "bold"
        fontSize = "20"
        backgroundColor = "magenta"
        hoverFontStyle = "bold"
        justification = "center"
        hoverForegroundColor = "white"
        onClick = "JScript:player.controls.stop();"
    />

    <TEXT
        id = "position_display"
        top = "110"
        left = "80"
        value="wmpprop:player.controls.currentPositionString"
        enabled = "false"
    />

    <TEXT
        id = "label03"
        top = "110"
        left = "10"
```

```
            value = "Position:"
            enabled = "false"
    />

    <TEXT
        id = "duration_display"
        top = "110"
        left = "265"
        value="wmpprop:player.currentMedia.DurationString"
        enabled = "false"
    />

    <TEXT
        id = "label04"
        top = "110"
        left = "200"
        value = "Duration:"
        enabled = "false"
    />

    <EFFECTS
        id = "visualization_window"
        top = "140"
        left = "10"
        width = "130"
        height = "130"
     />

    <VIDEO
        id = "video_display"
        top = "140"
        left = "170"
        width = "130"
        height = "130"
     />

    <TEXT
        id = "status_display"
        top = "290"
        left = "10"
        width = "290"
        scrolling = "true"
        backgroundColor = "gold"
        value = "wmpprop:player.status"
    />

    </VIEW>
</THEME>
```

Adding the Auxiliary JScript Code

You have already added lines of embedded JScript code to some elements such as the stop_button element. But the code needed for the play_button element is too complex to fit into one line of embedded code. You must create an auxiliary JScript file to contain the code that will play a media file. The code for the auxiliary JScript file must perform the following tasks:

1. Create a new playlist using the default name or one supplied by the user.

2. Add a new digital media file to the playlist using a default path and name or ones supplied by the user.

3. Add the playlist to the Windows Media Player Media Library.

4. Play the new playlist.

5. Check whether the playlist has already been added; if it has, don't add it again, just play the file. You want to do this if the user clicks PLAY again after clicking PAUSE or STOP.

Creating the JScript File

Create an ASCII text file with the same name as the skin file, but give it the extension .js.

Adding a Flag to Check for Duplicate Entries

Add the following code at the beginning of the JScript file to set up a flag to determine whether the user has already added a playlist.

```
var itemFlag = false;
```

This code initializes a variable that will be checked before the playlist is created.

Adding the getNewItem Function

Add the following code to create a function called getNewItem that will perform the tasks needed to play a file.

```
function getNewItem() {

}
```

This function will be called by the *onClick* property of the play_button TEXT element.

Preventing Duplicate Entries

You must be sure that the code that adds the playlist is executed only once. You don't want to add a copy of the playlist every time the user clicks the PLAY button. That is why the itemFlag variable was created earlier in the JScript file.

Set up an *if* statement to test the value of the flag. Put the following code inside the body of the getNewItem function.

```
if (itemFlag == false)
{

itemFlag = true;
}
```

This tests whether itemFlag is false. If it is, then the code inside the *if* statement is run. After it is run, itemFlag will be set to true. The next time the function is called, the code inside the *if* statement will not be run.

The code inside the *if* statement creates the playlist, adds a file to it, and adds the playlist to the Windows Media Player Media Library.

Creating the Playlist

Add the following code inside the *if* statement in the getNewItem function.

```
var NewList =
    player.playlistCollection.newPlaylist(playlist_name.value);
```

This creates a playlist object named NewList. The name of the playlist is obtained from the playlist_name EDITBOX. The playlist is added to the Media Library by using the *newPlaylist* method of the *playlistCollection* object, which is part of the *player* object.

You must use the keyword *var* to create a playlist object. If you do not create an object, you can't use it later in your code.

Finding the Media File

Add the following line of code to make the new digital media file the current media.

```
player.currentMedia =
    player.mediaCollection.add(filepath_name.value);
```

This gets the file name and path from the value of the filepath_name EDITBOX. The media file is added to the media collection by using the *add* method of the *mediaCollection* object. The media file is then assigned to the *currentMedia* property of the *player* object.

Adding the Media File to the Playlist

Now that you have added a playlist and a media file to Windows Media Player, you need to associate the new file with the new playlist. Add the following code to make that association.

```
NewList.appendItem(player.currentMedia);
```

This code takes the current media and adds it to the end of the new playlist you created, named NewList. The *appendItem* method adds the current media, which was defined as the file you wanted to add.

Adding the PLAY Code

Now that the media file has been added to the playlist, all you need to do is make the Player start playing. Add the following code after the *if* statement, as the last line in the getNewItem function. You want this code to run every time the PLAY button is clicked.

```
player.controls.play();
```

This code plays the current playlist by using the *play* method of the *controls* object, which is part of the *player* object.

Complete JScript Code for the Advanced Skin

Here is the complete code for the JScript file.

```
var itemFlag = false;

function getNewItem() {
    if (itemFlag == false)
    {
    var NewList =
        player.playlistCollection.newPlaylist(playlist_name.value);
    player.currentMedia =
        player.mediaCollection.add(filepath_name.value);

    NewList.appendItem(player.currentMedia);

    itemFlag = true;
    }

    player.controls.play();
}
```

Viewing the Skin

Figure 17.2 shows the custom Advanced Skin.

Figure 17.2   Advanced Skin for Windows Media Player.

Testing the Advanced Skin

To test the Advanced Skin, use the following procedure:

1.   In Windows Explorer, double-click the name of the .wms file to start Windows Media Player with the Advanced Skin. It should look something like Figure 17.2.

2.   Choose a playlist and a file to play.

3.   Click the PLAY button. You will see the video or, if no video is present, a visualization. You should also hear audio if the file contains audio. The duration of the file should be displayed, and the current position should change every second to indicate how many seconds of the file have been played.

4.   Click the PAUSE, PLAY, and STOP buttons. The status of the Player should be displayed at the bottom of the skin.

Complete copies of the source code and digital media for this application are on the companion CD.

18

Using Banners, Embedded Web Pages, and Borders

This chapter will show you three applications for customizing the Video and Visualization pane of Windows Media Player. These applications use Player features called banners, embedded Web pages, and borders. Each one lets you add additional graphic capabilities to the Player's video pane.

Introduction to Three Interactive Features of the Player

Windows Media Player has dozens of enhancement features you can use to customize it. This chapter covers three features that let you add graphic and interactive elements to animate and expand the capabilities of the Video and Visualization pane.

First you will learn how to create a *banner* that appears in a narrow strip at the bottom of the video pane of the Player. This strip can contain text or images that a user can click to go to a Web site. You can also display an additional text message when a user hovers a mouse over the banner.

Next you will see how to embed a Web page in the Video and Visualization pane. With this technique you can make your Player more interactive because you can add all the possibilities of a Web page to the Player. For example, while users are listening to music with the Player on their screens, they can call up any Web page you want them to have access to, or they can use the Player as a portal to anything on the Internet. This feature can also be used to provide more specific details about the music being played, as well as more information about the artist, concert dates, locations, and so on.

The third feature is called *borders*. In this section you will learn how to use the skin programming language to develop artwork that you can put inside the Video and Visualization pane. This is done by putting a skin inside the Player. The skin is a graphic feature that, when it is put inside the Player, enables you to add additional buttons, windows, and artwork inside your Player. With this feature you can add extra windows for viewing videos or visualizations, links to Web sites, and interactive artwork.

To create the banner, embedded Web page, and border examples for this chapter, you will create text files using the text editor of your choice. No later examples in this book will build on these three, but you may want to save them for further use, modification, and study.

Setting Up Your Programming Environment

Before you begin programming, be sure you have installed the following software.

Installing the Required Software

The following software must be installed on your computer before you can develop the examples in this chapter:

- Windows Media Player 9 Series, if it is not already installed.

- Unless you are using art that someone else has supplied, you will need an art creation program such as Microsoft Paint.

- While it is not required, a text editor such as Microsoft Notepad is recommend. You must save text files in the ASCII file format. Do not use a word processor such as Microsoft Word that saves formatting along with text.

> **Note** You should go to the Windows Update Web site and download any updates available for the required software.

Understanding the User Interface of Windows Media Player

The previous three chapters showed how to create custom user interfaces for Windows Media Player. In those chapters, the user interface for the Player was provided by Visual Basic, Internet Explorer, or a custom skin for Windows Media Player. This chapter shows you how to create embedded visual elements that appear inside the standard Player user interface.

The user interface of the Player includes several panes and buttons, and several different feature areas such as Now Playing, Media Guide, and so on. Figure 18.1 shows the Now Playing area in the Full Mode of Windows Media Player.

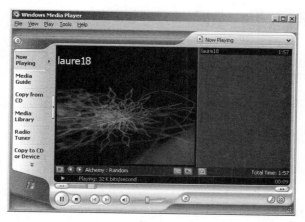

Figure 18.1   Now Playing area of Windows Media Player.

The Now Playing feature of the Player contains two major areas. On the right is the Playlist pane that shows the playlist that is currently playing. On the left is the Video and Visualization pane that displays video and visualizations. You can resize the Player and change the relative sizes of both areas. Also, the Video and Visualization pane can be split into two panes to allow the display of additional features such as a graphic equalizer, video settings, or a color chooser.

The rest of this chapter discusses custom visual elements that can be placed in the Video and Visualization pane. A developer can use these visual elements to customize the familiar user interface of the standard Windows Media Player.

There are three types of custom visual elements you can put in the Video and Visualization pane:

- Banners (clickable pictures)
- Embedded Web pages
- Borders (embedded skins)

Advantages of Using Banners

Although the capabilities of banners are more limited than those of embedded Web pages or embedded skins, they have the advantage of providing a quick and simple way to let the user click on a picture and navigate to a Web site. Banners are displayed in their own area, the banner bar, that usually appears in the Player only when a banner is present. Banners are most useful when you want to add a small unobtrusive image that will provide a link to a Web page.

Advantages of Embedding a Web Page

When you embed a Web page inside the Video and Visualization pane of Windows Media Player, you can leverage all the power of HTML, XML, Dynamic HTML, CSS, DOM, and other Internet programming techniques. Your Web page can communicate with the Player through events, and it can communicate with other applications and sites on a network or the Web. You can also embed the Windows Media Player ActiveX control in your Web page to provide further options such as synchronizing still images and captions to a video. You can use an embedded Web page to create a Web portal that is integrated with the Player, allowing a user to listen to music while surfing the Web for information related to the music that is currently playing.

Advantages of Embedding Skins

You can also embed a skin inside the Video and Visualization pane. This is called a border, and lets you use the skin technologies to provide a rich and complex user interface. Because skins are connected to the Player at a deeper layer of programming, you have more options for controlling the Player with more efficient timing. Borders are useful for adding extra controls and windows to the Player. For example, you could have one window for a video and another for a visualization.

Using Banners

Web pages on the Internet often use banners to display advertisements at the top of the page. You can click on a banner to learn more about the advertised product by navigating to a new Web page.

Windows Media Player has a similar technology. Player banners consist of a small graphic that appears in a special area called the banner bar at the bottom of the Video and Visualization pane. You can make a banner interactive and let the user click the banner to display a Web page in the default Web browser.

Viewing the Banner Bar

By default, the banner bar is hidden from view. When it is time to display a banner, the banner bar will pop up and display the banner at the bottom of the Video and Visualization pane. Figure 18.2 shows the Video and Visualization pane with the banner bar below it. The banner displays the word "EVERYTHING" in a long, narrow bitmap.

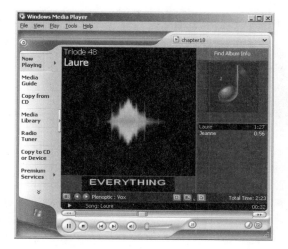

Figure 18.2   Video and Visualization pane with the banner bar below it.

> **Note**   The banner bar can be set programmatically in the playlist to remain open all the time that a playlist is playing, even when no banner is displayed. This setting is not recommended unless you are playing a series of short clips where some have banners and some do not. Otherwise it can be distracting to have a blank area at the bottom of the Video and Visualization pane. If you leave the banner bar setting on, the banner bar will still disappear when a new playlist is played if the new playlist doesn't open the banner bar. See the Windows Media Player SDK for more information about playlists and the banner bar.

Creating Banner Art

The artwork for a banner is long and narrow. The size of the banner can be no larger than 32 pixels high and 194 pixels wide. This is the largest banner that can fit into the smallest resizing of the Full Mode Windows Media Player. Figure 18.3 shows the Player resized to the smallest size possible. The user can click and drag the lower-right corner of the Player to make it smaller or larger.

Figure 18.3 Full-mode Windows Media Player resized to the smallest size possible.

Banners can use any of the following art file formats:

- BMP
- JPG
- PNG
- GIF

To create art for a banner, you can use Microsoft Paint or any other art program, such as Adobe Photoshop or Jasc Paint Shop Pro. The JPG file format is used in these examples because it is a widely known compressed graphic file format.

When creating your banner art, the prime concern is that your finished art file be no larger than 32 pixels high and 194 pixels wide.

Figure 18.4 shows a typical banner graphic.

EVERYTHING

Figure 18.4 Typical banner graphic.

Using Playlists with Banners

Windows Media Player uses XML (Extensible Markup Language) programming for playlists. The main purpose of a playlist is to provide a list of digital media items that the Player can play in order. However, one of the additional functions of playlists is to store information about banners: when they will be displayed, what media the banner will be synchronized to, and what link will be used when the user clicks the banner.

The following information provides an overview of XML as used in Player playlists. For more detailed information about XML and playlists in the Player, see Windows Media Metafiles in the Windows Media Player SDK.

Using XML for Playlists

A playlist is coded in XML and stores the playlist information in a logical manner. XML provides a structure for playlist information. The playlist structure must have exactly one header element and one or more entry elements.

Adding the Header Element

Every playlist must start with an opening ASX tag and close with an ending ASX tag. The following code shows the required tags. All other playlist code must be placed between these two lines.

```
<ASX>

</ASX>
```

While not required, it is highly recommended that you add the version attribute to the ASX element. The following code shows how to add the version information. Version 3.0 is the latest, as of the writing of this book.

```
<ASX version = "3.0">

</ASX>
```

Adding the version attribute ensures that your playlist will be recognized by future versions of Windows Media Player.

Adding Entry Elements

Each playlist must have one or more ENTRY elements. Each entry element consists of all the information needed to play one media item. The following code shows how to set up an ENTRY element. All details about the entry must be placed between these two lines.

```
<ENTRY>

</ENTRY>
```

For example, to create a minimum entry to play an audio file called laure18.wma, insert the following line between the opening and closing ENTRY tags.

```
<REF href = "laure18.wma" />
```

Creating a Minimum Playlist Example

The following lines show the minimum code needed to create a playlist containing one item. The item is the audio file laure18.wma.

```
<ASX version = "3.0">
    <ENTRY>
        <REF href = "laure18.wma" />
    </ENTRY>
</ASX>
```

Save this code to a file with the name chapter18a.asx. Be sure that the file laure18.wma is in the same folder as the playlist file. These files are on the companion CD.

To test your minimum playlist, in Windows Explorer double-click the name of the playlist file. Windows Media Player will start and the playlist will be displayed on the right side of the Now Playing area.

> **Note**   Playlists are also known as Windows Media metafiles. Do not confuse them with Windows Metafiles (WMF), which are vector graphic files that have nothing to do with Windows Media.

Using Playlist File Name Extensions

A playlist file must have one of the following extensions for the Player to recognize it as a playlist. All playlists are simple text files.

- **.asx**   This is the most common file name extension for playlists and will be used exclusively in this chapter.

- **.wax**   These files use the same file format as ASX but are used for playlists of audio (WMA) files.

- **.wvx**   These files use the same file format as ASX but are used for playlists of video (WMV) files.

> **Note**   Other file extensions may work for Windows Media Playlists, but the .asx, .wax, and .wvx extensions are supported for all Windows Media applications. Technically there is no difference between files using these three different extensions, and .wax and .wvx are only a convenience for sorting files by type.

Adding Banner Information to a Playlist

Banner programming information is stored in the BANNER element of a playlist. The BANNER element has an *href* attribute that defines a URL path to the banner artwork. A typical BANNER element might look like this.

```
<BANNER href = "laure18.jpg" />
```

The *href* attribute refers to an art file that is in the same folder as the playlist. You can also use any other URL that points to a valid art file.

Displaying the Banner Bar

To display a banner in Windows Media Player, you must add a *bannerbar* attribute to the ASX element. The *bannerbar* attribute determines how the banner bar is displayed. The two choices are:

- ■ *fixed*, which will always display the banner bar, whether there is a banner or not. This mode is usually not recommended, but you may want to use it if some items in the playlist have a banner and others do not.

- ■ *auto*, which will display the banner bar only when a banner exists. This is the default and is recommended.

To be sure that the banner bar is displayed automatically, find the following line in the playlist file.

```
<ASX version = "3.0">
```

Replace it with this line.

```
<ASX version = "3.0" bannerbar = "auto">
```

Placing Banner Elements

Banners can be displayed for a single item in a playlist or for the whole playlist. When creating banners, you have two choices:

- ■ You can create a banner that will be displayed in the banner bar the entire time the playlist is playing.

- ■ You can create a banner that will be displayed only for the duration of an individual item in the playlist. You can have a different banner for every item in the playlist, if desired.

Applying One Banner to the Whole Playlist

To add a banner that will be displayed for the entire time the playlist is playing, you must put the BANNER element outside of any specific ENTRY element.

For example, to display a banner for the minimum playlist shown previously under "Creating a Minimum Playlist Example," add the following line of code before the ENTRY element.

```
<BANNER href = "everything18.jpg" />
```

This will display a banner using the art file everything18.jpg. The complete code to display a banner for the duration of a two-item playlist would look like the following.

```
<ASX version = "3.0" bannerbar = "auto">
    <BANNER href = "everything18.jpg" />

    <ENTRY>
        <REF href = "laure18.wma" />
    </ENTRY>

    <ENTRY>
        <REF href = "jeanne18.wma" />
    </ENTRY>
</ASX>
```

This playlist provides a banner that will be displayed for the duration of the entire playlist. The playlist consists of two media items, laure18.wma and jeanne18.wma. Save the playlist and name it chapter18b.asx. This playlist and both of the media files are on the companion CD. Be sure that the playlist and the two media files are all in the same folder when you run the playlist.

Applying Banners to Individual Items in a Playlist

By inserting banner information inside each ENTRY element of a playlist, you can display a different banner for each item in the playlist.

To add a banner for each item in the preceding list, first remove the existing banner element by removing the following line.

```
<BANNER href = "everything18.jpg" />
```

Then add the following line as the first line inside the entry for the laure18.wma element.

```
<BANNER href = "laure18.jpg" />
```

Next add the following line as the first line inside the entry for the jeanne18.wma element.

```
<BANNER href = "jeanne18.jpg" />
```

Here is the complete code for a playlist that will display different banners for each item in the playlist.

```
<ASX version = "3.0" bannerbar = "auto">
    <ENTRY>
        <BANNER href = "laure18.jpg" />
        <REF href = "laure18.wma" />
    </ENTRY>

    <ENTRY>
        <BANNER href = "jeanne18.jpg" />
        <REF href = "jeanne18.wma" />
    </ENTRY>
</ASX>
```

This playlist requires two audio files, laure18.wma and jeanne18.wma, and two art files, laure18.jpg and jeanne18.jpg. The playlist is named chapter18c.asx, and the two media and two art files are on the companion CD. The media and art files must be in the same folder as the playlist file. For example, if you copied all your media files to c:\media, you should copy the playlist file and art files to c:\media as well.

Enhancing Banner Capabilities

A banner can be more than just a graphic displayed at the bottom of the Video and Visualization pane of the Player. The main purpose of banners is to provide extra information for the user by using pop-up ToolTip information windows and links to Web pages.

You can add programming information to a playlist to provide the user with additional information when the user hovers a mouse over the banner. This additional information uses the ABSTRACT element in a playlist and displays a standard Windows ToolTip.

You can also program the banner with a link that displays a Web page in the default browser when the user clicks the banner. The link is stored in a playlist by using the MOREINFO element.

The ABSTRACT and MOREINFO elements can be used for banners that apply to entire playlists or to banners that apply to individual items in a playlist.

Adding ABSTRACT Information to a Banner.

You can create text that will be displayed when the user hovers a mouse over the banner. The information will be displayed in a ToolTip window.

To add this additional information, you must insert an ABSTRACT element inside the BANNER element. Normally the BANNER element opens and closes in the same line by using the following syntax.

```
<BANNER href = "filename.jpg" />
```

But XML syntax allows placing an element inside another element by creating opening and closing tags.

Use these two lines for banners that will contain additional elements.

```
<BANNER href = "filename.jpg">

</BANNER>
```

The opening BANNER tag contains the *href* attribute.

The ABSTRACT element defines a text string that will be displayed when the user hovers a mouse over the banner. The text to be displayed is enclosed by opening and closing ABSTRACT tags.

The following line shows how to use a text string with the ABSTRACT element.

```
<ABSTRACT>Click on this banner for more information.</ABSTRACT>
```

To see how this works, start with the following code from earlier in this section, which was saved as chapter18b.asx.

```
<ASX version = "3.0" bannerbar = "auto">
    <BANNER href = "everything18.jpg" />

    <ENTRY>
        <REF href = "laure18.wma" />
    </ENTRY>

    <ENTRY>
        <REF href = "jeanne18.wma" />
    </ENTRY>
</ASX>
```

Remove the following line.

```
<BANNER href = "everything18.jpg" />
```

Replace it with the following lines.

```
<BANNER href = "everything18.jpg">

</BANNER>
```

Insert the following line between the opening and closing BANNER tags.

```
<ABSTRACT>Click on this banner for more information.</ABSTRACT>
```

The new code should look like this.

```
<ASX version = "3.0" BANNERBAR = "Auto">
    <BANNER href = "everything18.jpg">
        <ABSTRACT>Click on this banner for more information.</ABSTRACT>
    </BANNER>

    <ENTRY>
        <REF href = "laure18.wma" />
    </ENTRY>

    <ENTRY>
        <REF href = "jeanne18.wma" />
    </ENTRY>
</ASX>
```

When you double-click the file name, the Player opens and the banner is displayed while the media plays. When you hover your mouse over the banner, a ToolTip is displayed that reads "Click this banner for more information." Nothing will happen when you click the banner until you add a MOREINFO element to create a link.

Adding a MOREINFO Link to a Banner.

You can add a link that will start the default Web browser on the user's computer and display a Web page. The syntax and placement of the MOREINFO element is similar to the ABSTRACT element. The main difference is that instead of supplying text, the MOREINFO element supplies a URL.

To create a MOREINFO element that links to a Web page, insert the element inside a BANNER element and provide a URL for the *href* attribute. The following line shows a typical use of the MOREINFO element.

```
<MOREINFO href = "http://www.microsoft.com" />
```

You will often want to add the MOREINFO element right below a corresponding ABSTRACT element.

The following code shows a playlist with a banner that contains ABSTRACT and MOREINFO elements.

```
<ASX version = "3.0" bannerbar = "auto">

    <BANNER href = "everything18.jpg">
        <ABSTRACT>Click on this banner for more information.</ABSTRACT>
        <MOREINFO href = "http://www.microsoft.com" />
    </BANNER>

    <ENTRY>
        <REF href = "laure18.wma" />
    </ENTRY>

    <ENTRY>
        <REF href = "jeanne18.wma" />
    </ENTRY>
</ASX>
```

Save this code to a file with the name chapter18d.asx and double-click the file name. The files will start playing and the banner will be displayed. If you hover over the banner, a ToolTip will appear that reads "Click on this banner for more information." If you click the banner, the home page of the Microsoft Web site will be displayed.

Embedding a Web Page in Windows Media Player

Chapter 16 showed how to embed Windows Media Player in a Web page. You can also do the opposite and display a Web page in the Player. The Web page will be displayed in the Video and Visualization pane of the Now Playing area. This allows the user to have all the familiarity of the default Player, but gives the developer the ability to use all the power and functionality of Internet Explorer.

You can insert a Web page inside the Video and Visualization pane by adding new information to a playlist.

Using a Playlist to Embed a Web Page in the Player

To embed a Web page in the Video and Visualization pane, you must use the PARAM element in a playlist. The PARAM element is used to provide customized information to the Player. In this case, you need to tell the Player what Web page you want to embed in the Video and Visualization pane.

The PARAM element has a name attribute and a value attribute. To embed a Web page in the Player, you need to define the name attribute as "HTMLView" and the value attribute as the URL of the Web page you want to display.

The syntax to use the PARAM element to load a Web page into the Video and Visualization pane will look similar to the following line.

```
<PARAM name = "HTMLView" value = "http://www.microsoft.com" />
```

You can use any valid URL to link to a Web page.

> **Note**   The PARAM element enables Windows Media Player to receive custom attributes. This chapter uses the PARAM element for a specific custom attribute that uses the HTMLView name. But this and other kinds of custom attributes can be used by the Player to provide several kinds of additional functionality. For example, Windows Media Encoder can embed custom attributes in a media stream, and they could be used to embed Web pages in the Player at regular intervals, perhaps to provide identification every hour for a radio station. For more information about using the encoder to send custom attributes to the Player, see Chapter 5.

Placing the HTMLView Custom Attribute

You can use the HTMLView custom attribute to define a Web page that will be displayed for the duration of the entire playlist or for an individual item in the playlist. Place the HTMLView PARAM tag before the first entry to make it valid for the entire playlist; otherwise, put it inside the particular entry you want to display a Web page with. In this example, only the playlist-wide HTMLView option will be used.

To display the Web page for the duration of a playlist, insert the PARAM element outside of any ENTRY element. For example, use a simple playlist like this.

```
<ASX version = "3.0">
  <ENTRY>
    <REF href = "laure18.wma" />
  </ENTRY>

  <ENTRY>
    <REF href = "jeanne18.wma" />
  </ENTRY>
</ASX>
```

Then add the following line before the first ENTRY element.

```
<PARAM name = "HTMLView" value = "http://localhost/goodmusic18.htm" />
```

The complete code example will look like this.

```
<ASX version = "3.0">
  <PARAM name = "HTMLView" value = "http://localhost/goodmusic18.htm" />

  <ENTRY>
    <REF href = "laure18.wma" />
  </ENTRY>

  <ENTRY>
    <REF href = "jeanne18.wma" />
  </ENTRY>
</ASX>
```

This assumes that you have two media files, laure18.wma and jeanne18.wma, in the same folder as the playlist. It also assumes that you have a Web page called goodmusic18.htm that is on the local Web server. If the *localhost* variable does not work in the HTTP URL string for this example, substitute the name of your computer. For example, if your computer were named laureserver, you would type: http://laureserver/goodmusic18.htm instead of http://localhost/goodmusic18.htm. Save the playlist to a file with the name chapter18e.asx and double-click the file name. The goodmusic18.htm Web page will be displayed in the Video and Visualization pane of the Player. See Figure 18.5 for an example of a Web page displayed in the Player.

Figure 18.5 Windows Media Player displaying a Web page in the Video and Visualization pane.

Note that the Playlist pane has disappeared from the Now Playing area. Windows Media Player does this automatically when a Web page is loaded, to save more room for the Web page. You can restore the playlist by clicking the Restore The Video And Visualization Pane button at the lower-right corner of the enlarged Video and Visualization pane. Figure 18.6 shows the location of the button.

Figure 18.6 Restore The Video And Visualization Pane button.

Using a Player Inside the Player

Chapter 16 showed how to embed Windows Media Player in a Web page using ActiveX technology. The previous section of this chapter showed how to embed a Web page in the Video and Visualization pane of the Player. If you combine these two techniques, you can put the Windows Media Player ActiveX control in a Web page that runs inside the Player. In other words, you have a Player inside a Web page inside the Player!

All you have to do is create a Web page that uses the Windows Media Player ActiveX control and then create a playlist that instructs the Player to display the Web page in its Video and Visualization pane.

Creating a Web Page with an Embedded Player

The following code creates a simple Web page that contains the Player as an ActiveX object.

```
<HTML>
<HEAD>
</HEAD>
<BODY bgcolor = "#AFAFAF">

<DIV style = "top:50;left:50;position:absolute">
<H1>Player in a Web Page</H1>
<OBJECT id = "Player" Height = "150" Width = "150"
  classid = "CLSID:6BF52A52-394A-11D3-B153-00C04F79FAA6">
    <PARAM name = "uiMode" value = "none" />
    <PARAM name = "autoStart" value = "true" />
</OBJECT>
</DIV>

</BODY>
</HTML>
```

These lines of code accomplish the following tasks:

1. Set the background color of the Web page to gray.

2. Define the Windows Media Player ActiveX control with the following parameters:

    ❑   The *uiMode* property is set to "none" so that only the video window of the control will be displayed.

    ❑   The *autoStart* property is set to "true" so that the Player can start playing as soon as an item in the playlist is encountered.

3. Position the Player on the Web page, by using a DIV element, so that there are left and top margins of 50 pixels each.

If you load this Web page in a browser, the Web page will look like Figure 18.7. Nothing will play because there are no media items assigned to the Player yet. Save this Web page to a file called embedded18.htm and put it in the root folder of your local Web server.

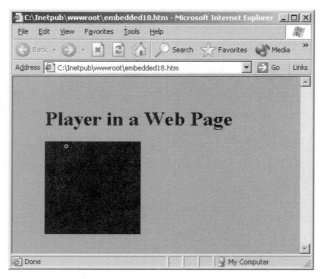

Figure 18.7 Windows Media Player in a Web Page.

Creating the Playlist to Display the Web Page in the Player

You must next create a playlist that will load the Web page into the Video and Visualization pane and also provide digital media files for the Windows Media Player ActiveX control to play.

Use the following code to create a sample playlist that will instruct the Player to embed a Web page in the Video and Visualization pane and then play the songs Laure and Jeanne.

```
<ASX version = "3.0">
    <PARAM name = "HTMLView"
            value = "http://localhost/embedded18.htm" />

    <ENTRY>
        <REF href = "http://localhost/laure18.wma" />
    </ENTRY>

    <ENTRY>
        <REF href = "http://localhost/jeanne18.wma" />
    </ENTRY>
</ASX>
```

This playlist consists of the following three elements:

1.   The header, which consists of the ASX element. Every playlist must start and end with the ASX tag.

2.   The PARAM element which uses the HTMLView custom parameter to define the Web page that will be displayed. In this example, the Web page will be the embedded.htm page that was shown in the previous section of this chapter.

3.   The ENTRY elements for the two media items, laure18.wma and jeanne18.wma.

Save this playlist with the name chapter18f.asx. The media files and the Web page should be in the root folder of your Web server, which is typically c:\inetpub\wwwroot. If the *localhost* variable does not work in the HTTP URL string for this example, substitute the name of your computer. For example, if your computer were named laureserver, you would type: http://laureserver/embedded18.htm instead of http://localhost/embedded18.htm.

Figure 18.8 shows the Player displaying a Web page in the Video and Visualization pane. The Web page is displaying a video or visualization in a small square window by using the Windows Media Player ActiveX control.

Figure 18.8   Windows Media Player displaying a Web page that contains an embedded Player.

Using Borders

Chapter 17 demonstrated how to create custom user interfaces for Windows Media Player by using skins. Skin technology can also be used to display a custom user interface inside the Video and Visualization pane. When you create a custom skin and place it inside the Player, the skin is called a border.

The border technology requires two parts:

- A skin, which consists of a skin definition file, any art files required, and any JScript files required.

- A playlist that instructs the Player to load the skin into the Video and Visualization pane, making the skin into a border.

Creating a Skin for a Border

Borders use Windows Media Player skin technology to create a custom interface. To see how borders operate, type the following skin code.

```
<THEME>
    <VIEW>
        <EFFECTS
            id = "visualization_window"
            top = "50"
            left = "10"
            width = "130"
            height = "130"
         />

        <VIDEO
            id = "video_display"
            top = "50"
            left = "170"
            width = "130"
            height = "130"
         />

        <TEXT
            id = "status_display"
            top = "20"
            left = "10"
            width = "290"
            scrolling = "true"
            backgroundColor = "Gold"
            value="wmpprop:player.currentMedia.name"
         />

    </VIEW>
</THEME>
```

This skin consists of the following parts:

1. The THEME and VIEW elements. Every skin must open and close with THEME tags and every skin must have at least one VIEW element. All other code must be placed in a view.

2. An EFFECTS element. It is used to display a visualization in a window on the skin. The visualization will be synchronized to the audio portion of the media.

3. A VIDEO element. It is used to display the video portion of the media. You should always provide a video ELEMENT in a skin. If you do not, and the Player starts playing video, the Player will enter the Full Mode and the skin will not be used.

4. A TEXT element. It is used to display the name of the current media in a scrolling text element.

Save the skin with the name border18.wms, and then double-click the file name. A skin will be displayed. Because there are no controls, it will not automatically play. However, you can right-click on the VIDEO element window, open a file, and play it, by selecting options from the shortcut menu.

Figure 18.9 shows the skin that will be used for a border.

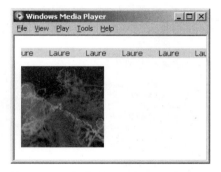

Figure 18.9   Skin that will be used for a border.

Using a Playlist to Load the Border

To change a skin into a border, you must use a playlist that contains a SKIN element. The SKIN element instructs the Player to display the skin in the Video and Visualization pane.

To load a border, use the *href* attribute of the SKIN element to define the URL of the skin file. A typical SKIN element would look like this.

```
<SKIN href = "border18.wms" />
```

The SKIN element must be placed in the playlist before any ENTRY element. Skins that are used for borders always apply to all items in a playlist.

To create a border, create a playlist and then add a SKIN element.

Start by typing the following code for a simple playlist.

```
<ASX version = "3.0">
    <ENTRY>
        <REF href = "laure18.wma" />
    </ENTRY>
</ASX>
```

This playlist has one entry, which will play the media file laure18.wma.

Add the SKIN element immediately before the first ENTRY element. The resulting code should now look like this.

```
<ASX version = "3.0">
    <SKIN href = "border18.wms" />
    <ENTRY>
        <REF href = "laure18.wma" />
    </ENTRY>
</ASX>
```

Save the playlist with the name chapter18g.asx. Be sure that the chapter18g.asx, laure18.wma, and border18.wms files are all in the same folder. Double-click the ASX file to test the example. The Player will start and the skin will be displayed in the Video and Visualization pane.

Figure 18.10 shows the Player displaying a border.

Figure 18.10 A Border in the Video and Visualization pane of Windows Media Player.

Using Windows Media Download Packages

Windows Media Player provides a technology that lets you package audio and video media with a border into one file. After users download the file, they automatically see your border when they play the media content in the file. This is often used for marketing and branding.

To create a Windows Media Download package, you must assemble the following files:

- A playlist that defines the border skin. The playlist must have the file extension .asx.

- A compressed border skin package that has the file name extension .wmz. This package contains the skin definition file and any associated art and JScript files. Use a program like WinZip to compress the skin files into a single package and then change the file name extension from .zip to .wmz.

- Any audio and video media that you want to reference in the playlist.

After these items are gathered, you must compress them into one file. Use a program like PKZIP or WinZip to compress all the files (including the border skin package that has already been "zipped") into a single package. Change the file name extension from .zip to .wmd.

When the file is downloaded, the media files are loaded into the Player, the border is displayed in the Video and Visualization pane, and the Player starts playing what's on the playlist.

For more information about Windows Media Download packages, see the Windows Media Player SDK.

Part V

Complete Radio Station Application

This final part of the book combines many of the Windows Media programming techniques you learned in previous chapters into one application that you can use to put digital media content on your computer and distribute it over a network. Chapter 19 will give you step-by-step directions for every line of code needed to develop an Internet radio station that will encode files, add them to a playlist, and stream them to users. This application has been designed to demonstrate how the major components of the Windows Media platform work together. It uses Windows Media Encoder to translate music files into Windows Media Format that a server running Windows Media Services can stream through a network to Windows Media Player. After you complete the Radio Station application, you can adapt it easily for a wide variety of uses, making it possible to put the highest quality audio and video on the Internet with ease and efficiency. This sample application includes custom automation techniques that simplify the user interfaces of the Windows Media components and reduce the number of tasks needed to make the components work together.

19

Creating an Internet Radio Station

This chapter will show you how to create an Internet broadcasting workstation that you can use to stream digital media across a network. The new application is called Radio Station, and it will combine the major components of the Windows Media platform into a simple and efficient program that will enable you to stream music over the Internet or a corporate intranet.

Introduction to the Radio Station Application

This chapter will use what you learned in previous chapters to develop an end-to-end streaming media radio station application that will let you encode digital media files with Windows Media Encoder, add the files to a playlist, create a publishing point on a server running Windows Media Services, and stream the playlist to Windows Media Player. The Radio Station application will let you create custom playlists of music selections that you can organize any way you want, to provide unique programming possibilities for a wide variety of audiences. This application contains the basic programming techniques for preparing digital media files and streaming them across a network. These basic techniques enable you to give users a unique playlist of music that can be made available on a Web site. Because these playlists are streamed on demand, the user can receive them at any time, and can fast forward and rewind through the music selections.

The Radio Station application can be adapted easily to create other types of streaming media software solutions for broadcasting over the Internet or a corporate intranet. For example, by substituting the appropriate video encoding profile, you can set up an Internet TV station and stream video over the Internet. By making simple modifications to the Radio Station application, you can develop programs to add streaming audio and video to community, school, and family Web sites. You could stream live, high-school football games, provide on-demand videos of your child's school play, or multicast freeway traffic reports. A streaming media Web site can provide videos about new products and audio product support for specific problems. Streaming media can be used on your corporate intranet for training, communicating messages from management to employees, and allowing people who are off site to "attend" a meeting from anywhere in the world. As more and more people are able to use broadband connections, the audience for streaming media will continue to grow. The World Wide Web has changed the lives of people all over the globe, and streaming media can be used on the Web to provide information that can be tailored to either individuals or large numbers of users anywhere.

The Radio Station application uses programming techniques that were presented in previous chapters. You will use what you learned in Chapter 2 to encode files, Chapter 3 to test the files, Chapter 14 to add the files to a playlist, Chapter 10 to create a publishing point to stream the playlist over the Internet, and Chapter 11 to test the resulting stream on the Player. When you compile all these techniques into the Radio Station application, you will have a complete Internet broadcasting workstation. This application will save dozens of steps that you would need to take if you were working with the full user interfaces of Windows Media Encoder, Windows Media Services, and Windows Media Player. Saving steps is very important if you want to create new playlists frequently. As a result, this program can make the creation and operation of an Internet radio station fun and easy.

When you have assembled the Radio Station application, it will be very simple to run. First you choose the name of your publishing point on a server running Windows Media Services. Similar to the call letters of an AM or FM radio station, the publishing point is used by your listeners to "tune in" to your station by using Windows Media Player. Next choose files that you want to distribute and encode them into Windows Media Format so that they will stream more efficiently over the Internet. After you encode each file, you can listen to the results by using the Player to make sure the encoded file sounds the way you want it to. When you're happy with the results of the encoded file, you can add it to a master playlist. When you have added all the files to your Internet radio show, you are ready to audition your playlist to make sure you have the songs in the right order. After your playlist is ready to go, all you have to do is click a button to put your Internet radio station "on the air." Now each listener can "tune in" to your radio station by using the Player to request your playlist from the server publishing point. Unlike an AM or FM radio station that broadcasts a program only at a specific time, the listeners to your Internet radio station will be able to tune in whenever they want and receive the entire playlist of songs. They will also be able to rewind or fast forward through the playlist at their convenience.

To develop the Radio Station application for this chapter, you will create a Visual Basic form and add controls and code to perform the programming tasks required.

There are no later applications in this book to build on the Radio Station application, but you may want to save it for further use, modification, and study.

The Radio Station application will perform the following tasks:

- Let the operator choose the source media path that will be associated with the on-demand publishing point. A default file path will be provided. The server can serve files with the following extensions: .wav, .jpg, and .mp3, as well as .asf and the standard Windows Media formats, .wma and .wmv. Files that have been encoded into Windows Media Format will provide better quality audio and video.

- Let the operator select a publishing-point name that the server will use for on-demand publishing. A default will be provided. Any valid publishing-point name can be used.

- When the operator has chosen a file path and publishing-point name, let the operator click a button to start the publishing point. The code will verify that the publishing point has not already been created. If another publishing point exists with the same name, the previous publishing point will be deleted and the operator will be notified.

- Let the operator select an encoding profile from a file. A default encoding profile will be provided. Any valid encoding profile can be used.

- Let the operator choose the source media file for encoding into Windows Media Format. A default file path and name will be provided. The encoder can convert files with the following extensions: .wav, .avi, .mpg, and .mp3, as well as .asf and the standard Windows Media formats, .wma and .wmv.

- Let the operator choose the path and name for the destination media file that will be created by the encoding process. A default path and file name will be provided. Use a standard Windows Media file name extension: .wma for audio or .wmv for video.

- After choosing file names and a profile, let the operator click a button to start the encoding process. The data in the chosen source file will then be converted to raw data and encoded into Windows Media Format, as specified by the chosen profile.

- When the encoding is finished, let the operator click a button to audition the file that was encoded. The operator can mute the file audition at any time.

- If satisfied with the newly encoded file, the operator can add it to a master playlist. The process of encoding a file and adding it to the playlist can be repeated as many times as necessary to create a complete master playlist. A default pre-encoded file of the operator's choice will also be included as the first item in the playlist.

- When the master playlist is complete, let the operator audition the complete playlist to be sure that all media items are in the correct order. The operator can mute the playlist audition at any time.

- When the playlist is ready to be streamed over the Internet, let the operator click a button to let clients connect and begin receiving the music in the streaming media playlist. A second button is provided to stop new clients from connecting.

Setting Up Your Programming Environment

Before you begin programming, be sure you have installed the following software and configured it properly.

Installing the Required Software

The following software must be installed on your computer before you can develop the Radio Station application:

- Windows Server 2003, Standard Edition; Windows Server 2003, Enterprise Edition; or Windows Server 2003, Datacenter Edition. Windows Media Services is a component of all three versions.

- Windows Media Encoder 9 Series. You can install Windows Media Encoder from the companion CD.

- Windows Media Profile Editor. When you install Windows Media Encoder, the profile editor is also installed.

- Windows Media Player 9 Series, if it is not already installed.

- Microsoft Visual Basic 6.0.

> **Note**   You should go to the Windows Update Web site and download any updates available for the required software.

Configuring Visual Basic

To configure Visual Basic for the Radio Station application, follow these steps:

1. Start Visual Basic and create a new programming project by selecting New Project from the File menu and selecting the Standard EXE option. Click OK.

2. Add a reference to a COM object that contains the Windows Media Services functionality. Add the reference by selecting References from the Project menu and scrolling down to Windows Media Services. Select the services check box and click OK.

3. Add a reference to a COM object that contains the Microsoft XML functionality. Add the reference by selecting References from the Project menu and scrolling down to Microsoft XML. Select the XML 3.0 check box and click OK. (Use XML version 3.0 or later.) You will use XML to create a playlist for the server to send to the Player.

4. Add a reference to a COM object that contains the Windows Media Encoder functionality. Add the reference by selecting References from the Project menu and scrolling down to Windows Media Encoder. Select the encoder check box and click OK.

5. Add the Windows Media Player ActiveX control to the Visual Basic toolbox. Add the Player control by selecting Components from the Project menu and then selecting the Windows Media Player check box. After you click OK in the Components dialog box, the Windows Media Player icon is displayed in the toolbox.

Creating a Visual Basic Form for the Radio Station Application

Because the Radio Station application combines material from several chapters, it will be easier to start with a blank form instead of using a previous one. Start Visual Basic and begin with the empty default form provided for a Standard EXE project.

As you move through this chapter, you will divide the form into four areas that represent the major tasks required to run an Internet radio station. The four areas of the form are, from top to bottom:

1. **Publishing-point area**   This area is used to set up the on-demand publishing point on the server. The publishing point is set up by the operator only once.

2. **Profile area**   This area is used to select a profile for all encoding. The operator of the radio station will need to do this only once.

3. **Encoding area**   This area is used to control the encoding of all individual files for potential inclusion in the master playlist. After a file is encoded, it can be added to the playlist of songs that will be delivered to listeners when they tune in to the radio station. The operator can encode as many files as desired and add them to the master playlist or save them for later. Encoded files can also be tested here to be sure that they were properly encoded.

4.   **Monitoring and Connections area**   This area is used to check the final playlist and put the radio station "on the air." The left side of the area will let the operator audition the master playlist for a final check. After the playlist has been auditioned, the right side of this area permits the operator to allow clients to connect, making it possible for them to request and receive the contents of the playlist as a continuous stream.

Note   Each listener receives the complete playlist of songs from beginning to end, no matter when they tune in, as long as the publishing point has been started and clients are allowed to connect. Unlike an AM or FM radio station, each listener to this Internet radio station receives the complete broadcast from the beginning of the playlist whenever they tune in. Windows Media allows the emulation of traditional radio stations through the use of multicast technology, but for reasons outlined in Chapters 1 and 13, unicast technology is more practical for the average Internet streaming media application. The Radio Station application in this chapter uses on-demand publishing to deliver a playlist of songs to the listener. The delivery uses unicast streaming to transmit the content, but does not use unicast broadcasting. Receiving a playlist on demand allows the listener to fast forward or rewind to any place in the playlist, which would not be possible with a unicast broadcast.

Detailed instructions for adding the controls to the Visual Basic form will be provided in the sections of this chapter covering the tasks associated with the four areas of the form. The layout of the form will correspond, from top to bottom, to the order of the major tasks that must be performed by the radio station operator.

Task 1: Creating a Publishing Point

To begin setting up a Windows Media–based radio station for broadcasting on the Internet, the first thing you must do is start a publishing point on a server running Windows Media Services. This publishing point will use a master playlist to contain the audio media that the radio station will broadcast. A listener will "tune in" by using Windows Media Player to send a request to the publishing point, and the server will send the audio media to the Player and use the master playlist to determine which on-demand files to send in what order.

To create the publishing point, you must first add controls to a form and then add the relevant code procedures.

Adding Controls to Create a Publishing Point

To create the portion of the user interface that will let the radio station operator create a publishing point, you must add the following eight controls to a new blank form in Visual Basic:

- **PubPointPath**   A TextBox box control named PubPointPath. It will contain the path to the publishing-point folder. The operator can modify this path before the publishing point is created.

- **Label1**   A Label control to the left of the PubPointPath text box. This label describes the contents of the publishing-point area. Give it a caption of "Set Up Publishing Point".

- **PubPointName**   A TextBox control to the right of the PubPointPath text box. It will contain the name of the publishing point. The operator can modify this name before the publishing point is created.

- **PlaylistName**   A TextBox control below the PubPointPath text box. It will contain the name of the master playlist. The operator can modify this name before the publishing point is created.

- **FirstFile**   A TextBox control to the right of the PlaylistName text box. It will contain the path and name of the first file in the playlist. The purpose of this file is to provide a station identification to listeners so they will know they are receiving the correct broadcast. The operator can modify this value before the publishing point is created.

- **Timer1**   A Timer control that will be used to determine when the publishing point has been created. Because this control is not visible at run time, you can place this control anywhere on the form.

- **AddPub**   A CommandButton control below the PlaylistName text box. This button will let the operator add a publishing point with the path and name specified in the PubPointPath and PubPointName text boxes. Give it a caption of "Add PubPoint".

- **PubPointStatus**   A Label control to the right of the AddPub button. This label will display the status of the publishing point. The Timer1 timer will check the publishing-point status every second, and this label will show the operator when the publishing point is running. Give it a caption of "PubPoint Status" to show the operator what it is for, and that the value will be changed by code when the application runs.

Figure 19.1 shows the first part of the form for the Radio Station application with the controls on it. These controls will be used to add a publishing point for the radio station broadcast.

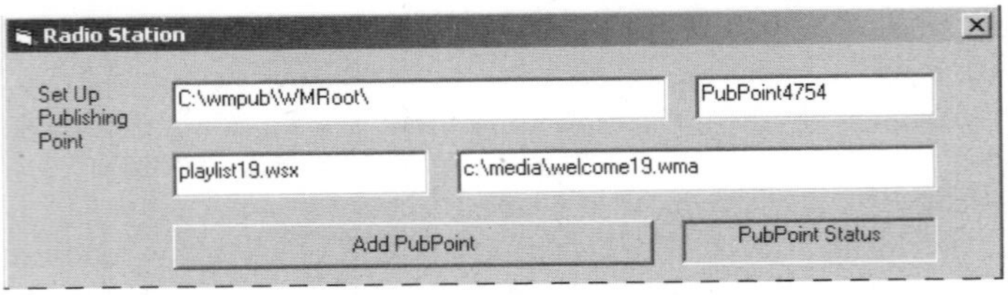

Figure 19.1 Partial Radio Station form with publishing-point controls added.

Designing the Code to Create a Publishing Point

The code for the publishing-point portion of the Radio Station application must perform the following tasks:

1. Let the operator specify a publishing-point path and name. Defaults will be provided.

2. Let the operator specify a name for the master playlist and a path and file name for the first media item in the playlist. Defaults will be provided.

3. Add the publishing point.

4. Display the status of the publishing point by using a timer to poll the server at one-second intervals.

Adding the Code to Create a Publishing Point

The code for the publishing-point portion of the Radio Station application will be added in the following four blocks:

- **General declarations** Variables that can be used in any procedure need to be declared in this block. Variables defined inside a procedure are not available in any other procedure.

- **Form_Load procedure** This is code that runs when the application starts. After this code has been executed, the application is ready for operator input.

- **AddPub_Click procedure** This is code that runs when the operator clicks the AddPub button to start the publishing point.

■   **Timer1_Timer procedure**   This is code that runs at intervals determined by the *Interval* property of the Timer1 control.

Adding the Declarations Code for the Publishing Point

To define the global variables that you will use to create a publishing point, several lines must be added to the declarations section of the Visual Basic form module. You must add code to define the server objects, the XML objects that are used to create a playlist, and a flag variable.

Adding the Server Declarations

To define the objects needed for the server, add the following lines of code at the beginning of the declarations area of the form module.

```
Dim Server As WMSServer
Dim MyPubPoint As IWMSOnDemandPublishingPoint
Dim MyPubPoints As IWMSPublishingPoints
```

These lines create the server object, the objects needed for the publishing-point collection, and the individual publishing point. For more information about server objects, see Chapter 11.

Adding the XML Playlist Declarations

To define the objects needed for playlists, add the following lines of code immediately after the lines you just added.

```
Dim MyPlaylist As IXMLDOMDocument
Dim MyProcNode As IXMLDOMNode
Dim Root As IXMLDOMNode
Dim Node As IXMLDOMNode
Dim Seq As IXMLDOMNode
Dim RootElement As IXMLDOMElement
Dim SequenceElement As IXMLDOMElement
Dim MediaItem As IXMLDOMElement
```

These lines define the XML objects needed for playlists. For more information about using XML to create server playlists, see Chapter 14.

Adding the PubPoint Flag

To define a global variable that will be used to determine whether the publishing point has been started, add the following line of code immediately after the lines you just added.

```
Dim PubPointFlag As Boolean
```

This variable will be used to be sure that the operator does not attempt to add an item to the playlist before the publishing point has been started.

Adding the Form_Load Code for the Publishing Point

Several lines of code must be put into the Form_Load procedure to create objects, initialize variables, and set properties that will be used to create a publishing point. Double-click the form to create a shell for the Form_Load procedure that looks like this.

```
Private Sub Form_Load()

End Sub
```

Creating the Server Objects

To create the objects needed for the server, add the following lines of code as the first lines inside the Form_Load procedure.

```
Set Server = New WMSServer
Set MyPubPoints = Server.PublishingPoints
```

These lines create the server object and the server's collection of publishing points. For more information about creating server objects, see Chapter 10.

Setting the Default Values

To define the default values for the publishing point, add the following lines of code immediately after the lines you just added.

```
PubPointPath.Text = "C:\wmpub\WMRoot\"
PubPointName.Text = "PubPoint4754"
```

These lines define default values for the publishing-point path and publishing-point name. Be sure that the path is a valid path for a publishing point. For more information about publishing points, see Chapter 10.

Beginning the Master Playlist

To create the first part of the master playlist, add the following lines of code to the Form_Load procedure immediately after the lines you just added.

```
Set MyPlaylist = Server.CreatePlaylist
Set MyProcNode = MyPlaylist.createNode(7, "wsx", "")
MyPlaylist.appendChild MyProcNode
MyProcNode.Text = "version = '1.0'"
Set RootElement = MyPlaylist.createElement("smil")
Set Root = MyPlaylist.appendChild(RootElement)
Set SequenceElement = MyPlaylist.createElement("seq")
Set Seq = Root.appendChild(SequenceElement)
PlayListName.Text = "playlist19.wsx"
FirstFile.Text = "C:\media\welcome19.wma"
```

These lines assemble the first part of the master playlist and perform the following tasks:

1.   Create the playlist object.

2.   Create an XML node that defines the XML document as a playlist and specifies the Windows Media metafile version number.

3.   Create a root element for the playlist that defines the playlist as being compatible with the Synchronized Multimedia Integration Language (SMIL).

4.   Create an element that further defines the playlist as consisting of a sequence of items that will be played in order.

5.   Set the default name of the playlist in a text box. The operator can change the name before the playlist is created.

6.   Set the default file name and path to a file that will be used as the first file in the playlist. This file should be properly encoded and can be used as a station-identification audio clip to let listeners know whose stream (signal) they are receiving. The default path and name for the first file can be changed by the operator.

The first part of the playlist has now been created, but the playlist will not be complete until the operator adds one or more media items and saves the playlist to a file.

If the playlist were saved at this point, it would look like this.

```
<?wsx version = '1.0'?>
<smil>
    <seq>
        <media src="C:\media\welcome19.wma" />
    </seq>
</smil>
```

For more information about XML playlists, see Chapter 14.

Setting the Timer Properties

To set the timer properties, add the following lines of code immediately after the lines you just added.

```
Timer1.Interval = 1000
Timer1.Enabled = False
```

The first line sets the timer interval to 1000 milliseconds (one second). Once per second the timer will trigger a request to obtain status information from the publishing point.

The second line disables the timer. The timer will not be enabled until the request is sent to Windows Media Services to start the publishing point. If the timer were enabled before then, an error might result because the publishing-point object might not yet exist.

Setting the PubPoint Flag

To set the publishing-point flag variable, add the following line of code to the Form_Load procedure immediately after the lines you just added.

```
PubPointFlag = False
```

This line sets the flag variable to **False**. This flag will be used to prevent the operator from adding any files to the master playlist before the publishing point has been started. This will prevent the operator from adding any other files to the master playlist before the station-identification file is added.

Adding the AddPub_Click Procedure

You must now add a new procedure to the module that will be attached to the AddPub command button. Double-click the AddPub button on the form. This creates a new empty procedure called AddPub_Click.

Several lines must be added to this procedure to create objects, initialize variables, and set properties that will be used to create a publishing point.

Avoiding Duplicate Publishing Points

To avoid duplicate names for publishing points on the server, insert the following lines of code inside the empty AddPub_Click procedure.

```
Dim i As Integer
Dim CheckName As String
For i = 0 To (MyPubPoints.Count - 1)
    CheckName = MyPubPoints.Item(i).Name
    If (CheckName = PubPointName.Text) Then
        MyPubPoints.Remove (PubPointName.Text)
        MsgBox ("Deleting previous " & PubPointName.Text)
    End If
Next i
```

These lines examine all the publishing points in the publishing-point collection to determine whether any of them has the same name as the default publishing point stored in the *Text* property of the PubPointName text box. If there is a match, the existing publishing point will be removed so that the new one can be added.

> **Note**   You may want to write code to let the operator decide whether to delete the old publishing point or supply a different name for the new one. In this application it will be assumed that the operator knows the names of any previous publishing points.

Creating the Publishing-Point Object

To create the publishing-point object, add the following line of code immediately after the lines you just added.

```
Set MyPubPoint = Server.PublishingPoints.Add(PubPointName.Text, _
    WMS_PUBLISHING_POINT_CATEGORY.WMS_PUBLISHING_POINT_ON_DEMAND, _
    PubPointPath.Text)
```

Note that this is a single line of code. It creates the publishing-point object, gives it the name provided by the PubPointName text box, specifies that it is an on-demand publishing point, and gives it the path stored in the PubPointPath text box. For more information about on-demand publishing points, see Chapter 11.

Finishing the Default Playlist

To finish creating the default playlist and make it available to listeners, add the following lines of code immediately after the line you just added.

```
Set MediaItem = MyPlaylist.createElement("media")
MediaItem.SetAttribute "src", FirstFile.Text
Set Node = Seq.appendChild(MediaItem)
MyPlaylist.Save (PubPointPath.Text & PlayListName.Text)
```

The first three lines create an XML node that contains the default media item for the master playlist. The XML media item is created, the source attribute is set to the file path and name defined in the FirstFile text box, and the media item is added to the master playlist.

The fourth line saves the master playlist to the publishing point that is defined in the PubPointPath text box and gives it the name defined in the PlayListName text box.

For more information about playlists, see Chapter 14.

Preventing Client Connections

Next add the following line of code to the AddPub_Click procedure immediately after the lines you just added.

```
MyPubPoint.AllowClientsToConnect = False
```

This line prevents listeners from connecting to the publishing point until the operator is ready for them to connect.

Enabling the Timer

To enable the timer to begin displaying the status of the publishing point, add the following line of code immediately after the line you just added.

```
Timer1.Enabled = True
```

This enables the timer procedure and runs the timer code at one-second intervals.

Adding the Timer Code for the Publishing Point

You must now add a new procedure that will be attached to the Timer1 timer control. Double-click the Timer control. This creates a new procedure called Timer1_Timer.

Lines must be added to display the publishing-point status and to set the *PubPointFlag* so that new items can later be added to the master playlist.

Displaying the Publishing-Point Status

To display the publishing-point status, add the following lines of code inside the empty Timer1_Timer procedure.

```
If (MyPubPoint.Status = WMS_PUBLISHING_POINT_RUNNING) Then
    PubPointStatus.Caption = "Running"
End If
```

These lines will test the status of the publishing point every 1000 milliseconds (one second). If the publishing point is running, the status of "Running" will be displayed in the PubPointStatus label.

Setting the PubPointFlag

To set the *PubPointFlag* variable, find the following line in the Timer1_Timer procedure.

```
    PubPointStatus.Caption = "Running"
```

Add the following line immediately after it.

```
    PubPointFlag = True
```

The *PubPointFlag* will be used to determine whether a new item can be added to the master playlist. When the publishing point is started, the station-identification item is automatically added as the first item in the playlist. Only when the publishing point is running do you want to allow adding a new item to the playlist. If an operator can add an item to the playlist before the publishing point is started, the desired station-identification media item will not be the first item on the master playlist. Using flags helps you to be sure that all operations take place in the correct sequence.

The complete Timer1_Timer procedure looks like this.

```
Private Sub Timer1_Timer()
    If (MyPubPoint.Status = WMS_PUBLISHING_POINT_RUNNING) Then
        PubPointStatus.Caption = "Running"
        PubPointFlag = True
    End If
End Sub
```

You now have all the code needed to create and add a publishing point and a default master playlist.

Task 2: Creating a Custom Encoding Profile

Before the operator can start encoding files and adding them to the master playlist, an encoding profile must be chosen. In this chapter a custom profile will be loaded from disk automatically, to simplify the code. In a typical radio station, after the proper profile setting has been determined for all files, it would be better to use a profile stored on disk so that an operator couldn't select the wrong one.

Before you can load a custom profile, you must create it by using the Windows Media Profile Editor. Then you will add controls and code to the Radio Station application to load the profile so that Windows Media Encoder will use it to encode all files.

The custom profile portion of the form is used only to let the operator choose the file name and path of the profile to be used. The custom profile name and path will not be used until the encoding begins—then the name of the profile that was chosen will be displayed in this part of the form.

Creating the Encoding Profile

When you start Windows Media Profile Editor, be sure that you choose an audio profile in the media types, and choose at least one bit rate. When you have chosen an encoding profile that includes at least one audio bit rate, save the file as chapter19.prx, because that is the file named used by the Radio Station application. Encoding profiles are always stored with the .prx file name extension, but any file name can be used as long as your application loads the file with that name. A default encoding profile named chapter19.prx is on the companion CD, but your choice of profile should be determined by the needs of your listeners. When you are setting up your own Internet radio station, you should perform several tests using different profiles to see what works best. The documentation for Windows Media Encoder provides detailed information to help you choose a profile. The profile provided with this book is an average profile that will not fill the needs of all developers.

Adding Controls for the Encoding Profile

To create the portion of the user interface that will let the radio station operator use a custom encoder profile, add the following four controls below the controls you added to create a publishing point in Task 1:

- **Line1**   A Line control named Line1 that divides the publishing-point area of the form from the encoding profile area.

- **ProfilePath**   A TextBox control to hold the path to the profile file. The operator can modify this path before the encoding begins.

- **Label2**   A Label control that describes the contents of the custom profile area of the form. Put it to the left of the ProfilePath text box, and give it a caption of "Profile Path and Name".

- **ProfileName**   A Label control to the right of the ProfilePath text box. When the encoding profile is loaded, the profile name will be displayed in this label. The profile name might not be the same as the file name of the profile.

Figure 19.2 shows the second part of the Radio Station form with the controls on it. These controls will be used to add a custom profile for encoding all digital media files for the radio station broadcast. After the first file is encoded in the encoding area, the operator cannot change the path or name of the profile.

Figure 19.2   Partial Radio Station form with custom profile controls added.

The code for the profile controls will be added in Task 3.

Task 3: Encoding Files and Adding Them to the Playlist

Now that the controls and code for the publishing-point area and the controls for the encoding profile area have been added to the Radio Station application, the next task is to add controls and code to encode one or more files and to let the operator add them to the master playlist. This section also includes controls and code for testing a newly encoded file to be sure it sounds the way the operator expects before adding it to the master playlist.

Important   A copyright gives certain exclusive ownership rights to the person who creates an original work. These rights are protected by U.S. and international laws. It is illegal to reproduce copyrighted material without the permission of the copyright owner.

Whenever you copy music or a video that you did not create, consider that it may be copyrighted. Ownership of a CD or licensed digital media files that you downloaded from the Internet does not necessarily constitute the right to redistribute or share the content. If you intend to redistribute or share content, be sure you have the necessary permissions to do so.

To encode and test files and then add them to the master playlist, you must first add controls to the form and then add code procedures relevant to those controls.

Adding Controls for Windows Media Encoder

To create the portion of the user interface that will let the radio station operator encode files, add the following 11 controls below the controls you have already added to the Radio Station form:

- **Line2**   A Line control named Line2 to divide the custom profile area of the form from the encoding area.

- **MySourcePath**   A TextBox control to hold the path to the source file to be encoded. The operator can modify the path.

- **MyDestinationPath**   A TextBox control to hold the path to the destination (encoded) file. The operator can modify the path.

- **Label3A**   A Label control that describes the contents of the MySourcePath text box. Put it to the left of the MySourcePath text box and give it a caption of "Encode From:"

- **Label3B**   A Label control that describes the contents of the My DestinationPath text box. Put it to the left of the MyDestinationPath text box and give it a caption of "Encode To:"

- **StartEncoder**   A CommandButton control to start the encoding process for the source file and place the result in the destination file. Give this button a caption of "Start Encoding".

- **MyState**   A Label control to display the status of the encoding process.

- **Player1**   A WindowsMediaPlayer ActiveX control to display the encoded file.

- **TestFile**   A CommandButton control to play the encoded file. Give it a caption of "Audition".

- **StopTestFile**   A CommandButton control to stop the playing of the encoded file. Give it a caption of "Mute".

- **AddToPlaylist**   A CommandButton control to add the newly encoded file to the master playlist. Give this button a caption of "Add to Playlist".

Figure 19.3 shows the third part of the Radio Station form with the controls on it. These controls will be used to encode files, audition them, and add them to the master playlist for the radio station broadcast.

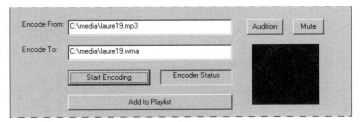

Figure 19.3 Partial Radio Station form with the controls needed to encode and audition files and add them to the master playlist.

Designing the Code for the Encoder

The code for the encoding portion of the Radio Station application needs to perform the following tasks:

1. Let the operator select a source path and file name for the file to be encoded. Defaults will be provided.

2. Let the operator select a destination path and file name for the newly encoded file. Defaults will be provided.

3. Start the encoding process and display the progress of the encoding.

4. Audition the newly created file by playing it in the Windows Media Player control.

5. Add the file to the master playlist, if desired.

Adding the Code for the Encoder

The code for the encoding portion of the Radio Station application will be added in the following seven blocks. The first two blocks were created in the Task 1 section of this chapter, and you will be adding code to them. The remaining blocks will be created in this section:

- **General declarations** You will add code to the existing declarations area of the code module to declare global variables that will be used to encode and audition files and add them to the master playlist.

- **Form_Load procedure** You will add code to the existing Form_Load procedure to create objects, initialize variables, and set properties that will be used to encode and audition files and add them to the master playlist.

- **StartEncoder_Click procedure** This is code that runs when the operator clicks the StartEncoder button to encode a digital media file.

- **TestFile_Click procedure** This is code that runs when the operator clicks the TestFile button to test an encoded file.

- **StopTestFile_Click procedure** This is code that runs when the operator clicks the StopTestFile button to stop playing the encoded file.

- **AddToPlaylist_Click procedure** This is code that runs when the operator clicks the AddToPlaylist button to add the encoded file to the master playlist.

- **MyEncoder_OnStateChange procedure** This is code that runs when Windows Media Encoder changes its state. This is an event procedure and does not have a control attached to it. This code displays the state of the encoder and sets and resets the encoder flags to control program flow and avoid errors.

Adding the Declarations Code for the Encoder

To define the global variables used to encode and audition files and add them to the master playlist, several lines must be added to the declarations section of the Visual Basic code module.

Defining the Encoder Objects

To define the objects that are used for encoding, add the following lines of code to the end of the existing declarations section of the Radio Station code module.

```
Dim WithEvents MyEncoder As WMEncoder
Dim MyProColl As IWMEncProfileCollection
Dim MySrcGrpColl As IWMEncSourceGroupCollection
Dim MySrcGrp As IWMEncSourceGroup
Dim MyAudioSource As IWMEncSource
Dim MyProfile As IWMEncProfile
Dim MyFile As IWMEncFile
```

These lines define the objects that are used to encode files. For more information about using encoder objects, see Chapter 2.

Defining the Encoder Flags

To define flags that indicate the state of the encoder, add the following lines of code immediately after the lines you just added.

```
Dim EncodingFlag As Boolean
Dim EncodedFlag As Boolean
```

These lines define two flags that will be used to avoid operator errors in the Radio Station application. The *EncodingFlag* variable will be used to test whether the encoder is in the process of encoding. The *EncodedFlag* will be used to test whether the encoding is finished.

Adding the Form_Load Code for the Encoder

Several lines need to be added to the existing Form_Load procedure to create objects, initialize variables, and set properties that will be used to encode and test files and add them to the master playlist.

Creating the Encoder Objects

To create the encoder objects, find the following line in the Form_Load procedure.

```
PubPointFlag = False
```

Add the following lines immediately after it.

```
Set MyEncoder = New WMEncoder
Set MyProColl = MyEncoder.ProfileCollection
Set MySrcGrpColl = MyEncoder.SourceGroupCollection
Set MySrcGrp = MySrcGrpColl.Add("SG_1")
Set MyAudioSource = MySrcGrp.AddSource(WMENC_AUDIO)
Set MyFile = MyEncoder.File
```

These lines create the encoder objects needed for encoding audio files and saving them to a file. For more information about encoder objects, see Chapter 2.

Setting Default Paths and Files

To set the default values in text boxes related to encoding, add the following lines immediately after the lines you just added.

```
MySourcePath.Text = "C:\media\laure19.mp3"
MyDestinationPath.Text = "C:\media\laure19.wma"
ProfilePath.Text = "C:\media\chapter19.prx"
```

The first two lines set the default values for the source and destination paths that will be used by the encoding process. Be sure you use valid file names and paths.

The third line is the default value for the path and file name of the custom encoding profile that you created earlier in this chapter. Be sure this is a valid path and file name.

Defining the uiMode Property of Windows Media Player

To set the *uiMode* property of the Player control, add the following two lines immediately after the lines you just added.

```
Player1.uiMode = "none"
Player2.uiMode = "none"
```

These two lines set the *uiMode* of the Player to "none" so that only the Video and Visualization pane of the Player control will be displayed. This hides the transport controls.

Note that you are setting the *uiMode* of two different instances of the Windows Media Player control. Player1 displays the newly encoded file. Player2 displays the final result of a request from the Player to the server for the contents of the master playlist. Player2 is discussed later in this chapter.

Initializing the Encoder Flags

To initialize the default values of the two encoder flag variables, add the following two lines immediately after the lines you just added.

```
EncodingFlag = False
EncodedFlag = False
```

These lines set the initial values of the flags to **False**. They will be used later to prevent operator error.

Adding Code to Start the Encoder

To encode files, you must add a new procedure that is attached to the StartEncoder command button. Double-click the StartEncoder button on the form. That creates a new procedure called StartEncoder_Click that looks like this.

```
Private Sub StartEncoder_Click()

End Sub
```

Several lines must be added to this procedure to create objects, initialize variables, and set properties that will be used to encode a file.

Determining Whether the Encoder Is Already Encoding

To prevent the operator from trying to encode a file that is already in the process of being encoded, add the following lines of code inside the empty StartEncoder_Click procedure.

```
If (EncodingFlag = True) Then
    Exit Sub
End If
```

These lines determine whether the *EncodingFlag* has been set to **True**. Initially it was set to **False** in the Form_Load procedure, but it will be set to **True** after the file begins encoding.

Changing the EncodingFlag Value

To change the *EncodingFlag* variable, add the following line of code immediately after the lines you just added.

```
EncodingFlag = True
```

This line is used to prevent the operator from trying to encode a file if that file is already in the process of being encoded. The value of *EncodingFlag* is checked at the beginning of the StartEncoder_Click procedure, and if it is *True*, the procedure is exited. The value of *EncodingFlag* will be set to *False* in the MyEncoder_OnStateChange event procedure after the encoder has stopped encoding.

Changing the EncodedFlag Value

To change the *EncodedFlag* variable, add the following line of code to the StartEncoder_Click procedure immediately after the line you just added.

```
EncodedFlag = False
```

This line is used to prevent the operator from trying to play a file before it has been encoded. The *EncodedFlag* is tested in the TestFile_Click procedure, and no attempt to play the file is made if *EncodedFlag* is *False*. The value of *EncodedFlag* will be set to *True* in the MyEncoder_OnStateChange event procedure after the encoder has stopped encoding.

Defining the Encoding Source File

To specify the audio source to be encoded, add the following line of code immediately after the line you just added.

```
MyAudioSource.SetInput (MySourcePath.Text)
```

This line sets the source for audio encoding to the path and file name defined in the MySourcePath text box.

Defining the Encoding Destination File

To specify the file for the encoded output, add the following line of code immediately after the line you just added.

```
MyFile.LocalFileName = MyDestinationPath.Text
```

This line sets the destination of the encoded content to the path and file name defined in the MyDestinationPath text box.

Defining the Encoding Profile File

To set the path and file name of the custom encoder profile, add the following line of code to the StartEncoder_Click procedure immediately after the line you just added.

```
MySrcGrp.Profile = ProfilePath.Text
```

This line sets the path and file name of the custom encoder profile to the path and file name defined in the ProfilePath text box.

Displaying the Profile Name

To display the name of the profile you just loaded, add the following line of code immediately after the line you just added.

```
ProfileName.Caption = MySrcGrp.Profile.Name
```

This line gets the name of the profile from the profile file and displays it in the Profile-Name label. Note that the profile name may not be the same as the name of the profile file.

Starting the Encoder

To start the encoder, add this line of code immediately after the line you just added.

```
MyEncoder.Start
```

This line starts the encoding process.

Adding Code to Process Encoder Events

You must now add an event procedure to process events that take place in Windows Media Encoder. Because the event procedure is not attached to a control, you must add the event code in a new procedure that is not inside any other procedure.

Add the following two lines of code at the end of the code module after all other procedures.

```
Private Sub MyEncoder_OnStateChange(ByVal enumState As _
        WMEncoderLib.WMENC_ENCODER_STATE)


End Sub
```

These lines define the event procedure that will process encoder events. Every time the encoder changes its state, the code in this procedure will be called. Leave space between these two lines to add more code to the procedure.

Adding Code to Display the Encoder Status

To display the current state of Windows Media Encoder, add the following lines inside the blank MyEncoder_OnStateChange procedure.

```
Select Case enumState
    Case WMENC_ENCODER_RUNNING
        MyState.Caption = "Running"
    Case WMENC_ENCODER_STOPPED
        MyState.Caption = "Stopped"
End Select
```

These lines set up a Select Case block to test the value of the enumerated encoder state. For each state value, a text equivalent will be displayed in the MyState label.

Changing the Encoder Flags

To change the value of the encoder flags, find the following line in the MyEncoder_On-StateChange procedure.

```
MyState.Caption = "Stopped"
```

Add the following two lines immediately after it.

```
EncodedFlag = True
EncodingFlag = False
```

These flags are used to determine the state of the encoding process. After the encoder has stopped, the encoding process is finished (*EncodingFlag* = False) and the file is encoded (*EncodedFlag* = True). These flags are used to prevent operator error in the StartEncoder_Click and TestFile_Click procedures.

Adding Code to Test the Encoded File

To test encoded files, you must add a new procedure to the module that will be attached to the TestFile command button. Double-click the TestFile button. This creates a new procedure called TestFile_Click.

A few lines must be added to the TestFile_Click procedure to play the newly encoded file in the Player.

Determining Whether the Encoding Is Finished

To prevent the operator from trying to play a file before it has been encoded, add the following lines of code inside the empty TestFile_Click procedure.

```
If (EncodedFlag = False) Then
    MsgBox ("File not encoded yet.")
    Exit Sub
End If
```

These lines check the *EncodedFlag* value to determine whether the encoder has finished encoding. If it hasn't finished yet, the *EncodedFlag* value will still be **False**. It will be set to **True** only when the encoder event handler determines that the encoder has finished encoding and has stopped.

Testing the Encoded File

To play the newly encoded file, add the following line immediately after the lines you just added.

```
Player1.URL = MyDestinationPath.Text
```

This line instructs the first Windows Media Player control to play the file indicated in the MyDestinationPath text box.

Adding Code to Stop Testing the Encoded File

To stop playing the newly encoded file, you must add a new procedure that will be attached to the StopTestFile command button. Double-click the StopTestFile button. This creates a new procedure called StopTestFile_Click.

To make the first Player stop playing the newly encoded file, add the following line of code inside the empty TestFile_Click procedure.

```
Player1.Controls.Stop
```

This line stops the first Player.

Adding Code to Add the Encoded File to the Master Playlist

To add the encoded file to the master playlist, you must add a new procedure that will be attached to the AddToPlaylist command button. Double-click the AddToPlaylist button. This creates a new procedure called AddToPlaylist_Click.

Several lines must be added to the procedure to add the newly encoded file to the master playlist.

Determining Whether the Publishing Point Has Started

To prevent the operator from trying to add a file to the playlist before the publishing point has started, add the following lines of code inside the empty AddToPlaylist_Click procedure.

```
If (PubPointFlag = False) Then
    MsgBox ("Please start the publishing point first.")
    Exit Sub
End If
```

These lines check the *PubPointFlag* value to determine whether the publishing point has been started. If it hasn't, the *EncodedFlag* value will still be **False**. It will be set to **True** only when the publishing point is started. If the flag is **False**, the procedure will be exited.

Adding the New File to the Playlist

To add the newly encoded digital media file to the master playlist, add the following lines immediately after the lines you just added.

```
Set MediaItem = MyPlaylist.createElement("media")
MediaItem.SetAttribute "src", MyDestinationPath.Text
Set Node = Seq.appendChild(MediaItem)
```

These lines create a new XML element and add the newly encoded file as the source of the media item in the new element. The element is then added to the existing sequence node of the master playlist.

Saving the New Playlist

To save the new playlist, add the following line immediately after the line you just added.

```
MyPlaylist.Save (PubPointPath.Text & PlayListName.Text)
```

This saves the master playlist to the path and file name defined in the PubPointPath and PlayListName text boxes.

> **Note**   The master playlist is stored in memory. When you add a new node to the playlist, the playlist in memory is modified. When the playlist is saved to a file, it overwrites whatever values were in the master playlist file previously. When a client connects to the server and asks for the playlist in the publishing point, it will receive whatever playlist value is stored in the file, not in memory. To give the radio station operator a chance to be sure the playlist in the file is up to date before any clients connect, this application does not allow client connections until the operator gives explicit permission with the click of a button.

Task 4: Monitoring the Playlist and Allowing Connections

After the operator has started the publishing point, encoded the files that are to be played, and added those files to the master playlist, it is time to let listeners connect to your Internet radio station.

Before you do so, you will want to listen to the master playlist and monitor the output to be sure that your listeners will be hearing what you want them to.

After you are sure that the master playlist is ready, the final step is to let clients connect to the server and request the playlist from your radio station. You also need to prevent clients from connecting before the radio station is ready.

To monitor the radio station output and allow clients to connect to your station, you must add a few more controls and procedures.

Adding Controls to Allow Client Connections and Monitoring

To create the portion of the user interface that will let the radio station operator allow or stop client connections and also monitor the output of the radio station, you must add the following controls below the controls you have already added to the Radio Station form. Place the client connection controls on the right and the monitoring controls on the left.

- **Line3**   A Line control named Line3 that divides the encoding area from the client connection and monitoring area of the form.

Client Connection Controls

The following controls will be used to allow and stop client connections:

- **AllowConnect**   A CommandButton control that allows clients to connect to the publishing point. Give it a caption of "Allow Connections".

- **StopConnect**   A CommandButton control that stops clients from connecting to the publishing point. Give it a caption of "Stop Connections".

- **Label4**   A Label control that describes the contents of the connections area of the form. Put it to the left of the AllowConnect button and give it a caption of "Allow Users to Connect".

Playlist Monitoring Controls

The following controls will be used to monitor the final playlist:

- **TestPlaylist**   A CommandButton control that plays the complete playlist in the Player. Give it a caption of "Audition".

- **StopTestPlaylist**   A CommandButton control that stops the Player. Give it a caption of "Mute".

- **Player2**   A WindowsMediaPlayer ActiveX control to play the complete master playlist.

- **Label5**   A Label control that describes the contents of the testing area of the form. Put it to the left of the TestPlaylist button and give it a caption of "Audition Playlist".

Figure 19.4 shows the fourth part of the Radio Station form with the controls on it. These controls will allow client connections and monitoring of the radio station broadcast.

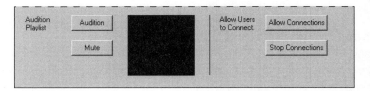

Figure 19.4   Partial Radio Station form with the controls needed to allow client connections and monitoring of the radio station output.

Designing the Code to Allow Client Connections and Monitoring

The code for the final portion of the Radio Station application needs to perform the following tasks:

1.   Let the operator allow or stop client connections. You do not want to allow client connections until all your files are encoded and your playlist is complete.

2.   Let the operator monitor the complete playlist by playing it in the Player control.

Adding the Code to Allow Client Connections and Monitoring

The code for the final area of the Radio Station form will be added in the following four blocks. The first two blocks will control client connections, and the second two will let the operator monitor the master playlist:

- **AllowConnect_Click**   This is code that runs when the operator clicks the AllowConnect button to start allowing client connections.

- **StopConnect_Click**   This is code that runs when the operator clicks the StopConnect button to stop allowing client connections.

- **TestPlaylist_Click**   This is code that runs when the operator clicks the TestPlaylist button to play the master playlist in the Player control.

- **StopTestPlaylist**   This is code that runs when the operator clicks the StopTestPlaylist button to stop the Player.

Adding Code to Allow Client Connections

To allow client connections, you must add a new procedure that will be attached to the AllowConnect command button. Double-click the AllowConnect button. This creates a new procedure called AllowConnect_Click.

Next add the following line of code inside the empty AllowConnect_Click procedure.

```
MyPubPoint.AllowClientsToConnect = True
```

This line allows clients to connect to the publishing point of the radio station.

Adding Code to Prevent Client Connections

To prevent client connections, you must add a new procedure that will be attached to the StopConnect command button. Double-click the StopConnect button. This creates a new procedure called StopConnect_Click.

Then add the following line of code inside the empty StopConnect_Click procedure.

```
MyPubPoint.AllowClientsToConnect = False
```

This line stops clients from connecting to the publishing point of the radio station.

Adding Code to Monitor the Final Playlist

To test and monitor the final playlist, you must add a new procedure that will be attached to the TestPlaylist command button. Double-click the TestPlaylist button. This creates a new procedure called TestPlaylist_Click.

You must add a few lines to this procedure to play the playlist in the Player.

Testing the Publishing-Point Status

To prevent the operator from trying to test the playlist before the publishing point has started, add the following lines of code inside the empty TestPlaylist_Click procedure.

```
If (MyPubPoint.Status <> WMS_PUBLISHING_POINT_RUNNING) Then
    Exit Sub
End If
```

These lines check whether the publishing point is running. If it is not, the procedure will be exited.

Playing the Playlist

To play the final playlist, add the following lines immediately after the lines you just added.

```
Dim MyURLPath As String
MyURLPath = "mms://" & Environ("COMPUTERNAME") & "/" _
            & PubPointName.Text & "/"
    Player2.URL = MyURLPath & PlayListName.Text
```

These lines play the final playlist as determined by the publishing-point name and the playlist name.

Adding Code to Mute the Final Playlist

To stop the final playlist from playing, you must add a new procedure that will be attached to the StopTestPlaylist command button. Double-click the StopTestPlaylist button. This creates a new procedure called StopTestPlaylist_Click.

To stop playing the final playlist, add the following line inside the empty StopTestPlaylist_Click procedure.

```
Player2.Controls.Stop
```

This line stops the second Player to mute the playlist. And with that, your Radio Station application is complete and ready for testing.

Running the Radio Station Application

After you have entered all the code, run the project in Visual Basic. From the Run menu, select Start. If there are no errors, the user interface of your application should look like Figure 19.5. You can compare your code to the complete code listing in the next section.

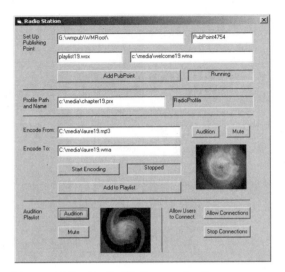

Figure 19.5 Radio Station application.

Use the following procedure to test your application:

1. Change the default values of the publishing-point path and name, if desired.

2. Change the name of the playlist and the path and name of the station-identification file, if desired.

3. Click the Add PubPoint button to create and start the publishing point. You will see the status of the publishing point change to "Running".

4. Change the path and file name of the custom profile, if desired.

5. Change the source and destination files for the encoding, if desired.

6. Click the Start Encoding button. The encoder status will change to "Running" and then to "Stopped" a few seconds later.

7. After the encoding has stopped, click the Audition button to audition your newly encoded file and see whether the encoding worked properly. When you are finished auditioning, click the Mute button.

8. If you want to add the encoded file to the master playlist, click the Add To Playlist button. (If you click the button more than once, the file will be added to the playlist again each time you click.)

9. You can now repeat steps 5, 6, and 7 to encode and add as many files as you want to the master playlist.

10. When you are finished creating the playlist, click the Allow Connections button. Your listeners can now connect to the publishing point of your radio

station. Be sure that you have supplied them with the correct link to the radio station. It should use the following format: mms://servername/pubpoint-name/playlistname.

11. Test the final playlist by clicking the Audition button. The Player should play the complete playlist. You can stop the playlist test by clicking the Mute button.

12. Click the Stop Connections button. If you were auditioning a file, it would not stop, but if you try to audition it again by clicking the Audition button, the Player will not be able to connect. Because the Player saves only the playlist file, it will need to go to the server again if a new connection is requested. Only the playlist file is saved by the Player, not the digital media files that are listed in the playlist.

Complete copies of the source code and media for the Radio Station application are on the companion CD.

Source Code for the Radio Station Application

Here is the complete source code listing for the Radio Station application.

```
Dim Server As WMSServer
Dim MyPubPoint As IWMSOnDemandPublishingPoint
Dim MyPubPoints As IWMSPublishingPoints

Dim MyPlaylist As IXMLDOMDocument

Dim MyProcNode As IXMLDOMNode
Dim Root As IXMLDOMNode
Dim Node As IXMLDOMNode
Dim Seq As IXMLDOMNode

Dim RootElement As IXMLDOMElement
Dim SequenceElement As IXMLDOMElement
Dim MediaItem As IXMLDOMElement

Dim PubPointFlag As Boolean

Dim WithEvents MyEncoder As WMEncoder
Dim MyProColl As IWMEncProfileCollection
Dim MySrcGrpColl As IWMEncSourceGroupCollection
Dim MySrcGrp As IWMEncSourceGroup
Dim MyAudioSource As IWMEncSource
Dim MyProfile As IWMEncProfile
Dim MyFile As IWMEncFile
```

(continued)

```vb
Dim EncodingFlag As Boolean
Dim EncodedFlag As Boolean

Private Sub Form_Load()
    Set Server = New WMSServer
    Set MyPubPoints = Server.PublishingPoints

    PubPointPath.Text = "C:\wmpub\WMRoot\"
    PubPointName.Text = "PubPoint4754"

    Set MyPlaylist = Server.CreatePlaylist
    Set MyProcNode = MyPlaylist.createNode(7, "wsx", "")
    MyPlaylist.appendChild MyProcNode
    MyProcNode.Text = "version = '1.0'"
    Set RootElement = MyPlaylist.createElement("smil")
    Set Root = MyPlaylist.appendChild(RootElement)
    Set SequenceElement = MyPlaylist.createElement("seq")
    Set Seq = Root.appendChild(SequenceElement)

    PlayListName.Text = "playlist19.wsx"
    FirstFile.Text = "C:\media\welcome19.wma"

    Timer1.Interval = 1000
    Timer1.Enabled = False

    PubPointFlag = False

    Set MyEncoder = New WMEncoder
    Set MyProColl = MyEncoder.ProfileCollection
    Set MySrcGrpColl = MyEncoder.SourceGroupCollection
    Set MySrcGrp = MySrcGrpColl.Add("SG_1")
    Set MyAudioSource = MySrcGrp.AddSource(WMENC_AUDIO)

    Set MyFile = MyEncoder.File

    MySourcePath.Text = "C:\media\laure19.mp3"
    MyDestinationPath.Text = "C:\media\laure19.wma"
    ProfilePath.Text = "C:\media\chapter19.prx"

    Player1.uiMode = "none"
    Player2.uiMode = "none"

    EncodingFlag = False
    EncodedFlag = False
End Sub
```

```
Private Sub AddPub_Click()
    Dim i As Integer
    Dim CheckName As String
    For i = 0 To (MyPubPoints.Count - 1)
        CheckName = MyPubPoints.Item(i).Name
        If (CheckName = PubPointName.Text) Then
            MyPubPoints.Remove (PubPointName.Text)
            MsgBox ("Deleting previous " & PubPointName.Text)
        End If
    Next i

    Set MyPubPoint = Server.PublishingPoints.Add(PubPointName.Text, _
        WMS_PUBLISHING_POINT_CATEGORY.WMS_PUBLISHING_POINT_ON_DEMAND, _
        PubPointPath.Text)

    Set MediaItem = MyPlaylist.createElement("media")
    MediaItem.SetAttribute "src", FirstFile.Text
    Set Node = Seq.appendChild(MediaItem)
    MyPlaylist.Save (PubPointPath.Text & PlayListName.Text)

    MyPubPoint.AllowClientsToConnect = False

    Timer1.Enabled = True
End Sub

Private Sub Timer1_Timer()
    If (MyPubPoint.Status = WMS_PUBLISHING_POINT_RUNNING) Then
        PubPointStatus.Caption = "Running"
        PubPointFlag = True
    End If
End Sub

Private Sub StartEncoder_Click()
    If (EncodingFlag = True) Then
        Exit Sub
    End If

    EncodingFlag = True
    EncodedFlag = False

    MyAudioSource.SetInput (MySourcePath.Text)
    MyFile.LocalFileName = MyDestinationPath.Text
    MySrcGrp.Profile = ProfilePath.Text

    ProfileName.Caption = MySrcGrp.Profile.Name

    MyEncoder.Start
End Sub
```

(continued)

```vb
Private Sub MyEncoder_OnStateChange(ByVal enumState As _
        WMEncoderLib.WMENC_ENCODER_STATE)
    Select Case enumState
        Case WMENC_ENCODER_RUNNING
            MyState.Caption = "Running"
        Case WMENC_ENCODER_STOPPED
            MyState.Caption = "Stopped"
            EncodedFlag = True
            EncodingFlag = False
    End Select
End Sub

Private Sub TestFile_Click()
    If (EncodedFlag = False) Then
        MsgBox ("File not encoded yet.")
        Exit Sub
    End If

    Player1.URL = MyDestinationPath.Text
End Sub

Private Sub StopTestFile_Click()
    Player1.Controls.Stop
End Sub

Private Sub AddToPlaylist_Click()
    If (PubPointFlag = False) Then
        MsgBox ("Please start the publishing point first.")
        Exit Sub
    End If

    Set MediaItem = MyPlaylist.createElement("media")
    MediaItem.SetAttribute "src", MyDestinationPath.Text
    Set Node = Seq.appendChild(MediaItem)

    MyPlaylist.Save (PubPointPath.Text & PlayListName.Text)
End Sub

Private Sub AllowConnect_Click()
    MyPubPoint.AllowClientsToConnect = True
End Sub

Private Sub StopConnect_Click()
    MyPubPoint.AllowClientsToConnect = False
End Sub
```

```
Private Sub TestPlaylist_Click()
    If (MyPubPoint.Status <> WMS_PUBLISHING_POINT_RUNNING) Then
        Exit Sub
    End If

    Dim MyURLPath As String
    MyURLPath = "mms://" & Environ("COMPUTERNAME") & "/" _
                & PubPointName.Text & "/"
    Player2.URL = MyURLPath & PlayListName.Text
End Sub

Private Sub StopTestPlaylist_Click()
    Player2.Controls.Stop
End Sub
```

Appendix

Programming an Encoding Profile

This appendix presents advanced programming techniques for creating encoding profiles. It includes a sample application called Encoder Profile that shows you how to develop a custom encoding profile with Visual Basic.

Introduction to the Encoder Profile Application

Each time you use Windows Media Encoder to convert a digital media file, you must choose an encoding profile to specify the level and type of compression required to convert the file. Encoding profiles are numeric templates that specify the compression settings of bit rate, video frame rate and size, codec, and so on. There are three different methods you can use to specify an encoding profile. This appendix shows you advanced programming techniques for creating custom profiles that can help you automate your encoder applications more efficiently. Earlier chapters in this book have already covered two other methods of specifying profiles. Chapter 2 explained how to choose a profile from the system profiles that are installed with the encoder. Chapter 8 showed you how to create and use an external specification file that contained a custom profile created with Windows Media Profile Editor. All three profile specification methods have their advantages and disadvantages.

The advantage of using system profiles is that they are conveniently installed with the encoder. You can easily determine which system profiles are installed and choose one from the list. However, if an encoder operator chooses an inappropriate profile, unexpected results may occur. For example, if an operator chooses a video profile when encoding an audio stream, an exception will be raised and, as a result, your application will need to include additional code to handle that exception. In addition, the system profiles do not cover all possible profile requirements, so an encoder operator may have to choose a system profile that doesn't exactly fit the desired encoding scenario.

Creating a profile specification file by using the Profile Editor is an advantageous method to use in repetitive situations where the files to be encoded are always in the same format. When the profile requirements are known in advance, profile specification files are more efficient than system or custom profiles. This method makes it possible to create different profile specification files for different needs and can help to reduce errors. For example, an application could check the file name extension of a file to determine the type of file, and then automatically choose audio profiles for audio files and video profiles for video files. However, if the operator must choose a file, errors might occur, and it might also become difficult to keep track of all the different files.

Using programming code to create custom profiles is the most comprehensive solution for specifying profiles. This method, presented in this appendix, is the most flexible and efficient way to tailor your application precisely. However, when you are developing this complex solution, you might need to write additional code to verify the encoded results. This appendix shows you advanced programming techniques for creating three complete profile settings, which can be presented to the operator in the form of an option box. As a result, the operator can choose only one of three options, and the option chosen will determine the appropriate profile based on the desired bit rate and number of frames per second (fps). The programming code you will write to develop the Encoder Profile application defines the codec, channels, sample rate, bit rate, and bit depth for the audio portion of the file to be encoded, as well as the codec, bit rate, width, height, fps, buffer, smoothness, and key-frame interval for the video.

To create the Encoder Profile application, you will use the Visual Basic form you created in Chapter 4 and add new controls and code to perform the new programming tasks required.

The Encoder Profile application will perform the following tasks:

- Let the operator choose the source media file for encoding into Windows Media Format. A default file path and name will be provided. The encoder can convert files with the following extensions: .wav, .avi, and .mp3, as well as .asf and the standard Windows Media formats, .wma and .wmv.

- Let the operator choose the desired number of frames per second for the video frame rate. A default value will be provided. Higher frame rates display motion more smoothly but result in larger files.

- Let the operator choose an HTTP port number for broadcasting the encoded stream to Windows Media Player. A default port number will be provided. Any valid port number is permissible.

- Let the operator select a basic profile by clicking one of three grouped options. One of the options will be selected. The options enable the operator to choose one of three bit rates.

- Let the operator click a button to start the encoding process after they have chosen a source file name, port number, fps value, and bit rate. The data in the source file will be encoded into a stream using the profile that is generated based on the operator's choices.

- After encoding has begun, display the status of the encoding process.

- At any time after the encoding process has begun, let the operator click a button to play the encoded stream with Windows Media Player by using the HTTP port specified.

- After the Player begins playing, display the bit rate of the encoded stream.

- Let the operator stop the encoding process at any time by clicking a button.

- Let the operator stop the Player at any time by clicking a button.

Setting Up Your Programming Environment

Before you begin programming, be sure you have installed the following software and configured it properly.

Installing the Required Software

The following software must be installed on your computer before you can develop the Encoder Profile sample application. If you created the Encoder Broadcast application in Chapter 4, all of these are installed already:

- Windows Server 2003, Standard Edition; Windows Server 2003, Enterprise Edition; or Windows Server 2003, Datacenter Edition. Windows Media Services is a component of all three versions. (The example application in this chapter does not require the server functionality, but using this operating system here enables you to use the same operating system for all example applications in this book.)

- Windows Media Encoder 9 Series. You can install the encoder from the companion CD.

- Windows Media Player 9 Series, if it is not already installed.

- Microsoft Visual Basic 6.0.

> **Note**   You should go to the Windows Update Web site and download any updates available for the required software.

Configuring Visual Basic

To configure Visual Basic for the Encoder Profile application, follow these steps:

1. Start Visual Basic and create a new programming project by selecting New Project from the File menu and selecting the Standard EXE option. Click OK.

2. Add a reference to a COM object that contains the Windows Media Encoder functionality. Add the reference by selecting References from the Project menu and scrolling down to Windows Media Encoder. Select the encoder check box and click OK.

3. Add the Windows Media Player ActiveX control to the Visual Basic toolbox. Add the Player control by selecting Components from the Project menu and then selecting the Windows Media Player check box. After you click OK in the Components dialog box, the Windows Media Player icon is displayed in the toolbox.

Creating a Visual Basic Form for the Encoder Profile Application

To build the Encoder Profile application, you will build on the Encoder Broadcast form that was created in Chapter 4. The Encoder Broadcast application lets the operator choose an encoding format and a file to encode, and then broadcast the encoded file directly to Windows Media Player without using a server. This chapter uses most of the same form, but modifies it to use a custom profile that is defined programmatically.

Using the Encoder Broadcast Form from Chapter 4

You can start by making a copy of the form that was created in Chapter 4. That form contains the following 10 controls:

- **ProfileComboBox**   A ComboBox control to hold all the default encoding profiles.

- **MySourcePath**   A TextBox control to hold the path to the file that is to be encoded. The operator can enter a new source path in this control.

- **StartEncoder**   A CommandButton control to start the encoding process. It has a caption of "Start Encoding".

- **StopEncoder**   A CommandButton control to stop the encoding process. It has a caption of "Stop Encoding".

- **MyState**   A Label control to display the current status of the encoder.

- **Address** A TextBox control to display the default network port that the broadcast will use. The operator can change this to another port if needed.

- **PlayPlayer** A CommandButton control to make Windows Media Player start playing. The button-click procedure checks whether Windows Media Encoder has finished encoding; if it has not finished, the Player will not play.

- **StopPlayer** A CommandButton control to stop the Player.

- **BitRate** A Label control to display the bit rate of the encoded file. The bit-rate data will be supplied by the Player.

- **Player** A WindowsMediaPlayer ActiveX control to display the default visualization of the audio file that is playing. This will give the operator a visual cue that the file is playing.

Figure A.1 shows the Encoder Broadcast form created in Chapter 4.

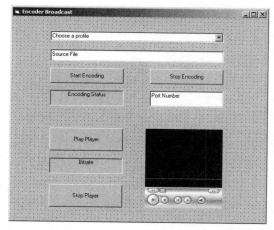

Figure A.1   Encoder Broadcast form from Chapter 4.

Modifying the Form

Most of the user interface controls on the Encoder Profile form will be the same as on the Encoder Broadcast form in Chapter 4. One old control will be removed from the form and five new ones will be added.

Removing Old Controls

Begin modifying the form by removing the following control:

- **ProfileComboBox** In chapter 4, this control was used to list all of the system profiles on the machine. Since this example creates a profile programmatically, this control is no longer needed.

Adding New Controls

Next add the following five controls to the form to provide the new functionality needed to programmatically define a new profile. You will need to resize the form to make room for the new controls.

- **Frame1** A Frame control named Frame1 will contain three option buttons for selecting the bit rate of the encoded file. Give this control a caption of "Bit Rate".

- **Option1** An OptionButton control named Option1. Set the Tag property to 28 and set the caption to "28 kbps". This will allow the operator to choose a 28 kbps bit rate.

- **Option2** An OptionButton control named Option2. Set the Tag property to 300 and set the caption to "300 kbps". This will allow the operator to choose a 300 kbps bit rate.

- **Option3** An OptionButton control named Option3. Set the Tag property to 1000 and set the caption to "1000 kbps". This will allow the operator to choose a 1000 kbps bit rate.

- **FPS** A TextBox control named FPS. Set the Text property to 30. This will enable the operator to select the frames per second (FPS) at which to encode the file.

Figure A.2 shows the Encoder Profile form with the new controls on it.

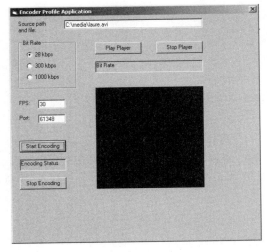

Figure A.2 Encoder Profile form.

Designing the Code for the Encoder Profile Application

The code in the Encoder Profile application begins with the same code that was used by the Encoder Broadcast application in Chapter 4. The Encoder Broadcast code lets the operator define a profile, change the default path to the source file for the encoding, and specify a port number for the broadcast. After Windows Media Encoder begins encoding the file, the operator can start Windows Media Player and begin receiving the broadcast.

In order to create the Encoder Profile application, new code must be added to perform the following tasks:

1. Define a custom profile object.

2. Define an audience for the profile object. A profile consists of one or more audiences. Each audience defines the audio and video settings for a specified stream. While a profile can contain more than one audience, this example creates only a single bit rate profile. When multiple audiences are defined, this is known as a multiple bit rate (MBR) profile.

Adding the Code

The Encoder Broadcast application in Chapter 4 included the following eight Visual Basic code blocks:

■   General declarations

■   Form_Load procedure

■   StartEncoder_Click procedure

■   StopEncoder_Click procedure

■   MyEncoder_OnStateChange procedure

■   PlayPlayer_Click procedure

■   StopPlayer_Click procedure

■   Player_PlayStateChange procedure

The Encoder Profile application will add four new procedures:

■   **SetupVideoAudience**   This procedure is called to define the video settings for the audience on the profile object.

■   **SetupAudioAudience**   This procedure is called to define the audio settings for the audience on the profile object.

■ **GetAudioCodecIndex** This is a helper function used by the SetupAudioAudience function to select the audio codec.

■ **GetVideoCodecIndex** This is a helper function used by the SetupVideoAudience function to select the video codec.

Reusing the Encoder Broadcast Application Code

Here is the code that will be reused from the Encoder Broadcast application in Chapter 4.

```
Dim WithEvents MyEncoder As WMEncoder
Dim MyProColl As IWMEncProfileCollection
Dim MySrcGrpColl As IWMEncSourceGroupCollection
Dim MySrcGrp As IWMEncSourceGroup
Dim MyAudioSource As IWMEncSource
Dim MyBroadcast As IWMEncBroadcast

Dim DummyText As String

Private Sub Form_Load()
    Set MyEncoder = New WMEncoder

    Dim i As Integer
    Set MyProColl = MyEncoder.ProfileCollection
    For i = 0 To (MyProColl.Count - 1)
      ProfileComboBox.AddItem MyProColl.Item(i).Name, i
    Next i

    Set MySrcGrpColl = MyEncoder.SourceGroupCollection
    Set MySrcGrp = MySrcGrpColl.Add("SG_1")
    Set MyAudioSource = MySrcGrp.AddSource(WMENC_AUDIO)
    MySourcePath.Text = "C:\media\laure04.mp3"

    DummyText = "Choose a profile first."
    ProfileComboBox.Text = DummyText

    Player.uiMode = "none"

    Address.Text = "8080"
End Sub

Private Sub StartEncoder_Click()
    MyAudioSource.SetInput (MySourcePath.Text)
    MyAudioSource.Repeat = True

    Dim MyProfileName As String
    MyProfileName = ProfileComboBox.Text
```

```
        If MyProfileName = DummyText Then
            MsgBox ("Please enter a profile before encoding.")
            Exit Sub
        End If


        Dim i As Integer
        Dim MyProfile As IWMEncProfile
        For i = 0 To (MyProColl.Count - 1)
            If MyProColl.Item(i).Name = MyProfileName Then
                Set MyProfile = MyProColl.Item(i)
                MySrcGrp.Profile = MyProfile
                Exit For
            End If
        Next i


        Set MyBroadcast = MyEncoder.Broadcast
        MyBroadcast.PortNumber(WMENC_PROTOCOL_HTTP) = Address.Text


        MyEncoder.Start
    End Sub

    Private Sub MyEncoder_OnStateChange(ByVal enumState As _
                    WMEncoderLib.WMENC_ENCODER_STATE)
        Select Case enumState
            Case WMENC_ENCODER_RUNNING
                MyState.Caption = "Running"
            Case WMENC_ENCODER_STOPPED
                MyState.Caption = "Stopped"
        End Select
    End Sub


    Private Sub PlayPlayer_Click()
        If MyState.Caption = "Running" Then
            Player.URL = "http://" & Environ("COMPUTERNAME")
                        & ":" & Address.Text
        Else
            MsgBox "Please start the encoding process."
        End If
    End Sub

    Private Sub StopEncoder_Click()
        MyEncoder.Stop
    End Sub

    Private Sub StopPlayer_Click()
        Player.Controls.Stop
    End Sub
```

(continued)

```
Private Sub Player_PlayStateChange(ByVal NewState As Long)
    If NewState = 3 Then
        Dim AC As Integer
        Dim MyRate As Long
        AC = Player.currentMedia.getAttributeCountByType _
                        ("Bitrate", "") - 1
        MyRate = Player.currentMedia.getItemInfoByType _
                        ("Bitrate", "", AC)
        BitRate.Caption = "Bitrate = " & CStr(MyRate) & _
                    " bits/second"
    End If
End Sub
```

Modifying the Encoder Broadcast Application Code

Several lines need to be added, removed, or modified to change the Encoder Broadcast code so that the Encoder Profile application can use a custom profile created with Visual Basic code.

The following code blocks from the Encoder Broadcast application must be modified:

■   General declarations

■   Form_Load procedure

■   StartEncoder_Click procedure

Changing the Declarations Code

The declaration for the type of encoder broadcast needs to be changed, and new declarations must be added for the video-source, profile, and audience objects.

Removing the ProfileCollection Declaration

Find the following line in the declarations block and remove it. Because the profile will not be chosen from a collection of system profiles, you do not need to declare the collection.

```
Dim MyProColl As IWMEncProfileCollection
```

Next find the following line in the declarations block and remove it, too. This line was part of the profile collection error checking process.

```
Dim DummyText As String
```

Adding the VideoSource, Profile, and Audience Declarations

Find the following line in the declarations block.

```
Dim MyBroadcast As IWMEncBroadcast
```

Add the following lines immediately after that line to define server objects for the Encoder Profile application.

```
Dim MyProfile As WMEncProfile2
Dim myAudience As IWMEncAudienceObj
Dim MyVideoSource As IWMEncSource
```

These lines declare the objects for the encoding profile, the audience, and the video source.

Changing the Form_Load Code

In this example, you will be creating a profile by using programming code, so you need to define the MyProfile object. Find the following line in the Form_Load procedure.

```
Set MyEncoder = New WMEncoder
```

Immediately after that line, add the following line.

```
Set MyProfile = New WMEncProfile2
```

In addition, you no longer need to populate the ComboBox control with the list of system profiles. Remove the following lines of code from the Form_Load procedure.

```
Dim i As Integer
Set MyProColl = MyEncoder.ProfileCollection
For i = 0 To (MyProColl.Count - 1)
  ProfileComboBox.AddItem MyProColl.Item(i).Name, i
Next i
```

Now remove the following lines, which were part of the error checking portion of the system profile selection process.

```
DummyText = "Choose a profile first."
ProfileComboBox.Text = DummyText
```

Adding a Video Source

Because this example will encode files with both audio and video, you need to add a video source to the source group collection. Find the following line.

```
Set MyAudioSource = MySrcGrp.AddSource(WMENC_AUDIO)
```

After that line add the following line.

```
Set MyVideoSource = MySrcGrp.AddSource(WMENC_VIDEO)
```

Changing the Source File for Encoding Both Audio and Video

This example encodes a file with both audio and video. You need to change the audio file listed in Chapter 4 to a file that contains both audio and video.

Find the following line.

```
MySourcePath.Text = "C:\media\laure04.mp3"
```

Change the file name as shown in the following line.

```
MySourcePath.Text = "C:\media\laure.avi"
```

Changing the StartEncoder_Click Code

The following changes need to be made in the Start_Encoder Click procedure. The original procedure only included an audio source, so you must add a video source. Next, you must remove the code that filled the combo box with system profile names because a different profile selection process is used in this application. Finally, you must add code to define the profile by using operator input.

Adding Support for Video Source Files

Find the following line.

```
MyAudioSource.SetInput (MySourcePath.Text)
```

Immediately after this line, add the following two lines.

```
MyVideoSource.SetInput (MySourcePath.Text)
MyVideoSource.Repeat = True
```

Removing the Profile Collection

Because the operator will be creating the profile, there is no need to select one of the system profiles. Remove the following lines from this procedure.

```
Dim MyProfileName As String
MyProfileName = ProfileComboBox.Text
If MyProfileName = DummyText Then
    MsgBox ("Please enter a profile before encoding.")
    Exit Sub
End If

Dim i As Integer
Dim MyProfile As IWMEncProfile
For i = 0 To (MyProColl.Count - 1)
    If MyProColl.Item(i).Name = MyProfileName Then
        Set MyProfile = MyProColl.Item(i)
        MySrcGrp.Profile = MyProfile
        Exit For
    End If
Next i
```

Defining a Custom Profile

Find the following line.

```
MyEncoder.Start
```

Add the following code immediately *before* that line. This code creates a built-in profile based on operator input that defines audio values for codec, channels, sample rate, bit rate, and bit depth, and video values for codec, bit rate, width, height, fps x 1000, buffer, smoothness, and key-frame interval. For more information about these settings, see the Windows Media Encoder SDK.

```
MyProfile.ContentType = 17
Set myAudience = MyProfile.AddAudience(100000)

If Option1.Value = True Then
    SetupAudioAudience "WMA9STD", 1, 8000, 5000, 16
    SetupVideoAudience "WMV9", 15000, 160, 120, 15000, _
                       5000, 75, 10000
ElseIf Option2.Value = True Then
    SetupAudioAudience "WMA9STD", 2, 32000, 48000, 16
    SetupVideoAudience "WMV9", 302000, 320, 240, 30000, 5000, 75, 10000
ElseIf Option3.Value = True Then
    SetupAudioAudience "WMA9STD", 2, 44100, 128040, 16
    SetupVideoAudience "WMV9", 1272000, 320, 240, 30000, 5000, 75, 10000
End If

MyProfile.ProfileName = "SampleProfile"
MySrcGrp.Profile = MyProfile
```

This code defines the profile that will be used during the encoding session. The first line sets the encoding type. Because you are encoding both audio and video, the content type is set to 17.

The next line adds an audience to the profile. This line adds an audience with the bit rate of 100 kilobits per second (kbps), but this value will be overwritten when SetupVideoAudience is called.

Next the code calls SetupAudioAudience and SetupVideoAudience with parameters that differ depending on which option button is selected. These two procedures are responsible for setting all of the needed parameters on the profile and audience objects.

Finally you set the profile on the SourceGroup.

SetupVideoAudience and SetupAudioAudience are two functions that are very helpful when defining custom profiles. By using these functions, provided in the following section, you can easily create strings that can be loaded into other programs to define specific profiles.

Adding New Procedures for the Encoder Profile Application

The following four new function procedures must be added. These procedures are called by the StartEncoder_Click procedure and are used to define the profile.

The first function, SetupAudioAudience, defines the audio stream for the audience. The function GetAudioCodecIndex converts a string value, such as "WMA9", into the appropriate codec index value. This codec index value specifies the audio codec. Finally, myAudience.SetAudioConfig is called to set the number of channels, sample rate, bit rate and bits per sample.

The second function, SetupVideoAudience, is very similar to SetupAudioAudience, but it defines the video settings for the stream instead of the audio. This lookup function determines the video codec's index value and then sets the video codec accordingly. Next, the bit rate, width, height, fps, buffer window and key-frame interval are set. Finally, depending on the encoding mode, the function will choose either VBR compression quality for variable-bit-rate content or the image sharpness setting for CBR. This example uses CBR and requires additional code to specify a different encoding mode. For additional information on how to set the encoding mode, see the *VBRMode* property of the *WMEncProfile2* topic in the Windows Media Encoder SDK.

The next two functions, GetVideoCodecIndex and GetAudioCodecIndex, are lookup functions that convert the string value passed into the correct codec index value.

```
Function SetupAudioAudience(strAudioCodec, intChannels, _
            intSampleRate, intBitrate, intBitsPerSample)
    Dim intAudioCodecIndex

    intAudioCodecIndex = GetAudioCodecIndex(strAudioCodec)


    myAudience.AudioCodec(0) = intAudioCodecIndex
    myAudience.SetAudioConfig 0, intChannels, intSampleRate, _
                        intBitrate, intBitsPerSample
End Function

Function SetupVideoAudience(strVideoCodec, intBitrate, _
            intWidth, intHeight, intFps, intBufferWindow, _
            intSmoothness, intKeyFrame)
    Dim intVideoCodecIndex

    intVideoCodecIndex = GetVideoCodecIndex(strVideoCodec)

    myAudience.VideoCodec(0) = intVideoCodecIndex
    myAudience.VideoBitrate(0) = intBitrate
    myAudience.VideoWidth(0) = intWidth
    myAudience.VideoHeight(0) = intHeight
    myAudience.VideoFPS(0) = intFps
    myAudience.VideoKeyFrameDistance(0) = intKeyFrame
    myAudience.VideoBufferSize(0) = intBufferWindow

    If MyProfile.VBRMode(WMENC_VIDEO, 0) = WMENC_PVM_UNCONSTRAINED Then
        myAudience.VideoCompressionQuality(0) = intSmoothness
    Else
        myAudience.VideoImageSharpness(0) = intSmoothness
    End If
End Function
```

```
Function GetVideoCodecIndex(strVideoCodec)
    Dim intFourCC

    WMV7_FOURCC = 827739479
    WMV8_FOURCC = 844516695
    WMV9_FOURCC = 861293911
    WMS9_FOURCC = 844321613
    MP41_FOURCC = 1395937357
    UNCOMP_FOURCC = 0

    Select Case strVideoCodec
        Case "WMV7"
            intFourCC = WMV7_FOURCC

        Case "WMV8"
            intFourCC = WMV8_FOURCC

        Case "WMV9"
            intFourCC = WMV9_FOURCC

        Case "WMS9"
            intFourCC = WMS9_FOURCC

        Case "MP41"
            intFourCC = MP41_FOURCC

        Case "UNCOMP"
            intFourCC = UNCOMP_FOURCC

        Case Else
            intFourCC = WMV9_FOURCC
    End Select

    GetVideoCodecIndex = MyProfile.GetCodecIndexFromFourCC( _
                                    WMENC_VIDEO, intFourCC)
End Function

Function GetAudioCodecIndex(strAudioCodec)
    Dim intFourCC

    WMA9STD_FOURCC = 353
    WMA9PRO_FOURCC = 354
    WMA9LSL_FOURCC = 355
    WMSPEECH_FOURCC = 10
    PCM_FOURCC = 0

    Select Case strAudioCodec
        Case "WMA9STD"
            intFourCC = WMA9STD_FOURCC
```

(continued)

```
        Case "WMA9PRO"
            intFourCC = WMA9PRO_FOURCC

        Case "WMA9LSL"
            intFourCC = WMA9LSL_FOURCC

        Case "WMSPEECH"
            intFourCC = WMSPEECH_FOURCC

        Case "PCM"
            intFourCC = PCM_FOURCC

        Case Else
            intFourCC = WMA9STD_FOURCC
    End Select

    GetAudioCodecIndex = MyProfile.GetCodecIndexFromFourCC( _
                                    WMENC_AUDIO, intFourCC)
End Function
```

Running the Encoder Profile Application

After you have entered all the code, run the project in Visual Basic. From the Run menu, select Start. If there are no errors, the user interface of your application should look like Figure A.3. You can compare your code to the complete code listing in the next section.

Figure A.3   Encoder Profile application broadcasting.

Use the following procedure to test your application:

1. Choose one of the three bit rates by clicking on one of the bit rate options.

2. Change the frame rate (FPS), if desired.

3. Change the HTTP port number, if desired.

4. Change the path to the source file you want encoded, if different from the default.

5. Click the Start Encoding button. After a moment, the encoder status should read "Running."

6. Any time after the encoder has begun encoding, click the Play Player button to display the encoded stream by using Windows Media Player.

7. After the Player begins playing the encoded stream, the bit rate of the stream is displayed.

8. You can stop the Player at any time by clicking the Stop Player button.

9. You can stop the encoder by clicking the Stop Encoding button.

Complete copies of the source code and digital media for this application are on the companion CD.

Source Code for the Encoder Profile Application

Here is the complete source code for the Encoder Profile application.

```
Dim WithEvents MyEncoder As WMEncoder
Dim MySrcGrpColl As IWMEncSourceGroupCollection
Dim MySrcGrp As IWMEncSourceGroup
Dim MyAudioSource As IWMEncSource
Dim MyBroadcast As IWMEncBroadcast
Dim MyProfile As WMEncProfile2
Dim myAudience As IWMEncAudienceObj
Dim MyVideoSource As IWMEncSource

Private Sub Form_Load()
    Set MyEncoder = New WMEncoder
    Set MyProfile = New WMEncProfile2

    Set MySrcGrpColl = MyEncoder.SourceGroupCollection
    Set MySrcGrp = MySrcGrpColl.Add("SG_1")
    Set MyAudioSource = MySrcGrp.AddSource(WMENC_AUDIO)
    Set MyVideoSource = MySrcGrp.AddSource(WMENC_VIDEO)
```

(continued)

```vb
        MySourcePath.Text = "C:\Media\laure.avi"

        Player.uiMode = "none"
        Address.Text = "8080"

    End Sub

    Private Sub StartEncoder_Click()
        MyAudioSource.SetInput (MySourcePath.Text)
        MyVideoSource.SetInput (MySourcePath.Text)

        MyVideoSource.Repeat = True
        MyAudioSource.Repeat = True

        Set MyBroadcast = MyEncoder.Broadcast
        MyBroadcast.PortNumber(WMENC_PROTOCOL_HTTP) = Address.Text

        MyProfile.ContentType = 17
        Set myAudience = MyProfile.AddAudience(100000)

        If Option1.Value = True Then
            SetupAudioAudience "WMA9STD", 1, 8000, 5000, 16
            SetupVideoAudience "WMV9", 15000, 160, 120, 15000, _
                            5000, 75, 10000
        ElseIf Option2.Value = True Then
            SetupAudioAudience "WMA9STD", 2, 32000, 48000, 16
            SetupVideoAudience "WMV9", 302000, 320, 240, 30000, 5000, 75, 10000
        ElseIf Option3.Value = True Then
            SetupAudioAudience "WMA9STD", 2, 44100, 128040, 16
            SetupVideoAudience "WMV9", 1272000, 320, 240, 30000, 5000, 75, 10000
        End If
        MyProfile.ProfileName = "SampleProfile"
        MySrcGrp.Profile = MyProfile

        MyEncoder.Start
    End Sub

    Private Sub MyEncoder_OnStateChange(ByVal enumState As _
            WMEncoderLib.WMENC_ENCODER_STATE)
        Select Case enumState
            Case WMENC_ENCODER_RUNNING
                MyState.Caption = "Running"
            Case WMENC_ENCODER_STOPPED
                MyState.Caption = "Stopped"
        End Select
    End Sub
```

```
Private Sub PlayPlayer_Click()
    If MyState.Caption = "Running" Then
        Player.URL = "http://" & Environ("COMPUTERNAME") & ":" _
                    & Address.Text
    Else
        MsgBox "Please start the encoding process."
    End If
End Sub

Private Sub StopEncoder_Click()
    MyEncoder.Stop
End Sub

Private Sub StopPlayer_Click()
    Player.Controls.Stop
End Sub

Private Sub Player_PlayStateChange(ByVal NewState As Long)
    If NewState = 3 Then
        Dim AC As Integer
        Dim MyRate As Long
        AC = Player.currentMedia.getAttributeCountByType _
                            ("Bitrate", "") - 1
        MyRate = Player.currentMedia.getItemInfoByType _
                            ("Bitrate", "", AC)
        BitRate.Caption = "Bitrate = " & CStr(MyRate) & _
                            " bits/second"
    End If
End Sub

Function SetupAudioAudience(strAudioCodec, intChannels, _
            intSampleRate, intBitrate, intBitsPerSample)
    Dim intAudioCodecIndex

    intAudioCodecIndex = GetAudioCodecIndex(strAudioCodec)

    myAudience.AudioCodec(0) = intAudioCodecIndex
    myAudience.SetAudioConfig 0, intChannels, intSampleRate, _
                            intBitrate, intBitsPerSample
End Function

Function SetupVideoAudience(strVideoCodec, intBitrate, _
            intWidth, intHeight, intFps, intBufferWindow, _
            intSmoothness, intKeyFrame)
    Dim intVideoCodecIndex

    intVideoCodecIndex = GetVideoCodecIndex(strVideoCodec)
    myAudience.VideoCodec(0) = intVideoCodecIndex
    myAudience.VideoBitrate(0) = intBitrate
```

(continued)

```
        myAudience.VideoWidth(0) = intWidth
        myAudience.VideoHeight(0) = intHeight
        myAudience.VideoFPS(0) = intFps
        myAudience.VideoKeyFrameDistance(0) = intKeyFrame
        myAudience.VideoBufferSize(0) = intBufferWindow

        If MyProfile.VBRMode(WMENC_VIDEO, 0) = WMENC_PVM_UNCONSTRAINED Then
            myAudience.VideoCompressionQuality(0) = intSmoothness
        Else
            myAudience.VideoImageSharpness(0) = intSmoothness
        End If
End Function


Function GetVideoCodecIndex(strVideoCodec)
    Dim intFourCC

    WMV7_FOURCC = 827739479
    WMV8_FOURCC = 844516695
    WMV9_FOURCC = 861293911
    WMS9_FOURCC = 844321613
    MP41_FOURCC = 1395937357
    UNCOMP_FOURCC = 0

    Select Case strVideoCodec
        Case "WMV7"
            intFourCC = WMV7_FOURCC

        Case "WMV8"
            intFourCC = WMV8_FOURCC

        Case "WMV9"
            intFourCC = WMV9_FOURCC

        Case "WMS9"
            intFourCC = WMS9_FOURCC

        Case "MP41"
            intFourCC = MP41_FOURCC

        Case "UNCOMP"
            intFourCC = UNCOMP_FOURCC

        Case Else
            intFourCC = WMV9_FOURCC
    End Select

    GetVideoCodecIndex = MyProfile.GetCodecIndexFromFourCC( _
                                    WMENC_VIDEO, intFourCC)
End Function
```

```
Function GetAudioCodecIndex(strAudioCodec)
    Dim intFourCC

    WMA9STD_FOURCC = 353
    WMA9PRO_FOURCC = 354
    WMA9LSL_FOURCC = 355
    WMSPEECH_FOURCC = 10
    PCM_FOURCC = 0

    Select Case strAudioCodec
        Case "WMA9STD"
            intFourCC = WMA9STD_FOURCC

        Case "WMA9PRO"
            intFourCC = WMA9PRO_FOURCC

        Case "WMA9LSL"
            intFourCC = WMA9LSL_FOURCC

        Case "WMSPEECH"
            intFourCC = WMSPEECH_FOURCC
        Case "PCM"
            intFourCC = PCM_FOURCC

        Case Else
            intFourCC = WMA9STD_FOURCC
    End Select

    GetAudioCodecIndex = MyProfile.GetCodecIndexFromFourCC( _
                            WMENC_AUDIO, intFourCC)
End Function
```

Index

Seth McEvoy

Seth McEvoy has over twenty-five years experience in the computer industry as a video game developer, programmer writer, and technical editor. He has specialized in learning over 30 computer languages, ranging from XML, COM, C++, ActiveX, Visual Basic, C#, and JScript, to 6 different assembly languages. In his 12 years at Microsoft, he has written the programming code and text for many Microsoft Software Development Kits, including Windows Media, Office, OLE, and Interactive Television.

In addition, he has written 35 computer and children's books for Simon & Schuster, Dell, Bantam, Scholastic, Compute, and Random House. One of his children's book series, *Not Quite Human*, was made into three TV movies by Disney.

Work smarter—*conquer your software from the inside out!*

Microsoft® Windows® XP Inside Out, Deluxe Edition	**Microsoft Office System Inside Out—2003 Edition**	**Microsoft Office Access 2003 Inside Out**	**Microsoft Office FrontPage® 2003 Inside Out**
ISBN: 0-7356-1805-4	ISBN: 0-7356-1512-8	ISBN: 0-7356-1513-6	ISBN: 0-7356-1510-1
U.S.A. $59.99	U.S.A. $49.99	U.S.A. $49.99	U.S.A. $49.99
Canada $86.99	Canada $72.99	Canada $72.99	Canada $72.99

Hey, you know your way around a desktop. Now dig into the new Microsoft Office products and the Windows XP operating system and *really* put your PC to work! These supremely organized software reference titles pack hundreds of timesaving solutions, troubleshooting tips and tricks, and handy workarounds into a concise, fast-answer format. They're all muscle and no fluff. All this comprehensive information goes deep into the nooks and crannies of each Office application and Windows XP feature. And every INSIDE OUT title includes a CD-ROM packed with bonus content such as tools and utilities, demo programs, sample scripts, batch programs, an eBook containing the book's complete text, and more! Discover the best and fastest ways to perform everyday tasks, and challenge yourself to new levels of software mastery!

Microsoft Press has other INSIDE OUT titles to help you get the job done every day:

Microsoft Office Excel 2003 Programming Inside Out
ISBN: 0-7356-1985-9

Microsoft Office Word 2003 Inside Out
ISBN: 0-7356-1515-2

Microsoft Office Excel 2003 Inside Out
ISBN: 0-7356-1511-X

Microsoft Office Outlook 2003® Inside Out
ISBN: 0-7356-1514-4

Microsoft Office Project 2003 Inside Out
ISBN: 0-7356-1958-1

Microsoft Office Visio® 2003 Inside Out
ISBN: 0-7356-1516-0

Microsoft Windows XP Networking Inside Out
ISBN: 0-7356-1652-3

Microsoft Windows Security Inside Out for Windows XP and Windows 2000
ISBN: 0-7356-1632-9

To learn more about the full line of Microsoft Press® products, please visit us at:

microsoft.com/mspress

Microsoft
Press

In-depth learning solutions *for every software user*

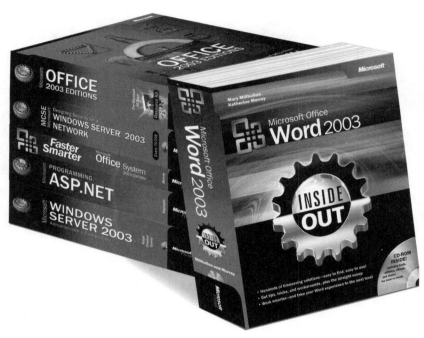

The tools you need to put technology to work.

Microsoft Press

Learn how to develop software at your own pace with the proven *Microsoft STEP BY STEP* method!

Microsoft® Visual Basic® .NET Step by Step— Version 2003
ISBN: 0-7356-1905-0
U.S.A. $39.99
Canada $57.99

Microsoft® Visual C#® .NET Step by Step— Version 2003
ISBN: 0-7356-1909-3
U.S.A. $39.99
Canada $57.99

Microsoft® Visual C++® .NET Step by Step— Version 2003
ISBN: 0-7356-1907-7
U.S.A. $39.99
Canada $57.99

Learn core programming skills with these hands-on, tutorial-based guides—all of them designed to walk any developer through the fundamentals of Microsoft's programming languages. Work through every lesson to complete the full course, or do just the lessons you want to learn exactly the skills you need. Either way, you receive professional development training at your own pace, with real-world examples and practice files to help you master core skills with the world's most popular programming languages and technologies. Throughout, you'll find insightful tips and expert explanations for rapid application development, increased productivity, and more powerful results.

To learn more about the full line of Microsoft Press® products for developers, please visit us at:

microsoft.com/mspress/developer